JAZZ

in the Time of the Novel

JAZZ

in the Time
of the Novel

The Temporal Politics of
American Race and Culture

BRUCE BARNHART

THE UNIVERSITY OF ALABAMA PRESS
Tuscaloosa

Typeface: Garamond and Gill Sans

Cover image: Copyright © Benjamin Haas, Dreamstime.com
Cover design: Erin Bradlry Dangar / Dangar Design

∞

The paper on which this book is printed meets the minimum requirements
of American National Standard for Information Sciences—Permanence of
Paper for Printed Library Materials, ANSI Z39.48-1984.

Library of Congress Cataloging-in-Publication Data

Barnhart, Bruce, 1966-
Jazz in the time of the novel : the temporal politics of American race and
culture / Bruce Barnhart.
pages cm
Includes bibliographical references and index.
ISBN 978-0-8173-1804-8 (trade cloth : alk. paper) —
ISBN 978-0-8173-8690-0 (e book)
1. American fiction—History and criticism. 2. Jazz in literature. 3. Music in
literature. 4. Rhythm in literature. 5. Time in literature. I. Title.
PS374.J38B37 2013
813'.509357—dc23
2013009278

For Linda D. Nichols and Lindon W. Barrett

Contents

Illustrations

Acknowledgments

This book owes the most to three exceptional teachers: Lindon Barrett, John Carlos Rowe, and Julian Priester. Their expansive vision of African American studies, American studies, and jazz has provided the model for all that I have tried to achieve here. The suppleness of their thought and intensity of their convictions continue to be a stimulating and sustaining resource for me.

I also would like to acknowledge the intellectual camaraderie of colleagues and friends at Irvine and Wake Forest. At Irvine, I had the good fortune of encountering a number of exciting and powerful thinkers: Jacques Derrida, Hortense Spillers, Angela Davis, and Fredric Jameson have all shaped my thinking in profound but uncategorizable ways.

My experience in the cultural studies reading group at Irvine was also invaluable. The group provided a combative and playful intellectual forum, which allowed me to test out my ideas and develop a methodology that took on board some of the group's capacious and dissonant energies: Leila Neti, Radha Radhakrishnan, Janet Neary, Mrinalini Chakravorty, Arnold Pan, and Amy Parsons were always quick to challenge my ideas and to refill my wine glass. My Wake Forest colleagues have also been terrific: Dean Franco, Patrick Moran, Andy Burkett, and Jamin Rowan have been particularly supportive.

Finally, my many listening sessions with Jeff Atteberry were crucial in allowing me to hear what the music was really saying.

Parts of this work were written with the assistance of grants from the University of California, Irvine, and the University of California Humanities Research Institute.

A portion of chapter 2 has appeared in *African American Review*, and a version of chapter 3 has appeared in *Callaloo*.

1

Jazz and the Novel in the Cultural and Imaginative Landscape

Jazz seeps into words.
    —Langston Hughes, "Jazz as Communication"

The also and also of the drummer signifying on the high-hat cymbal, even in the distance (and it is as if it were the also and also of time itself whispering red alert as if in blue italics).
    —Albert Murray, *Stomping the Blues*

The story I want to tell takes place in the first three decades of the twentieth century; it is the story of the interaction between two quite different aesthetic forms, jazz and the novel. Although the importance of this interaction has often been acknowledged, it has never been the central guiding concern of an extended critical investigation.[1] Given the simultaneity of the explosive development and dissemination of jazz with the production of a slew of important and innovative American novels, both African American and Anglo-American, the lack of attention given this relationship constitutes a major gap in our understanding of a critical period in American and African American cultural history. It is this gap that my study works to fill by investigating thematic allusions to, and representations of, jazz, as well as the temporal and formal schematics through which two sets of novels from the first three decades of the twentieth century, one African American and one Anglo-American, respond to jazz's form of temporality. A large part of my aim is to push for a less one-sided understanding of the relationship between jazz and the novel. Jazz is no passive object for literary appropriation. It talks back to the novel, often quite forcefully, and part of my goal here is to think about what it says. To this end, two of my chapters are direct analyses of jazz recordings: chapter 3 looks at James P. Johnson's "Carolina Shout," and chapter 5 looks at Bessie Smith and Louis Armstrong's "St. Louis Blues."

While my analysis focuses intensely on jazz and constantly returns to its formal arrangements and performance practices, it is primarily an examination of the way that the novel refracts, redacts, incorporates, and suppresses jazz and its aesthetic and social logic. Social because it quickly and necessarily moves to a consideration of how these forms, the novel and jazz, reflect and participate in the political and social struggles of the time period, conflicts that centered on questions such as the meaning of race, the proper economic organization of society, competing conceptions of the self, healthy modes of social interaction, and the definition and relevance of culture. The novelists (and other intellectuals) of the 1910s and 1920s did not see jazz primarily as a disembodied or detached aesthetic form. For them it was a manifestation of potent psychic, racial and/ or social energies, vital or disreputable eruptions of racial essence, repressed libido, or runaway modernity. As wrongheaded or overly simplistic as these readings of jazz may be, they have the virtue of keeping in sight the fact that form is never neutral, never entirely detached from the social situation out of which it emerges.

In his consideration of the role of improvisation in jazz, Albert Murray posits a definition of art that incorporates this insight regarding form. He writes, "art is the ultimate extension, elaboration, and refinement of the rituals that reenact the primary survival technology; and hence it conveys basic attitudes toward experience of a given people in a given time, place, circumstance, and predicament" ("Improvisation" 111). Defining art as a kind of "equipment for living," Murray's formulation insists that history is always implicit in aesthetic form, and hence that no form travels from one social situation to another without a degree of friction or dissonance. Every form embodies the specific survival rituals of a specific people and will be understood and received differently by people with a different pattern of ritual accommodation to reality. Despite Murray's emphasis elsewhere on the continuities of African American and Anglo-American experience and aesthetics, here he suggests that blacks and whites in twentieth-century America have fairly divergent "attitudes toward experience." African Americans and white Americans of the 1910s, 1920s, and 1930s might have shared the same time, but they rarely shared the same place and almost never shared the same circumstances. The "primary survival technologies" that jazz and the novel extend, elaborate, and refine are responses to different social situations and thus take radically different shapes. Jazz emerges from densely populated urban African American communities in the first decade and a half of the twentieth century; it is a function of the new opportunities for musicians in the secular recreational spaces created by the confluence of unprecedentedly high levels of demographic and economic fluidity.[2] The novel is the product of eighteenth-century England and the maturation of both capitalism and the self-assurance of a literate middle class.[3] Despite the difference of these two forms' genesis, the complex web of social and economic relations that have always existed between Anglo-Americans and African Americans make it a mistake to imagine that jazz has an absolute correspondence to an African American essence, racial or otherwise, or that the novel has remained unaltered by its transportation into the racially divided landscape of America. This fact makes any productive conception of the relationship between the novel and jazz quite difficult.

This difficulty is constructively addressed by Olly Wilson in his article "Black Music as an Art Form." In his outline of the conceptual approaches that define African American music, Wilson constructs two categories of African American music. These categories are not absolute categories of a pure African American musical tradition and a hybrid African American–European American tradition but, reflecting his observation that "cultural interaction more than cultural isolation has characterized the American experience," are categories based on relative degrees of "interaction and interpenetration" of an African American tradition and a Euro-American tradition (83). The complexity of these interactions is suggested by the fact that the example Wilson gives of "the tradition characterized by a greater interaction and interpenetration of African and Euro-American elements" (89) is a jazz performance, a 1959 recording of the Miles Davis sextet.[4] Following Wilson's model, the categories used to theorize the novels and jazz of the (expanded) Jazz Age will be relative poles of interaction between an African American mode of culture and a European American mode, a dialectical use of categories that doesn't deny the contact and interaction which constituted these categories in the first place.[5]

In "Repetition as a Figure of Black Culture" James Snead asserts that "one may readily classify cultural forms according to whether they tend to admit or cover up the repeating constituents within them" (63). Snead's assertion deftly cuts to the heart of the difference between European-influenced and African-influenced cultural art forms without reifying either culture or the difference(s) between them. His use of repetition as the key distinction between European and black culture is not one that makes a sharp division between a repetitive cyclical form of culture and a progressive, nonrepetitive one.[6] For Snead, repetition is an inevitably present component of all cultures, an unavoidable result of the fact that "culture as a reservoir of inexhaustible novelty is unthinkable" (63). All cultures partake of repetition; the difference is the extent to which a particular culture acknowledges or disavows its dependence on it. This difference manifests itself along "a scale of tendencies from culture to culture," with European culture tending to dress repetition in the masking terms of accumulation and growth and black culture tending to embrace repetition as a goalless circulation of elements in equilibrium. Snead sees jazz as one of the prime manifestations of this attitude toward repetition, whereas the novel, for him, is a genre based on the suppression of repetition and an evasion of "the need for 'repeated descriptions'"(73).

The tremors that resulted from the attempt of jazz and the novel to inhabit roughly the same cultural space spread out in ways that were blind to the borders between disciplinary and conceptual fields. This necessitates an approach that touches on the problematics of a number of fairly diverse fields: music, economics, literature, sociology, and cultural history. Because of this, I rely on the critical formulations of a fairly large array of critics from a number of different fields. This study starts with the juxtaposition of two distinct aesthetic forms, and while my conception of the novel is rooted in the writings of Paul de Man, Theodor Adorno,[7] and Georg Lukács, and my theorization of jazz attempts to build on Samuel A. Floyd Jr.'s transportation of Henry Louis Gates Jr.'s work on Signifyin(g) into the realm of music, my approach essentially grows out of a pair of formulations by Albert Murray and James Snead:

> Murray: "Art is the ultimate extension, elaboration, and refinement of the rituals that re-enact the primary survival technology; and hence it conveys basic attitudes toward experience of a given people in a given time, place, circumstance and predicament" ("Improvisation" 111).
> Snead: African American music contains "an essentially philosophical insight about the shape of time and history" (59–60).

Taken together, these two statements adumbrate the major presupposition of my study: that aesthetic forms enshrine a cultural rhythm, a cognitive and epistemological mode of moving from one situation to another that assigns value to certain intellectual and pragmatic maneuvers while repudiating others. It is this concept that allows a bridge to be made between jazz and the novel, a bridge that, despite the seemingly insuperable differences between the two forms, allows me to imagine them as both rivals and interlocutors. The arena in which they face each other is both the highly fluid cultural and intellectual landscape of early twentieth-century America and, as Snead points out, the realm of temporality. Part of what I am arguing here is a point forcefully made by Eric Porter in *What Is This Thing Called Jazz?*: that jazz musicians are intellectuals whose status has "seldom been acknowledged," but who play an important role "as arbiters of cultural tastes and cultural politics" (xiv). Porter's focus is on the writings of jazz musicians, but I share with Snead an approach that looks to the music itself as the source of musicians' influence and intellectual contributions. Like the novel, jazz is an intellectual force that critiques existing modes of temporality and argues that its treatment of time is the most productive way of translating the present into the future.

Foregrounding temporality as the link between these two forms allows for an analysis that sees the questions of aesthetic form raised by their juxtaposition as also questions of race, politics, culture, history, and economics. This is because the conception of time at work here, like the one utilized by Snead, is uncompromisingly materialist. Incorporating sociological (Durkheim) and Marxist (Marx, Lukács, and Adorno) theorizations, the notion of time that I employ is focused through the thinking of Johannes Fabian, an anthropologist who, in his work *Time and the Other*, asserts that "time belongs to the political economy of relations between individuals, classes and nations," and that "there is a 'Politics of Time'" (xii). For Fabian, time is always political because it governs the envisioning of otherness; the way in which it has traditionally done this in Western society is by imposing an apparently insurmountable conceptual barrier between subject and object, exercising what Fabian refers to as an "epistemological dictatorship" that licenses oppression by creating fixed hierarchical categories such as master and servant, white and black, primitive and civilized, worker and owner. Fabian labels this conceptual operation "allochronism," a denial of the dialectical relationship between subject and object that divests the object of knowledge (whether person, body, art form, culture, race, etc.) of the ability to occupy and act in the same temporal space of the observing subject of knowledge. Fabian's theorization of time is a call for a consideration of "the ideological nature of temporal concepts which inform our theories and our rhetoric" (xii), a call to which my analysis of jazz and the novel in the arena of nascent American consumer culture responds by unfolding the theoretical implications contained in the statement that "a clear conception of allochronism is the prerequisite and frame for a critique of racism" (182).

Fabian's project is primarily an investigation of the way that time is imposed on the other, which suggests a study of race that sees the structure of time as an agent of oppression. This is part of what I am engaged in here, but what is more important for my analysis is the way that Fabian's emphasis on the political aspect of time and his call for dialectical analysis enables a consideration of time as a cultural coefficient, an expression of Murray's "primary survival technology," as well as an imposed structure. Snead's reading of African American musical forms as expositions of alternative models of temporality provides the basis for an approach that not only recognizes the novels and jazz of the Jazz Age as participants and players in the "Politics of Time" but also sees in jazz and jazz-influenced novels a critique of allochronism and its attendant racism that precedes Fabian's call for such a critique. Combining the insights of Snead with those of Fabian opens up to us the truth of jazz's insights into the relationship between subject and object, relationships that subtend systems of subordination as well as systems of philosophical speculation.

This link is one that has best been theorized by Michael Hanchard in his essay "Afro-Modernity: Temporality, Politics, and the African Diaspora." Hanchard's meditations on race and alternative modernities extend Fabian's analysis of time by positing the existence of "racial time," a time defined by "the inequalities that result from power relations between dominant and subordinate groups" (253). Hanchard moves from the highly abstract level of Fabian's analysis to a concrete analysis of the real temporal constraints imposed on members of the African diaspora in the form of "unequal temporal access to institutions, goods, services, resources, power, and knowledge" (253). This move gives Fabian's theorizations a sharper social point; it also forwards important insights about the nature of racial community and about how the jazz emanating from the African American communities of the 1910s, 1920s, and 1930s came to contain such crucial insights into the social and temporal structure of American, as well as African American, culture. For Hanchard, the fact that members of African American communities had access to a sense of time distinct from that of mainstream America is not due to any biological racial essence but is a function of their sharing the same subordinate place in society. The tensions and social struggles arising from the interactions between those assigned to this place and those who imposed temporal (and other) restrictions on them, "along with the resentments, anger, and fears associated with their interactions, became the source for collective consciousness and, ultimately, strategies for organized and individuated resistance" (254). Hanchard posits an African American group identity that is not biological but is what he refers to as an "epistemological community," a community whose subordinate position gives it a unique insight into social structures of domination, temporal or otherwise. Recognizing the coercive nature of the relationship to time forced upon them, some members of this epistemological community were gifted with what one might call economic "second-sight." Aware of the necessity of orienting themselves to the form of time enshrined by the governing forces of society, and unwilling to give up the possibility of a noncoercive form of time and order, African Americans developed an extremely sophisticated survival technique, a conceptual strategy that Hanchard refers to as "time appropriation." Hanchard defines time appropriation as "the actual instance of social movement when group members who constitute a collective social formulation decide to intervene in public debate for the purpose of affecting positive change in their overall position and location in society" by attempting to "eradicat[e] the gulf in racial time" (256).

For Hanchard, time appropriation usually accompanies "periods of social upheaval and transformation," such as the Great Migration of the 1910s and 1920s, and is a sign of the kind of reflective self-conscious modernity that allowed African American artists and intellectuals to "utilize the very mechanisms of their subordination for their liberation" (246). This, I argue, is precisely what jazz does to the mechanisms and machinations of objective clock time; it is also what the influence of jazz enables novelists like James Weldon Johnson and Nella Larsen to do to both Western developmental time and the form of the novel. This goes a long way toward explaining the powerful charge that jazz had in the 1910s and 1920s, for this was the period when something akin to the kind of temporal regime that African Americans had long been subjected to extended its reach into the lives of all Americans in the form of urbanization, Taylorization, and increased rationalization of the workplace. Both groups are propelled toward an urban, rationalized workplace, but at radically different rates; the Great Migration took under two decades to urbanize the black population to the same extent that it had taken the white population a century to achieve.

In *Terrible Honesty* Ann Douglass notes two symptoms attendant to this extended rationalization of time. The first is the proliferation in the 1920s of a welter of new phrases embodying a new vernacular consciousness of time: "people 'buy time,' 'pass the time,' 'spend time,' 'borrow time,' 'steal time,' 'mark time,' 'waste time,' and even 'kill time'; people are 'on time,' 'in time,' 'doing time'" (39). The second is the growing urbanization of the population, indicated by the census of 1920 in which for the first time America was seen to be a predominantly urban, rather than rural, nation. As symptoms of a broad cultural and economic shift, the two facts are interdependent. Urbanization brought large and diverse groups of people into contact with each other, and the organization of their interactions and the coordination of the specialized functions they all performed brought about a more rigid conception of time, a shift from the flexibility of task-oriented time to the abstraction of calculable labor time.[8] Inevitably, this material organization of work (and recreational) life came to affect the shape of consciousness, and time came to be seen as a quantifiable object, subject to the same laws of scarcity as other objects. In other words, the alteration of economic patterns prompted cultural and, ultimately, aesthetic change. This is essentially the topic of Douglass's impressive study of Manhattan in the 1920s: the shape of the profound cultural shift that resulted from an interruption of America's traditional form of self-assurance. Douglass describes this interruption as a moment of openness and even freedom, characterizing the 1920s as "the first and perhaps the last moment when something like the practice of free will was possible in the consumer society and entertainment culture America was fast becoming" (70). For her, the terrible honesty of the 1920s is an occluded possibility, an examination of which might serve to uncover some of the possibilities for the exercise of free will latent in the culture that post-1920s America has become.

Douglass's approach is a productive one, but it partially works to obscure the fact that the cultural formations of the period are not *just* momentary structures effaced by subsequent historical tides; they are also the very basis for the formations that followed them, enabling agents whose shapes were at least partially retained in the historical process that has brought us to our current situation. In effect, Douglass's approach partakes of the kind of commodification of time characteristic of the period she studies, slighting both the historical antecedents of "terrible honesty" and its effect upon subsequent periods. What is missing is a sense that the shift of the 1910s and 1920s is an adaptation of the traditional form of American cultural self-consciousness to fit new conditions, as well as a breaking down of this form. Douglass brilliantly and exhaustively details the changes that the economic reorganization of society *allows* but does not pay enough attention to what this reorganization *demands*.

A comparison of Douglass's study to Chip Rhodes's analysis of the same period in his *Structures of the Jazz Age* clarifies the distinction between what social change allows and what it demands and shows the ways in which my approach diverges from Douglass's despite the very real debt that my analysis owes to *Terrible Honesty*. The difference between Rhodes and Douglass is essentially due to their diverging visions of the relationship between art and society or, in other terms, the relationship between superstructure and base. Ever since Marx's initial formulation of the concept of ideology, there has been a tension within it between the notion of ideology as the expression of a specific form of social existence and the notion of it as a mystificatory justification of the economic relations that govern social existence. The stress that Douglass places on openness and freedom betrays an understanding of ideology in the first sense, whereas Rhodes's study takes up the second sense of ideology.

While *Terrible Honesty* predominantly emphasizes the way that jazz age cultural production corresponds to new and potentially liberating social modes of existence, Rhodes's *Structure of the Jazz Age* places greater emphasis on the role of literature in preparing the way for the form of society least threatening to the continuity of both economic interests and American cultural identity. For Rhodes, the cultural production of the 1920s is ideological in the sense that it facilitates accommodation to the economic structures of society. Regardless of the intentions of its producers, this art serves to legitimate at least as much to critique. Rhodes differs from Douglass insofar as he senses that the primary causes of the flurry of change in the realm of the aesthetic were the changing ideological imperatives of capital rather than any movements entirely internal to the aesthetic realm. For him the central fact of the 1920s was that "the principal ideological imperative was no longer the construction of workers so much as it was the construction of consumers to enable the boom in consumer durables" (176). Here the economy is a central character, as it must be in any materialist critique. The stress that Rhodes puts on economic change and on the role that cultural production has in legitimating (and facilitating) this change is crucial to my understanding of the interaction between art and society in the 1910s and 1920s. Rhodes's articulation of the link between economic structures and aesthetic structures opens up the period to an analysis that takes into account not only its distinctiveness (as Douglass's study does) but also its continuity with the periods that precede and follow it. His consideration of how art serves the desire of society to retain its current divisions and relations of production as well as critiquing society is indispensable, but it is handicapped by his tendency to align these functions according to a division between what he calls "mass culture" and "high culture" (which almost always appears in the form of the novel), a division that was not nearly as firm in the 1920s as it is today, as well as a division that one might argue has never been as firmly established in America as it was in Europe.[9] In *Structures of the Jazz Age* it is consistently a relatively undifferentiated, under-analyzed mass culture that serves the ideological interests of capital, while only novels are imagined as having the capability of questioning these interests and of rising above them to indicate "the inseparability of economic, social, and cultural processes" (194). The implicit reliance on an unexamined division between high and mass culture prevents Rhodes's study from attaining the critical purchase that his framing of it promises, for the conclusions that he reaches depend on an understanding of the function of mass culture, an understanding unsupported by any direct analysis of specific mass cultural forms. His analysis of these forms is derived from the reflections of, and meditations on, them contained in the novels that are the focus of his work. What this means is that in a work titled "Structures of the Jazz Age," there is virtually no consideration of "jazz" itself. Like many other literary studies of the period, Rhodes's work runs up against disciplinary constraints that make any direct consideration of jazz quite difficult. These disciplinary constraints occlude important cultural connections and further a myopic vision of the period; any meaningful analysis must work to move beyond them.

In my study this attempt is made by way of recourse to Snead's meditation on the centrality of the role of repetition and rhythm to any full understanding of African American culture, European culture, and an American culture built on both. The work of a primarily literary critic on the form of music and its commonalities with the form of literature, Snead's "Repetition as a Figure of Black Culture" shows the way for a reading of jazz age society that extends the work of Rhodes and Douglass by focusing on the formal structure of jazz itself. This is crucial, because, without direct formal analysis, the specifics of jazz's innovative configurations of sound and experience, as well as its radical newness, are unavailable. Music is a medium in which form is of much greater significance than in literature; Henry Louis Gates Jr. even goes so far as to claim that it is "the audible embodiment of form" (*Figures in Black* 31). In laying stress on the importance of form, however, it must be made clear that form is being understood here not as an idealized container of content but in the way that Houston Baker defines it in *Modernism and the Harlem Renaissance*, that is, as "a symbolizing fluidity, . . . a family of concepts or a momentary and changing same array of images, figures and assumptions," something that can only be defined "from the perspective of action" (17).

To deprive ourselves of formal analysis of jazz is to deprive ourselves of any possible access to its self-understanding, leaving us only with the necessarily stunted understanding of it that comes from contemporary accounts, accounts distorted by the lenses of primitivism, white control of the media and other means of the music's propagation, and music's resistance to language. Looking at jazz in the way that Snead and the musicologist Samuel A. Floyd Jr. do allows an understanding of both what the music essentially was in the 1910s and 1920s and the way in which much of its popular acceptance was made possible by a misunderstanding of this essence.

Lawrence Levine speaks of this misunderstanding when he writes that "American society has done far more than merely neglect jazz; it has pigeonholed it, stereotyped it, denigrated it, distorted its meaning and its character" (432). Jazz entered onto the stage of mass culture under conditions primarily of other's making and thus was susceptible to being packaged as something it was not, namely a timeless survival of primal rhythm from a more primitive stage of mankind's development. Rhodes's insight that this figuration of jazz served the important ideological function of producing consumer desire is indispensable, but it must be supplemented by an investigation of jazz that starts with the realization that the significance of no important art form is identical with its ideological use. This is to say that there were (and are) different modes of listening to jazz. Not everyone heard in jazz the tom-toms of primitive essence, and the fact that so many were capable of hearing it in this way is a testament to the profound power of America's racialized epistemology to distort and efface. To begin to come to terms with this power, it is necessary to trace both modes of hearing jazz, to treat both mainstream primitivist visions of jazz and responses that were more open to the temporal revelations that speak from within jazz's manipulation of form. This is my strategy here, a strategy that investigates the novels of Fitzgerald and James Weldon Johnson, of Nella Larsen, Gertrude Stein, and Langston Hughes in order to excavate the crystallizations and appropriations of these modes of hearing jazz. The nature and focus of the attention these novels pay to jazz reveal a great deal about how they configure time and thus about their social and racial vision.

Using Jazz

The hierarchy of values that places the novel on a different and "higher" plane than jazz has meant that the relationship most often considered between these two forms has been one in which the novel makes some *use* of jazz. A turn to a consideration of F. Scott Fitzgerald's short story "The Offshore Pirate" and of one scene in James Weldon Johnson's novel *The Autobiography of an Ex-Colored Man* provides depictions of jazz that are not only examples of how jazz is used to advance the aims of narrative but are also instances of jazz being used *within* the narrative. That is, in these two works jazz is utilized by characters as well as by the authors who created these characters. Both employments of jazz and textual reflections on the employment of jazz, these works show us the strength of the impulse behind literary attempts to use jazz as a kind of raw material, as well as the reason why this conception of the relationship between the novel and jazz is ultimately inadequate.

In "The Offshore Pirate" Fitzgerald gives us a romantic vision of jazz as timeless and primitive utterance: "Over across the silver lake the figures of the negroes writhed and squirmed in the moonlight . . . now with their heads thrown back, now bent over their instruments like piping fauns. And from trombones and saxophone ceaselessly whined a blended melody, sometime riotous and jubilant, sometimes haunting and plaintive as a death-dance from the Congo's heart" (28). This description serves a very specific function in the economy of Fitzgerald's narrative, and in the economy of Fitzgerald's entire oeuvre, namely the function of signifying an exotic otherness that legitimates the authenticity of Fitzgerald and of a number of his characters.

We see this in the "offshore pirate" of Fitzgerald's narrative, the affluent Toby Moreland whose use of jazz parallels Fitzgerald's. In this narrative, Toby uses the alias of Curtis Carlyle to pose as a "ragtime bank robber" (27) who has abandoned an extremely successful career in jazz out of a revulsion for "gibbering round a stage with a lot of black men" and has absconded with a stolen fortune capable of propelling him into the ranks of what he calls "the aristocracy." The object of Toby's charade is to woo and win the rebellious flapper Ardita who has nothing but scorn for established social conventions. In order to appear to Ardita as "a romantic figure," Toby surrounds himself with six African American bandmates. According to the account that Toby/Carlyle gives of himself to Ardita, these men follow him out of deference to his superior musicianship and "peculiar sense of rhythm" (15). Toby uses the fiction of his mastery of African American music to build an image of himself as capable of evoking Ardita's admiration. In his wooing of Ardita, jazz is merely a prop intended to signify Toby/Carlyle's ability to see beyond what Ardita calls the "bleakness" and "dull gray mist" of the strictures of dominant society. Toby's tale of immersion in, and mastery of, African American music (and musicians—it is important that Carlyle/Toby's bandmates are said to follow him out of admiration and acknowledgment of his superiority) is enough to pique Ardita's interest but is not sufficient to arouse her emotions. If it were, this would mean that Ardita was capable of love for a black man, an impossibility in Fitzgerald's literary imagination and indeed in the white literary imagination of the period. Instead it is necessary for Toby to construct a narrative in which he triumphs in the field of jazz only to feel revulsion at his triumph and for the life that playing jazz creates for him. He makes it clear to Ardita that he was ashamed at "playing the role of the eternal monkey" and of being seen as "a damn, bobbing, squawking clown" (17).

What wins over Ardita is not Toby's imagined prowess at ragtime but his dream of rising out of the realm of ragtime and the companionship of black men to achieve "the luxury of leisure" that he calls "aristocracy." Toby constructs himself as a figure of otherness aspiring to sameness rather than as a figure of absolute otherness. His story succeeds because Ardita sees in him a figure that confirms her own values: scorn for convention coupled with worship of the prerogatives of wealth. To be a worthy mate for Ardita, Toby has to be a figure that passes through jazz in order to arrive at aristocracy. His attraction lies in his combination of unusual means with traditional ends, a combination that temporarily valorizes jazz only in order to ultimately denigrate it as unworthy: his story imagines a gradual accumulation of wealth through a career in jazz as less worthy than armed robbery.

Toby's use of jazz to woo Ardita evinces an attitude toward jazz that is a mixture of attraction and repulsion, an attitude shared not only by Fitzgerald but also by the majority of the white literary production of Fitzgerald's age. This attitude admires the vitality and alterity of jazz while sensing in it a threat to some of the most entrenched American convictions and values. As a result, jazz appears in the literature of the period almost exclusively as a symptom of mainstream society's discontents rather than as a structure embodying a unique set of values.[10] As in "The Offshore Pirate" and in Toby's ensconced narrative, jazz functions as a prop, a kind of raw material to power narrative flow as well as an arena for protagonists to test themselves in without fully risking themselves. Toby's uncle imagines his nephew as being at risk with "the six strange niggers" who he has hired to enact the drama that results in his winning of Ardita's affections. This is a fear that the reader is invited to share, for it is the only hint that Toby has risked anything in what is essentially a rather absurd charade. The presence of black jazz musicians in the tale legitimizes Toby as a protagonist as well as legitimizing him as a suitor to Ardita.

In Fitzgerald's story, jazz musicians enter the scene only through the dictates of white economic power. The same is true in the scene from James Weldon Johnson's *The Autobiography of an Ex-Colored Man* that I want to consider next. In this scene, which takes place in Berlin, the nameless narrator of the novel, who is traveling with his white patron, plays ragtime for "a party of men composed of artists, musicians[, and] writers" (140). The patron's intent at the party is to astonish his guests with a novel form of entertainment. Like Toby in "The Offshore Pirate," the narrator's patron uses jazz as a prop, as a form of exotic spice with which to flavor his dinner parties.

The patron and his guests are representatives of a class "who were ever expecting to find happiness in novelty" (119); for them this novelty is the chief value of ragtime.[11] The narrator's millionaire patron makes clear the importance that he places upon the music's novelty when he stipulates that the narrator perform exclusively for him. In doing this, the patron attempts to transform the narrator's ragtime into one of his own possessions, an object seen as having a novelty value that will wear out with overuse. The patron sees in jazz a raw material to be used, but not overused, in the dramas of self-presentation that he stages at his parties.

At his Berlin party, the patron intends to astonish and amaze his guests with "his" discovery, but instead of the astonishment and delight that had greeted the narrator's music in the United States, here the narrator's performance of "the most intricate rag-time [he] knew" is answered by an act of violent usurpation: "Before there was time for anybody to express an opinion on what I had done, a big bespectacled, bushy-headed man rushed over, and, shoving me out of the chair, exclaimed: 'Get up! Get up!' He seated himself at the piano, and, taking the theme of my rag-time, played it through first in straight chords; then varied and developed it through every known musical form" (141–42).

The patron's German guest may not have acted in the way that the patron would have expected or preferred, but he certainly acts in a manner that the patron should be familiar with, for his pianistic appropriation of the narrator's ragtime is a formal analog to the patron's appropriation of the same music. The German guest extracts what he sees as the essence of the narrator's performance (the theme) and transports it into the forms of the European classical tradition. He too treats the narrator's ragtime as a kind of raw material, a material that can be contained in classical forms and utilized to further the ends of these forms. In taking the narrator's place at the piano, he usurps not only the prerogative of the patron to use the narrator's music for his own ends but also the prerogative of the narrator to determine the fate of his piece's theme. No matter what the intent of the German guest is (and it is unclear whether his act is an admiring attempt at imitation or a dismissive demonstration of ragtime's rudimentary thematic construction), his usurpation of the narrator's place at the piano is an act of conceptual violence that reduces everything vital and unknown in the narrator's ragtime to the well-known forms of classical music. The ability of the German guest to do this depends not on any superiority of musical knowledge but only on the social relations that dictate that a guest of the narrator's employer take precedence over one of his employees. A comparison of what the narrator plays at the piano to what the German plays makes this dramatically clear: the narrator pulls from the piano a dazzling display of rhythmic ingenuity and vitality, while the German guest follows this with a bland academic exercise of theme and variation, the kind of exercise that students at music conservatories are routinely assigned. Unlike the cutting contests of the ragtime and stride scene in New York, where the narrator learned to play, here the competition of value is decided in advance by a cultural hierarchy that can value only innovations that take place within the categories of aesthetic form it already knows and cherishes. What Johnson dramatizes in this scene is the way that the forces embodied in existing social relations determine aesthetic values. Aesthetic values flow from the positions at the top of the social hierarchy, enabling a particular vision and particular myopia to represent itself as both universal and universally superior. It is this mechanism that renders the German guest capable of believing that he can legitimately take the narrator's place at the piano and that renders him deaf to ragtime's true character. The German guest sees the essence of this ragtime as thematic, but as Johnson writes in his preface to the *Book of American Negro Poetry*, "the chief characteristic of Ragtime is rhythm" (18), and anyone "familiar with Ragtime may note that its chief charm is not in melody, but in rhythms" (12). In concentrating on the main theme of the narrator's piece, the bespectacled German guest overlooks its most crucial aspect. He sees the music through the myopic lenses of the European classical tradition that he embodies, a tradition that is unable to grasp the unique rhythmic genius at the core of ragtime. His transportation of the theme of the narrator's piece into the forms of classical music, and the containment and subsumption of the narrator's piece that this transportation attempts, depend upon an avoidance or repression of the rhythmic aspects of this piece.

In this the German guest is not alone, as we can see from the tack taken by a denunciation of jazz that appeared in the New Orleans *Times Picayune* in 1918, a denunciation whose main strategy is to hammer home the point that "rhythm is not necessarily music" (O'Meally 436). The denunciation, avoidance, or repression of the music's manipulation of rhythm is the most constant and most important strategy governing hegemonic America's reaction to jazz and ragtime. Like the German at the piano, most Americans struggled to make sense of jazz by fitting it into narrative structures familiar to them, a process requiring that jazz be seen as an object not essentially different from objects encountered in the past. This is the strategy of the German and the classical music tradition that he represents, and it is also the strategy of the novel. Both conspire to make of jazz a raw material that can be incorporated or subsumed. The major shortcoming of this strategy is that it fails to comprehend jazz; for jazz is not an object but is itself a mode of relating to objects. To see it as an object is to ignore the rhythm that most defines jazz and gives it its own form of temporality. Rhythm cannot be accounted for as an object, for as Leopold Senghor writes, rhythm "is the most perceptible and least material thing" (qtd. in Chernoff 23). Rhythm is neither material nor an object but is in itself both a model for encountering and configuring objects and a mode of perception. The suppression of rhythm that characterizes the majority reaction to jazz misrecognizes the music as an object, a misrepresentation that fails to come to terms with the fact that jazz is a rival mode of knowledge.

Acknowledging this fact makes it clear that the strategies of Toby in Fitzgerald's "The Offshore Pirate," of Fitzgerald himself, of Johnson's German at the piano, and of any novel that attempts to make of jazz mere material for the advancement of plot must fail. Jazz cannot be only material or content, for it is itself a radical innovation in form. The encounter of jazz and the novel is an encounter of two forms, an encounter that inevitably alters the form of the novel. To account for the relationship between jazz and the novel, then, it is not enough to examine the way that jazz is represented in the novel. Attention must be shifted to the manipulations and rethinkings of form that the encounter between jazz and the novel necessitates, particularly in the area in which rhythm has its largest impact: the way in which novelistic form configures time. To do this, we must turn to a consideration of the way that the form of jazz and the form of the novel treat temporality.

Jazz

Jazz's insistent dependence on, and manipulation of, repetition manifests an attitude toward time that is both cyclical and social. Cyclical because in jazz chord progressions, rhythmic patterns, melodies, and riffs are repeated without any allusion to a goal outside of themselves. These repetitions have a meaning and weight separate from their position in a cohesive whole that would subsume them; because of this, they do not justify themselves as part of a developmental progression toward an ultimate goal. For Snead, this question of orientation toward a goal is key to understanding different cultural orientations toward repetition. "In European culture," he asserts, "the 'goal' is always clear," whereas in black culture the goal, "if there is a goal [an important if!] . . . is always deferred" (69). Insofar as there is a goal in the embrace of repetition that Snead sees as characteristic of black culture, its function is only to open up the space for the circulation of repetition. Jazz, and other African American musical forms, utilizes the horizon of the future only as an excuse for its insistent emphasis on the present. Though not without its own form of entanglement with the past and the future, jazz is the music of the present.

Jazz announces its tarrying with the present through its perpetual performance of a "continuous, implied, and sometimes-sounded pulse [that] serves as the reference" for everything that occurs in the music. This pulse grounds every melodic, rhythmic, and harmonic variation that a jazz performance creates, no matter how complex these variations are and how far they appear to move away from this pulse. In his article "Ring Shout, Signifyin(g), and Jazz Analysis," Samuel A. Floyd Jr. refers to this as "the time-line concept of African music" (407), pointing out the derivation of this aspect of jazz performance from the ring shouts performed by African Americans since at least the beginning of the nineteenth century but also pointing out that in adopting this concept jazz moves from the variable, accelerating tempo of the ring shout and substitutes a consistency that is virtually metronomic (but also, as we shall see, much more than metronomic). The great pianist James P. Johnson, who ruled the musical world of Manhattan throughout the 1920s and was a crucial figure in the transition from ragtime to jazz, described the solid bass lines he played in his left hand as "like a metronome" (Brown 87). This metronomic ticking out of the beat is an intrinsic aspect of virtually all jazz performance, and one that, like the ticking of a clock, insists on the primacy of the present moment and on its constant and never ending repetition. The improvised nature of jazz is another component of the music's powerful orientation to the present. The music forces each performer to play a part that is not determined in advance but that is created on the spot as the music unfolds, demanding from performers, listeners, and dancers a sharp focus on the present that is unlike that of any other art form. The intense excitement, bordering on hysteria, that jazz generated in the 1910s, 1920s, and 1930s is the result of the music's unprecedented ability to create a musical flow out of a seemingly endless series of sharply focused moments. This flow was the production of a new form of aesthetic continuity, a continuity that in Snead's words "attempts to confront accident and rupture not by covering them over but by making room for them inside the system itself" (69–70), that is, by confronting the truth that lived time is at least partially a mere succession of events with no necessary relationship to each other. This truth is one that cannot be confronted individually, for the result would be a desultory and haphazard succession without form or significance. The forbidding austerity of naked succession can only be approached collectively, through the maintenance of a metronomically objective community time. For Louis Armstrong or any other jazz musician to engage in their virtuousic significatory flights of improvisation, they have to have absolute assurance that the improvised accompaniment of the rest of the band will stay within the realm defined by the organizing principle of repetition. If they stray from this principle, if they attempt to progress away from their dwelling in and on the present, the rhythm will not be there for the soloist to return to. Jazz is a collective music embodying a collective form of time that is socially maintained so that there can be a series of collective or individual solos. Snead refers to this form of collectively performed time as the maintenance or sustenance of a thing (whether ritual, dance, or beat) "there for you to pick . . . up when you come back to get it" (69). The jazz imperative to never drop the beat keeps a collective time afloat so that each performer can depart from, return to, toy with, push, pull, or ride on the beat as the vicissitudes of the performative moment require.[12]

Jazz bases itself on repetitive cycles that allow any piece to be compressed or telescoped as the performance situation requires: three minutes for a recording session, one minute to signal a band's impending break, fifteen minutes for a really jumping dance hall, or all night for a Kansas City jam session. The repetitive maintenance of "a thing there for you to pick . . . up when you come back to get it" extends beyond the boundaries of any one performance. The implication at the end of any jazz piece is that the halt in rhythm is only temporary and that it will soon be picked up again by the same or a different group of musicians. This gives jazz form, especially its beginnings and endings, a different valence than the form of something like a novel or a symphony, where an ending is supposed to come at a necessary and fixed point that perfectly seals off the entire form and retroactively bestows on it a strongly felt cohesion. Jazz's beginnings and endings are, in a certain sense, arbitrary, as befits a form that reflects a vision of life that Albert Murray describes as "a *ceaseless* struggle for form against chaos" (*Hero and the Blues* 16). Because this struggle is ceaseless and because jazz's continuity is one that incorporates discontinuity within itself, the ending of a jazz piece does not signal the culmination of a uniquely necessary and never to be repeated developmental process. It signals a temporary and context-determined cessation of a particular collectively maintained form of repetitive rhythm. Jazz's utilization of repetition redefines form, transforming it into an open-ended and contingent vehicle.

Although repetition is crucial for jazz, it alone does not adequately characterize the music's treatment of rhythm or its configuration of temporality. Jazz performers like James P. Johnson and Duke Ellington consistently maintain a metronomic beat, *but* what is most uniquely important about jazz rhythm is its ability to create a rhythmic flow that is both metronomic and something excessively more than metronomic, in other words, its ability to swing. In his preface to the *Book of American Negro Spirituals*, James Weldon Johnson describes swing as a swaying of the body that marks "the regular beat or, better, surge, for it is something stronger than a beat, and is more or less, not precisely, strict in time" (Johnson 30). Here Johnson describes a rhythm that both marks a regular beat and, for lack of a better word, mocks it in its departure from it ("more or less"). Johnson goes on to say that "the Negro loves nothing better then to play with the fundamental time beat" (30) indicating a relationship to metronomic time that both acknowledges its power over the individual and allows the individual subject (whether musician, dancer, or listener) an expressive power that lies in his ability to play around (Andrews 52), or play with, the space within the beat. Note the hesitation in which Johnson replaces "beat" with "surge," indicating that swing is a way of playing a beat that highlights not its isolated regularly reproducible quality but its propensity to relate itself to the beats that follow or precede it, either surging ahead or dragging behind. According to Snead, "beat is an entity of relation" (68), and swing is an acknowledgement of this relational quality, a pushing or pulling on the beat so that individual beats lean (or "swing") toward each other.

Swing is a notoriously elusive quality. Symptomatic of this elusiveness are the multiple attempts that have been made to accurately notate swing eighth notes. Everything from eighth notes with legato and staccato markings to pairs of dotted eighth and sixteenth notes to tied groupings of triplets in 4/4 time have been tried. While the last seems to most clearly approximate the polymetric tension of swing, the important thing to recognize here is the fact that swing is a quality that eludes European musical notation's power of representation. Swing is both in excess of, and foreign to, the sense of time and rhythm embodied in European musical notation.

This is because, as Adorno puts it in *Minima Moralia*, "historically, the notion of time is itself formed on the basis of the order of ownership" (79). European musical notation is designed to function with a conception of time based on the model of possessive individualism, which assumes "that man is free and human by virtue of his sole proprietorship of his own person, and that human society is essentially a series of market relations" (Macpherson 43). Possessive individualism necessitates a construction of time that facilitates calculability, both of an individual's labor and of the future, while obscuring its own historical formulation by representing itself as transcendent rather than the function of relations between individuals. The time bound up with possessive individualism must configure the future as a quantifiable entity because of its imagination of the world as containing nothing that exceeds market relations, and because it makes the individual into a form of property that, at least since Bentham, has been thought in terms of expectation. According to Bentham, "property is nothing but the basis of expectation, consist[ing] in an established expectation, in the persuasion of being able to draw such and such advantage from the thing possessed" (qtd. in C. Harris 280). In a society based on possessive individualism, everything is based on property, and property is a form of extending the social structure of ownership into the future. In the twentieth century, the futural aspect of property takes on an increasing importance, for, as C. B. Macpherson notes, this period is one characterized by the increased preeminence of corporations, and "the rise of the corporation as the dominant form of business enterprise has meant that the dominant form of property is the *expectation* of revenue" (8). The stress that this places on a calculable future, compounded by the economic emergence of speculation on futures, conspires to promote and naturalize "a habit of mind in which the future is taken as if it were present" (Carroll 66). The epistemology and temporality of possessive individualism foster substantialist illusions by transforming everything, even the future, into discrete, possessible objects whose value is exhausted by the calculations of the market. In this vision, time is merely a measuring stick for market calculations and thus is willfully blind to anything outside the market, including the nonmarket origins of the material wealth produced by slavery.

Under slavery, African Americans were the content of market relations and prohibited from being actors in market society. Thus, the forms of sociality that they evolved coalesced around a quite different notion of individuality and humanity, a notion intimately familiar with the fact that men and women could be both human and free only in the sense of commodities freely bought and sold.[13] The enforced separation of individuals along the lines of the category of color guaranteed that the group on each side of the color line would have their own time. However, these different notions of time are not symmetrical, for African Americans were forced to be aware of and to conform to the time of their owners and were severely constrained in the kinds of social organization they were allowed to construct. As a result, the African American sense of time has a special relation to the dominant American sense of time, a relation that is both parasitic and parodic. African American time is constructed in the interstices of American time. This is, strictly speaking, only true of the slavery period, but both the cultural continuity of African American aesthetic forms and the continued oppression of African Americans makes it almost as true of the 1910s and 1920s. The emergence of jazz occurs in the wake of the Supreme Court's

1896 ruling in *Plessy v. Ferguson*, a ruling that not only licenses state-sanctioned apartheid but accepts Plessy's lawyer's argument that race is property and that property is a form of expectation. Swing is a rhythmic performance of a time-consciousness all too familiar with the paradoxes of a system in which persons either owned property or were themselves property. In this context, it makes perfect sense that swing exceeds and subverts the musical conception of time as a linear teleological process.[14]

Because the concepts derived from the European musical tradition are in-adequate to swing, one must turn elsewhere for resources capable of making its elusiveness speak. One such resource is the reading of a 1926 Jelly Roll Morton performance found in Samuel A. Floyd Jr.'s *The Power of Black Music*. In this reading, Floyd turns to Henry Louis Gates Jr.'s work on the African American rhetorical tradition of Signifyin(g) in order to define swing as "a quality that manifests itself when sound events Signify on the time line against the flow of its pulse, making the pulse freely lilt; this troping of the time line creates the slight resistances that result in the driving, *swinging*, rhythmic persistence that we find in all African American music but that is most vividly present in jazz" (115n13). Floyd defines swing as the result of a mode of troping, and in the "time line" concept of jazz the swing of the rhythm section tropes a fixed Western clock time by expressing it and critiquing it at the same time. Floyd refers to this dual attitude as "Call-Response," a musical principle that tropes what it performs. Call-Response, the "musical trope of tropes," drops the "and" of the musical device of call and response, which is one manifestation of Call-Response, in order to indicate the way swing transforms any musical note, phrase, rhythm, or sound into a manifestation of semantic value that is both a figure and its revision and a collapsing of the distinction between figure and revision. The temporal division of the "and" is excised, creating a restless, dynamic surge of a present fully divided from neither past nor future. The extent to which this repetitive, swung jazz time is subversive of teleological time cannot be overstated.

The Novel

The novel is the genre of linear, progressive time. Its burden is to transform crude unshaped succession into a teleological pattern imbued with meaning.[15] Its transformation of contingency into necessity relies on a strict adherence to a three-part schema of time in which the past, the present, and the future all are assigned specific and unequal tasks. Unequal because the novel is an essentially proleptic form, a form that stakes everything on the ability of the future to resolve the aporias of the present and of the past. In doing so the novel articulates the hegemonic form of Western capitalist subjectivity, a subjectivity that is futurally oriented and that, according to Adorno and Horkheimer, "owes its existence to the sacrifice of the present moment to the future" (51). For Adorno and Horkheimer, the novel is the story of a hero who "loses himself in order to find himself" (48). The ur-model for them is Odysseus, who finds himself only through a process of "estrangement from nature," which guarantees that the self that he refinds has none of the richness of the self that he has lost.[16] The condition of his, or of any other novelistic hero's, refinding of himself depends upon the transference of pleasure and fulfillment to a future that, like Althusser's "lonely hour of the last instance," never arrives.[17] Homer's *Odyssey*, and the line of novels that follow it, constructs a subjectivity that relates all its experiences to some future horizon, whether spiritual, economic, or utopian. It enshrines a model of time that cannot countenance repetition or mere succession. In the novel every step is either along an upward or downward path and can never be a mere marking time. This configuration of temporality with its slavish obedience to the dictates of the future gives short shrift to the past as well as to the present. While the present is transformed into a mere stepping stone to the future, the threefold schema that the novel enshrines negates "the past by referring [its] power behind the barrier of the unrepeatable and placing it at the disposal of the present as practicable knowledge" (Adorno and Horkheimer 32). The subjectivity produced by the novel does not acknowledge any power of the past over it but sees the past only as raw material for its own use. For Adorno and Horkheimer, this transformation of the past into a mere inert resource is part of the dialectic of enlightenment, the separation of a rational subject, powerful but self-defeating, from the mythic past in which it was a helpless object of the forces of nature. The mythic past is always characterized by repetition, and the novel polices the boundary between myth and enlightenment by enacting a ban on repetition and replacing it with either progress or decadence. Despite the fact that for Adorno and Horkheimer the subject precipitated by the novel is a false one, both swollen in its inflated and mistaken notion of its own power to shape itself and its surroundings and desiccated by its sacrificial estrangement from nature within and without, they share with the novel an outlook that sees repetition as an invidious and pernicious force, a mere capitulation to mythic enslavement.[18] This fact explains why Adorno and Horkheimer, despite their critique of the novel, look on jazz with suspicious eyes. According to them, the novel's attempt to free the individual from the mythic past of repetition is a valuable step, and the novel goes wrong not in its suppression of repetition but in its enshrinement of a stunted and ultimately irrational mode of rationality.

In this they differ sharply from the critique of James Snead with whom they otherwise share much. Like Adorno and Horkheimer, Snead sees repetition as the crucial point of difference between a culture whose cyclical view of time is linked to the observance of "periodic regeneration[s] of biological and agricultural systems" and a culture whose rationalized system of scientific and economic beliefs goes hand in hand with its linear view of time. Snead also sees the passage from one episteme and conception of temporality to another as the result of a kind of dialectic of enlightenment, an onward march of constricting rationalism that leads to a situation for European culture in which it is "never immediate, but mediated and separated from the present tense by its own future orientation" (64). Despite these important and telling similarities, Snead differs from Adorno and Horkheimer not only in his valuation of repetition but in his account of the emerging dominance of linear time. He places this time's origin not in any ur-text of Western culture but in the eighteenth-century nexus of nationalism, racism, and colonialism, a time he rightly describes as one when Europeans were "busy defining 'European culture' as separate from 'African culture,' the ultimate otherness, the final mass" (64). For Snead, the question of repetition is not only a question of history as single process, it is a question of histories both divided and conflictual, histories emerging out of the confrontations of peoples and cultures. What Snead shows us is that the European suppression and intellectual condemnation of repetition, which Adorno and Horkheimer—despite their telling critique of European thought—are a part of, is a reaction to the contacts between Europeans and Africans in the eighteenth century. The oppression, violence, and enslavement that constituted these contacts cried out for an ideological justification, and the condemnation of repetition that Adorno and Horkheimer repeat is an integral part of this justification. Taking this into account makes apparent the urgency involved in theorizing and critiquing the model of time embodied in the novel. Snead's insights allow us to see that the time of the novel sustains and focuses a mode of envisioning otherness as well as a mode of envisioning subjectivity. The link between time and the relationship of the other to the self is at least partially adumbrated in Adorno and Horkheimer; they note that the totality of Odysseus's ego can be realized "only in complete alienation from all other men, who meet [him] only in an alienated form—as enemies or as points of support, but always as tools, as things" (62). Odysseus's self-estrangement leaves him capable of seeing others only as possible profits or losses and not as individuals with their own past and future. This critique demonstrates the link between the developmental linear time of the novel and of the reifying, objectifying gaze that accompanies it, but it doesn't get at the way that this gaze depends on categories and groupings of otherness.[19]

The gaze of early twentieth-century white America may be one that sees all individuals as objects or tools, but this gaze recognizes degrees of object-hood, degrees predicated largely on what Hortense Spillers calls "the politics of melanin" ("Mama's Baby" 71). In her essay "Mama's Baby, Papa's Maybe: An American Grammar Book," Spillers makes explicit the link between a gaze determined by the politics of melanin and a specific cultural grammar, a grammar that relegates the racial other to a passive object position. This grammar draws its power from an ability to represent distinctions of force as distinctions of nature, transforming historical contingency into enshrined necessity.[20] In short, the American grammar of racial categorization is a novelistic grammar. Ascribing both cultural superiority and the power to determine cultural superiority to a position that is implicitly defined as rational, white, and upper class (and rational because white and upper class), this novelistic grammar situates African Americans in "earlier stages of either ontogenetic or phylogenetic development, or ascribe(s) to them a state of nature" (Reichardt 473). The linear progressive time of the novel needs to define alterity as inferior in order to define its own movement as a progression. The protagonist of the novel sees the situations and individuals that he encounters as elements in the process of becoming past, of becoming his past. In "Of Dogs Alive, Birds Dead, and Time to Tell a Story," Johannes Fabian points out the way this process of generating meaning partakes of the logic of the omen, a logic in which an event in the present gets constructed as "a past for narratives to build on" (192). It is the power of expectation (and here we should think of Bentham's characterization of property as expectation) that allows this to occur, both in the way that expectations shape the categories by which something seems "strange and distinctive," and thus can appear as an omen, and in the way that the expectation of later fulfillment, of the kind of meaningfulness that the endings of novels deliver, allows the dialectical encounter with experienced otherness to be suspended in favor of a future in which this otherness is overcome or assimilated. In order for novelistic encounters to be meaningful they have to be encounters between a developing subject and individuals or situations that this subject dialectically subsumes (usually by dismissing) and moves beyond. This developing subject sacrifices the present moment, both his and that of what he encounters, in order to achieve a contemplative taxonomic stance that envisions a fulfillment in the future by condemning alterity to the past. In America, the taxonomies that this process produces have always been predominately racial, figuring African Americans as "savages," "barbarians," "primitives," "atavistic," or "primal." At no time in American history has this insistent primitivist vision been more pronounced than in the 1910s and 1920s, a time in which the reaction to the increased mobility and visibility of the African American population combined with a popular understanding of Freud that moved from ontogeny to phylogeny in a way that led people to believe they could refind some (imagined) childhood exuberance and vitality in the expressions of a "younger" culture. This combination created an image of African Americans as the embodiment of a lost primitive past, which was absolutely compelling to the white imagination. Although this primitivist vision accompanied and licensed an intensification of violence against African Americans (more African Americans were lynched in the 1920s than in any other decade), it also was one of the enabling elements for the outburst of African American artistic production that characterized the Harlem Renaissance.

The dual impetus of this form of racial essentialism is at the heart of the paradoxical difficulties governing the production of both jazz and African American novels (and, in a different way, Anglo-American novels) during the first three decades of the century. In terms of both funding and dissemination, primitivism licensed African American cultural production but in a very specific and restrictive manner, placing constraints on the boundaries of this production that were shaped by assumptions of racial essence. James Reese Europe, whose career owed much to his association with the white dancing team of Vernon and Irene Castle, lamented this fact when he stated in 1919 that "the music world is controlled by a trust, and the Negro must submit to its demands or fail to have his compositions produced" (qtd. in O'Meally 419). The machinery of the production of culture was almost entirely in white hands, and this fact was not without its direct consequences for the shape that African American art took in the 1920s and 1930s. One need only think of white music reviews criticizing portions of Europe's Carnegie Hall concert for lacking authenticity,[21] or of John Hammond's later criticisms of Duke Ellington for getting away from the "Negroid roots" of his music to realize the serious barriers that primitivist conceptions placed in the way of aesthetic production.[22] Yet these primitivist conceptions were the dominant terrain, and artists mostly had to play within these conceptions or choose not to play at all (and here one thinks of Will Marion Cook smashing his violin against the desk of a journalist unable to think of him as anything other than "a Negro violinist"). Under such circumstances, the goal of many African American artists (musical or novelistic) became to work with these constraints as a way of struggling against them, an attempt to accept a given form only in order to deform or reform it. Characterizing it as one of the most urgent motivations of African American liberation, Hortense Spillers defines this goal as the attempt "to break apart, to rupture violently the laws of American behavior that make such syntax possible," that is, a syntax capable of listing African American bodies in a grammatical series alongside livestock and "a virtually endless profusion of domestic context from the culinary item to the book" ("Mama's Baby" 79). Stated in this way the question of the temporal implications of novelistic form attains its properly political valence and the burden of every novel, and particularly the novels of the period when the categories of race and time were being redefined, becomes clear: either to write with or against the developmental, taxonomic time, which since the eighteenth century has been the legacy and inheritance of the novel.

Conceived in this way, the novel becomes a potential weapon against racist epistemologies and the violent actions that they engender, which is exactly how James Weldon Johnson saw the African American production of novels. In the 1931 preface to *The Book of American Negro Poetry*, Johnson asserts that "the status of the Negro in the United States is more a question of national mental attitude toward the race than of actual conditions. And nothing will do more to change that mental attitude and raise his status than a demonstration of intellectual parity by the Negro through the production of literature and art" (9). For Johnson, the most effective response to the racism of a society in which African Americans were regularly lynched was for African Americans to produce art that could not be accounted for by the established racial hierarchies. Despite the fact that in this preface Johnson describes ragtime as one of the only true American artistic products, it is clear that ragtime (or jazz) cannot be the art form that raises the Negro's status. Because its form and logic are too radically dissimilar to the most venerated art forms of Euro-American high culture, and because it is a music associated more with the motion of dancing bodies than with intellectual contemplation, ragtime and the jazz that grew out of it are too easily dismissed as the manifestation of a primitive and natural racial essence. Only artistic products that conform to the established, valorized categories of American (and European) artistic value can achieve the status that Johnson desires.

While this makes clear the inefficacy of art that diverges too markedly from established models, art that conforms too closely to these models is not without its own problems. First of all, if it too slavishly recapitulates the form, logic, and temporality of the society from which recognition is desired, it fails to trouble the exclusionary machinations of this society and ends up reproducing these maneuvers and their underlying justifications. Too much conformity fails to produce the deformation and rupture that Spiller and Baker call for. Second, such conformity fails even in the terms that Johnson sets out, that is, it fails to register as "great literature [or] art." Despite the demand that art recognized as great reproduce cherished cultural norms and values, each "great" art work is expected to perform this task in an at least slightly innovative manner, one that expands on the tradition rather than merely repeating it. This expectation was even more pronounced in the 1910s and 1920s with their emphasis on the new. In addition there is a tendency going all the way back to Thomas Jefferson's comments on Phyllis Wheatley to see African American endeavors in literature or other traditional "high" art forms as mere imitation, a manifestation of only a parrot-like gift for mimicry. Taken together these two demands make Johnson's strategy of creating art that will raise the status of the race exceedingly difficult to execute. Art that can succeed at doing this has to conform closely enough to established aesthetic models to be recognizable as high art but diverge from these models enough to be recognized as significant contributions to this art. When you add to this the consideration that racialized epistemology is more likely to figure departures from convention as deficiencies rather than innovations, the virtual impossibility of unalloyed success becomes clear.

Confronted with these difficulties, one can easily imagine authors looking around anxiously for a possible path. What must have struck authors in such a position were the possibilities offered by the way in which jazz is able to combine repetition of what has gone before with the achievement of new combinations and effects. Samuel A Floyd Jr. ascribes this power of jazz to the fact that in it, "the how of a performance is more important than the *what*" (*Power of Black Music* 96–97). He states that "certainly African Americans have their favorite tunes, but it is what is done with and inside those tunes that the listeners look forward to, not the mere playing of them. The hearing of an old or a favorite tune may carry pleasant memories, but these memories and their quality—absent inquiry—are based in preference and nostalgia. With the *musical* experience, the expectation is that something musical will *happen* in the playing of the music, and it is the *something* that fascinates, that elevates the expectations and places the hearer in a critical mode" (97). Here it is the repetition of the same, rather than the suppression of repetition, that makes possible the emergence of something genuinely new. Jazz offers a suggestive model for negotiating the minefield of aesthetic production and the politics of cultural recognition, a model that offers a mode of linking the present and the possibility of the new to the past, which is absent from the novelistic tradition. Its emphasis on repetition evokes the past as a living and still present force rather than as an entombed body of cultural monuments available to the artist as a kind of raw material. This is crucial because, as Gerald Early has shown, the cultural struggles of the 1910s and 1920s were as much about the configuration of the past as they were about the present, the future, and the new.[23] African American artists had to shake off an image of themselves as being without any worthwhile past as a crucial part of their efforts to demonstrate their worthiness to participate in the culture of the present. Their attention to the relationship between the past and the future was an attempt to write themselves into the developmental history that America told about itself, but it was an attempt that also strove to disrupt, deform, and denaturalize this history and its reliance on racialized categories of alterity.

To do this it was necessary to attack the notion of time that subtends this developmental history, a notion of time that denies its own past. Time has a history just as much as societies, cultures, or individuals do. Time is not an ontological category but a social and historical one. Time is an instrument by and through which social life is ordered, and different socioeconomic structures engender different rhythms and lived experiences of time. Societies preserve themselves by fostering a belief that the notion of time they have created is a fixed and natural one, performing a fetishizing ritual that serves the goal of perpetuating existing economic and social relations by removing the structure of time that undergirds these relations from the realm of social and political struggle and placing it in the realm of the fixed, timeless, and immutable. The sense of natural timelessness that this process generates is what Lukács calls "phantom objectivity," a false objectivity and form of commodity fetishism that both blocks insight into the true nature of any social formation and impedes the imagining of any future that is qualitatively different from the present. Any attempt to transform society must also be an attempt to dispel this phantom objectivity, and the cultural politics that James Weldon Johnson adumbrates is no exception. The goal of the African American novelists of the 1910s, 1920s, and 1930s is at least partially the goal of breaking the stranglehold that the dominant notion of time had on the American cultural imagination by exposing the fetish as fetish and exorcising phantom objectivity by lifting the cloak of its naturalness. Before time can be appropriated or expropriated, its misrepresentation of itself as a natural form has to be translated back into the social register of relations between men. This is a necessary prerequisite to the task that Hanchard describes as "eradicat[ing] the chasm in racial time"(256).

The urgency of this goal is a second reason that jazz was so mesmerizing and important for the novelists of this period, for jazz's swing, its troping of the objective time line of an increasingly individualized and urban society, performs this demystification. Its performance of time mocks objective time, assailing its static objectivity by setting it in motion and bending it to its own will. It animates the seemingly inanimate by speaking to it in its own language, by performing a version of objective time that exposes its performative quality, dissolving its objectivity and injecting back into it the dynamics of its own making and institutionalization. The swing defined by Floyd as musical analog to Signifying tropes objective and developmental time in a particularly violent manner. Grasping this objective time, it shakes it and swings it until it yields the secrets of its violent self-enshrinement. In *Not Without Laughter*, Langston Hughes captures something of this violent urgency in his description of a specific point in a community dance when the music was no longer merely "pleasant," but "the drum-beats had become sharp with surly sound, *like* heavy waves that beat angrily on a granite rock" (100). Here the intensity of rhythm is directed against the rock-like (and the "like" is important) objectivity of time that, despite this antagonism, the drumbeats themselves still uphold, for Hughes is clear that the music is still "in" the time that it had nonchalantly "struck into" a page earlier. The point is that all the energy of opposition that swing brings to bear on an objective abstract time never leads swing totally away from this time. As a troping of this time, swing is dependant on it. It does not move away from this time to posit some absolutely other time, but tarries with it in order to toy with it. Jazz time acknowledges the powerfully inescapable hold of objective time as a governing principle because it is not governed by an aesthetic ideal that imagines a separation of art from the world. Jazz does not transcend in the way that a classical symphony attempts to but incorporates its imbrication with the social into its performance practice. In the music of Jelly Roll Morton, Duke Ellington, and Louis Armstrong we hear a virtuoso manipulation of time and rhythm harnessed both to the imperative of propelling bodies around a dance floor and to the articulation and embodiment of what Snead calls "an essentially philosophical insight about the shape of time and history" (63).

This dual imperative and dual attitude toward time is manifested most clearly in the way that James P. Johnson and the other great New York stride pianists played the function of each hand against one another. Ann Douglass describes this division as one in which the "pianist varied and mocked his traditional left-hand bass march time [which James P. Johnson insists is always "metronomic"] with his iconoclastic right-hand treble syncopation" (373). She points out that the etymology of ragtime comes from "'ragged [or broken] time' and meant 'tearing time apart'; the phrase 'to rag' also meant to tease" (368). The implication is that the interplay between the pianist's two hands is one in which the right hand teases the left, ragging and tearing at its metronomic base in order to create an effect in which objective time is both evoked and torn apart.[24] The overall effect is a deformation of time that acknowledges its power over the individual but also demonstrates that time is something performed and thus can be performed differently. A rigid, objective sense of time is a reified relation, and, as Marx insists, "these reified relations must be made to dance by singing to them their own melody" (Marx, "Contribution" 247). Jazz plays Marx's request, only in the rhythmic register rather than the melodic. With jazz's swing, the "phantom objectivity" of objective, developmental time is made to dance, to cut a caper to the mockery of its own form.

Two things follow from this. First, the magnetic pull of jazz's virtuosic engagement with form and time (and the form of time) cannot be underestimated. For a period in which the employment of traditional forms was becoming increasingly problematic, the aesthetic attitudes embodied in jazz were a revelation. Jazz's ability to build sophisticated and compelling structures without recourse to the established techniques of Western art held immense appeal to authors who saw Western art as either irredeemably corrupt or essentially moribund. With its power of creating new combinations without any need to build extended monumental forms (like the ones that Schoenberg was driven to construct at almost exactly the same time as jazz's emergence), jazz's strategies held a compelling attraction.[25] Although jazz grew out of a longstanding tradition of African American performance from which it drew its strategies, there is no question that the period of Jelly Roll Morton, James P. Johnson, James Reese Europe, Louis Armstrong, Fletcher Henderson, and Duke Ellington was a period in which these strategies were raised to a new level and given a heightened power and intensity.

The ragtime craze of the 1910s and the christening of the 1920s as the Jazz Age depended on new trends in social dancing and new forms of cultural dissemination, but these both depended on, as well as fostered, the growth of a group of professional musicians who gave the tradition of African American music making an increasingly potent edge. The flowering of jazz performance leading up to and continuing after the officially recognized Jazz Age was an unprecedented event in American history, and the urgency of this new sound and its cultural implications could not have failed to leave a mark on the aesthetic practices of the novelists who followed in its wake.

The second fact entailed by the signifying critique of objective time that jazz performs is that jazz could not have come upon the broad stage of widespread cultural recognition without being met by an intense resistance. Jazz challenges the notion of time that the dominant form of American identity based itself on. As cultural historians like Gerald Early and Kathy Ogren have pointed out, jazz in the 1920s was "an assault on Euro-centric cultural hegemony" (Early 403), and many critics were quick to recognize and denounce it as such. The spread of jazz engendered a large and pervasive body of criticism that excoriated jazz's pernicious effects, attaching signifiers such as "sinful," "barbaric," "decadent," savage," "soulless," and "mechanistic" to the music. This is the reception of jazz that is familiar to us due to the work of historians like Ogren and Leonard, a reception perhaps best summed up by the title of an article in The *Ladies' Home Journal*, "Does Jazz Put the Sin in Syncopation?"[26]

Despite this type of vehement resistance to jazz, the music grew rapidly in popularity, aided by the demands of the nascent recording and radio industries. Accompanying this rise in jazz's popularity was a form of resistance to it quite different than the outright denunciation that sees jazz as mere depravity. Much more insidious, this form of resistance acknowledges the vitality and staying power of jazz but sees in it a rough crudeness in need of refinement. When

Paul Whiteman stated his desire "to make an honest lady out of jazz" (116), he summed up this form of resistance and its intent to neutralize the most radical and unsettlingly critical aspects of the music through processes of appropriation, incorporation, and accommodation rather than overt resistance. The conductor Serge Koussevitsky, voicing an opinion similar to Whiteman's, compares this process to that of racial assimilation: jazz's "contribution to the music of the past will have the same revivifying effect as the injection of the new, and in the larger sense, vulgar blood into dying aristocracy" (Locke 221). Despite Koussevitsky's positive valorization of jazz, he takes it as self-evident that the music's proper role is as raw material to be incorporated or assimilated by these forms.[27] Koussevitsky relies on the traditional binary that figures the products of darker and "more primitive" races as content and reserves the prerogatives of form giving to "higher" and lighter races.[28] He is not alone in doing this, for even a critic like J. A. Rogers, the music critic for the *Messenger*, ends his essay on jazz in *The New Negro* with the advice that rather than protesting against jazz, it is wiser to "try to lift and divert it into nobler channels" (224). For both Koussevitsky and Rogers, the value of jazz lies not in its present shape, but in its future possibilities. Their statements exemplify a form of resistance that attempts to neutralize jazz's insistence on the present by figuring it as a crude potentiality whose true form lies in the future. Earlier in his *New Negro* article, Rogers states that "jazz has a great future. It is rapidly being sublimated" (221).

For Rogers, jazz's great future lies in its ability to be sublimated, that is, to be transformed into something less physical and more spiritual, to leave behind its childish insistence on instant gratification and develop into something more mature.[29] Rogers ties jazz's worth to its capability of fitting into a developmental form and of following the trajectory of progressive development epitomized in the bildungsroman. The impulse of the form of resistance to jazz that Koussevitsky's, Whiteman's, and Roger's statements are characteristic of is a narrativizing impulse. This impulse looks at jazz from the perspective of established Western cultural forms (the novel, the symphony, etc.) and willfully envisions it not as a contemporaneous rival to these forms but as something that lies, in a certain sense, behind these forms. Denied of coevalness, jazz is seen as a product that has not (and the product of a people who have not) shared the nineteenth and early twentieth century with the novel and the symphony (and their white creators) but has lingered in an atavistic timelessness and is now in need of catching up. This narrative vision looks upon threatening alterity and renders it recognizable by imposing a temporal veil between itself and its object, willfully constructing jazz as a holdover or survival from an earlier, less developed, and already surpassed form of existence. By situating jazz on a developmental time line whose fulfillment is entirely compatible with dominant society's own story, this primitivising vision blocked or forestalled the possibility of seeing in jazz challenges or possible alternatives to this story and the structuring of society that it underwrites. In short, jazz is figured as a belated development and as inert material to be fit into a progressive narrative.

Paul Whiteman's Aeolian Hall concert of 1924 is a perfect example of this kind of attempt to harness jazz to a developmental narrative. Whiteman's concert was an attempt to mollify critics who saw in jazz nothing but a degradation of all respectable values. Whiteman's bid to make an "honest lady" out of jazz took place in a concert hall associated with highbrow classical music and made use of a program structured like a novelistic narrative. Gerald Early writes that "starting from the earliest white jazz, 'Livery Stable Blues,' recorded by the Original Dixieland Jazz Band in 1917, the first jazz record, Whiteman's band worked its way in a clearly evolutionary manner to Victor Herbert's 'Serenades' and George Gershwin's 'Rhapsody in Blue,' before concluding with Elgar's 'Pomp and Circumstance'"(409).[30] Striving to demonstrate the temporal distance between the kind of "refined" and heavily arranged music that Whiteman's orchestra customarily played and the "crude" sounds of earlier jazz, the program of the concert was designed to show how jazz had progressed, had been "sublimated," in Roger's terms, and to demonstrate that Whiteman, the "king of jazz," had successfully tamed the wild beast, transforming it into a music compatible with even the most highbrow vision of culture and civilization. His concert told a developmental tale of jazz conforming itself to a shape that authenticated the existing shape of American society.

In sketching this self-authenticating tale of jazz's development, Whiteman creates what Early refers to as "a revisionist history that has excised the presence of blacks as creators of this music" (409). Whiteman's program starts with the white Original Dixieland Jazz Band and ends with the white Edward Elgar with no African American musicians or composers alluded to in between. His press release for the concert asserts that the "discordant jazz" with which the concert starts "sprang into existence about ten years ago from nowhere in particular." The narrative tale of jazz that Whiteman's concert tells is one in which the music emerges out of a no place that occludes its connection to either African American musicians and dancers or to changing African American attitudes and experiences. The Aeolian Hall concert exemplifies the strategy of containing and blunting the most unsettling and revolutionary aspects of jazz by harnessing the music in a developmental narrative that figures it as a "stepping stone" to a future palatable to white Americans, a future that is a reassuring continuation of the present and the past.[31]

Whiteman's concert attempted to sublimate jazz and fit it into a developmental narrative, but the concert did not succeed in the way that Whiteman had intended. Whiteman's intent was that the first section of the program, which started with the Original Dixieland Jazz Band's "Livery Stable Blues," serve as a demonstration of the artistic poverty and crudity of the early jazz antecedent to the "refined" music that Whiteman's orchestra had become famous playing. Intentionally exaggerating the tonal distortions, growls, animal noises, and sound effects that were an intrinsic part of the popularity of "Livery Stable Blues," Whiteman and his musicians played the piece in a manner that they were sure would elicit laughter and ridicule. Instead, the audience reacted with the same kind of applause and approval with which they responded to the rest of the pieces on the program. Whiteman's attempt to draw a sharp distinction between what he thought of as primitive jazz and his own style of symphonic jazz failed, largely because of Whiteman's inability to grasp the complexity of the cultural debate over jazz that his concert was entering into.

This debate, and the larger debate over the shape of early twentieth-century American culture that it is inextricably bound up with, was primarily a debate between traditionalists and modernists; Whiteman, despite his occupation as purveyor and "king" of jazz, belongs in the traditionalist camp. This is a point that Gerald Early makes convincingly in *The Culture of Bruising*. Early points to Whiteman's profound respect for classical music, his consistent reference to the composers in this tradition as "the masters," and his sense of himself as working on "the same job" as them (403). As a cultural traditionalist, Whiteman possessed a faith in progress that led him to imagine himself capable of embracing certain aspects of jazz while preserving the teleological, developmental thrust of traditional "high" art. In doing so, he overestimated the hegemonic hold that the ideals of high art had on his audience, an audience that responded positively rather than negatively to Whiteman's attempt to parody "crude" jazz because of their inability or unwillingness to appreciate this jazz merely as a "stepping stone" to future aesthetic pleasure. They expected a less delayed gratification, evidence of the fact that they were more attuned to the changing shape of culture and society than Whiteman was. As Alain Locke put it in *The New Negro*, published a year after Whiteman's concert, "a transformed and transforming psychology permeates the masses" (7). Neither high cultural ideals nor teleological conceptions of developmental progress had anything near the weight that transformation and change had in the American imagination of the period, both conceptually and experientially. The "unsettling demographic fluidities" of unprecedented external (until 1924) and internal migration, the rapid rise of new technologies of social recreation, and the increasing Fordism and Taylorization of working conditions all contributed to a flood of change that no clinging to traditionalist values, no matter how vehemently determined, could resist. In the face of this wave of change, Whiteman was in the paradoxical position of presenting to his audience the jazz whose vogue, Locke tells us, is "the symptom of a profound and cultural unrest and change" (Locke, *Negro and His Music,* 88); at the same time, Whiteman was presenting jazz from a traditionalist position, which the transfiguration of the American cultural landscape had already doomed to defeat. Whiteman's failure to get his audience to respond to his music in a way that confirmed the division between high and low art, between "crude" and "refined" jazz, is indicative of the inability of traditional, developmental, high art forms to respond to the sea change in American culture taking place at the time of his Aeolian Hall concert. For, as Houston Baker writes in *Modernism and the Harlem Renaissance,* this change "is most accurately defined as an acknowledgment of radical uncertainty" (3), an acknowledgment incompatible with the faith in progress that the developmental form of Whiteman's concert depends upon. In the face of this kind of change, only forms that can bend to accommodate "radical uncertainty" and its disruption of traditional notions of progress can have any claim to relevance or exert any influence on the imagination of an America gripped by the temporal implications of jazz rhythm.

To put it another way, the form of Whiteman's concert is like a novel in its attempt to tell a tale of developmental continuity, but it is unlike modernist novels in its failure to register the shifting valence of time and progress that accompanied American society's reconfiguration of itself. It exemplifies the impulse to harness and contain jazz temporality but uses a form nowhere near sophisticated enough to begin to do this. In effect, Whiteman's failure is the jumping off point for the American modernist novel, the formalist innovations of which can best be read as attempts to evolve structures equal to an encounter with the temporal sophistication of jazz.

Like Whiteman, and like Johnson's spectacled German and Fitzgerald's wealthy Toby, the Anglo-American novels of modernism strive to master and domesticate jazz, but unlike them, the most important of these novels recognize that jazz rhythm contains a truth about the future shape of culture insusceptible to the reinstatement of any master narrative of progress or development. The white modernists that I treat in this study saw jazz as Locke saw it, as the symptom of profound cultural unrest and change. They heard in its syncopation the death knell of traditional culture and learned from it that the aesthetic forms that would reign in the emerging landscape would not be the self-contained forms based on the total suspension of the present in favor of the future that had been dominant in the past. If the future was to regain its enshrined position as the approved repository of meaning in American culture, it could only do so by negotiating a pact with the present that gave it its due. Jazz signified that the future could no longer dominate the cultural imagination as it once had.

The change that gripped American society at the time of Whiteman's concert and James Weldon Johnson's novel was a change of temporal horizon, a shift of emphasis from the future to the present that resulted from imperatives both cultural and economic. The cultural causes of this shift have been treated extensively and are well summed up by Houston Baker in his description of what he calls "the profound shift in what can be taken as unquestionable assumptions about the meaning of human life" (5). If we accept Baker's characterization of this shift as "an acknowledgment of radical uncertainty"(3), then it is clear that this shift has to shake the subordination of the present to the future. If it is uncertain where the present leads to (or if it leads anywhere at all), then it makes little sense to value it only in terms of its future redemption. The present's value increases when it can no longer be reliably tied to an attractive or predictable future.

Economic Considerations

Less widely acknowledged are the economic causes of this temporal shift. These causes are perhaps best treated in Chip Rhodes's *Structures of the Jazz Age*, where Rhodes shows them to be the function of the demise of "a regime of extensive accumulation and the birth of a regime of intensive accumulation" (79). Following Michel Aglietta's thesis in *A Theory of Capitalist Regulation*, Rhodes describes the 1920s as the period in which the production and consumption of consumer durables (automobiles, Victrolas, radios, and so on) became the most crucial aspect of the American economy. For the first time, the importance of goods sold in the marketplace for direct consumption eclipsed the importance of the production of means of production or capital goods sold to other capitalists. The economy became increasingly driven by the sale of consumer goods, and this shift required a corresponding shift in the practices of both capitalists and laborers. For the capitalist the increased importance of consumer goods meant that "capital must no longer be hoarded; it must be invested," while for laborers it meant that their chief value in the economy came to lie not in their ability to produce but in their ability to consume (Rhodes 82). For both, a shift from an orientation toward the future to an orientation to the present was required if the demands of the new economic situation were to be met. As Rhodes points out, this temporal reorientation was necessarily accompanied by a reconfiguration of subjectivity, an ideologically motivated change that devalued the traditional virtues of hard work, thrift, and duty and valorized in their place the new skills of taste, discrimination, and self-fashioning. As the dictates of consumption increased their hegemony, these new skills crystallized in a new form of subjectivity and displaced what Rhodes calls the Puritan subject, a subject organized around the ability to earn and save capital. The Puritan, producing subject, in its orientation toward the future and denial of immediate gratification in favor of greater wealth to come, is gradually replaced by the subject of consumption who suspends Puritan self-denial in the belief that the future is at least partially accessible in the present in the form of commodities: the new, the fashionable, the up to date, and the latest model. The defining act of the consuming subject is the purchase of commodities, an act in which it participates in the future but also an act that must be continually re-performed as the new quickly becomes the not new.[32]

The modernist novel participates in this ideological shift both in its antipathy to traditional forms of causality and time and in its construction of meaningful literary form that incorporates the rising emphasis on the present without completely sacrificing the futural orientation on which both the novel and the structures of American society depend. Despite modernism's antagonistic stance toward established society, the modernist novel serves the ideological imperative of articulating and naturalizing the structure of a newly emergent consumption-oriented subject. It does so by enacting a formal compromise formation that retains crucial aspects of the traditional novelistic form that underwrote the ascension of the Puritan subject and combines them with the components of a repetitive and present-oriented temporality most susceptible to incorporation in such a form. Seen in this way, the modernist novel shares the domesticating impulse of the kind of reaction to jazz that we saw in Koussevitsky and Rogers, an impulse that looks enviously at jazz's vitality and power to captivate audiences but cannot fully embrace jazz as a rival aesthetic form out of a fear that the temporality embodied in it is incompatible with a society that reserves privileged positions for both the novel and for white, male, upper-class economic power.

Race plays an important part in the shape of the compromise formation enacted by the modernist novel and early twentieth-century culture. It was both the condition of the possibility of jazz's configuration of temporality and the foundation for the use of primitivism to license and naturalize "a new social norm of consumption" (Rhodes 176). Nothing was more important in the modernist novel's attempt to absorb and contain the rising tide of jazz than the trope of primitivism. An adaptation of already existing constructions of racial difference, primitivism made use of the increasingly pervasive discourses of Darwinism and Freudian psychoanalytic theory to code the socially enshrined phenotypical markers of race as signifiers of a primitive and natural human essence that civilization, for better or worse, had left behind. Primitivism made any gaze across the racial divide into a gaze into the past. The increasing visibility of African American experience and of African American modes of sociality, leisure, and aesthetic creation were explained by primitivism as traces not of any possible future but of a past stage of human and cultural development. While primitivism did not totally allay the "threat" that any African American presence was seen as by much of white America, it did do much to allow an appreciation or enjoyment of jazz (and other African American aesthetic forms) to coexist with a belief in white intellectual and cultural superiority. At the same time, primitivism also functioned as a rhetorical tool in the attempt to valorize the virtues of consumption over the virtues of production and self-denial. As Chip Rhodes writes in *Structures of the Jazz Age*, primitivism's fetishism of African Americans "emphasized their capacity and appetite for pleasure," a capacity and appetite antithetical to the "work-save-build Puritan ethos." Because this emphasis on "instant" pleasure was figured as natural—not only for blacks but also for whites, insofar as blacks were understood as representatives of a component of white essence that over-civilization had taught them to suppress—primitivism enabled an attack on the self-denial and futural orientation of Puritan subjectivity that regarded it as unnatural and thus unhealthy. Primitivism served the ideological imperative of shaping consumers for the rising flood of consumer products by figuring the consumption of these commodities as an instinctive enjoyment of the present without regard for the future.

The fact that this form came to have such a prominent place in American society says much about the tenacious hold that the Puritan emphasis on the future has on the American imagination. Despite the ideological portrayal of commodity consumption as an enjoyment of the present, such consumption is an activity with both imagined and actual ties to the future. Imagined because capitalism invites the purchaser of a commodity to see himself as transformed or completed by the object they purchase. The pleasure associated with each purchase is the pleasure of believing that what is being purchased is entry into an ideal future. The enshrining of a new social norm of consumption keeps a futural orientation alive by transposing the belief in a better future from the realm of saving to the realm of goods.

This imagined connection to the future was complemented by the economic connection to the future embodied in the debt that the consuming subject of the 1920s was likely to possess. In *Buy Now, Pay Later* Martha Olney describes the period's massive and unprecedented increase in individual debt. According to her, "total debt outstanding approximately doubled in each of the first two decades of the twentieth century . . . increasing from 3.3 billion in 1920 to over 7.6 billion in 1929" (86).[33] This growth in debt was the result of the embrace of "a new economic philosophy: buy now, pay later," an economic philosophy that required "a fundamental change in society's attitudes toward the propriety of incurring debt" (136). What had previously been seen as a kind of economic sin was now normalized as purchases beyond the amount of current cash balances became commonplace. In order to participate in consumption's emphasis on the now, consumers traded on their future earning power and in doing so yoked themselves to a future cycle of work and spend. Debt ensures that the future will repeat the present by foreclosing the possibility of any future activity not adequately sanctioned or rewarded by financial compensation.

These ties to the future make it clear that no matter how much a subject valued for its consumption of commodities might differ from a Puritan, production-oriented subject, this subject has not escaped from the logic of a system in which, to return to Adorno and Horkheimer's formulation, "the ego owes its existence to the sacrifice of the present to the future" (51). What the enshrinement of the subject of consumption represents is not a total suspension of the subordination of the present to the future but a new version of this subordination, a version that makes use of primitivism to figure the sacrifice of the present to the future as a primal enjoyment of the present. The priority given to the consumption of commodities served the purpose of forestalling any attempt to organize society around the goal of an enjoyment of the present not subservient to a fixed vision of the future and was thus a form of what Gary Cross calls an "unacknowledged social decision" (5).

In *Time and Money* Gary Cross delineates the connection between the emergence of consumer culture and "the often unacknowledged social decision to direct industrial innovation toward producing unlimited quantities of goods rather than leisure," a decision that "meant a culture of work and spend" and that transformed time into money "both on and off the job" (5). In the 1920s American industrial productivity rose rapidly (37 percent between 1919 and 1926), challenging the established equation between the amount of time devoted to labor and the amount reserved for leisure (Cross 30).[34] As we know, labor time and commodities won the day, but in the 1920s the choice of money over time was not an obvious one. In fact, if anything seemed obvious it was the choice of time over money; according to Cross, "the common assumption in 1920 [was] that free time, not the endless growth of consumption was the inevitable consequence of growth" (7). The valuation of money over time was one that took a great amount of cultural (and political) effort to enforce. As we have seen, despite the attack that certain attitudes figured as Puritan came under in the 1920s, this enforcement was a reenforcement of specific core values of America's irredeemably Puritan culture, a ploy to perpetuate the essential structure of American culture in a changed economic and social context. The aspects of America's puritan ethos most crucial in sanctioning the choice of money (in the form of commodities) over time (in the form of leisure) were a strong bias in favor of the quantifiable and the pervasiveness of Benjamin Franklin's equation, time is money.[35] Under the purview of these two tendencies, the present enjoyed in the form of a glistening new phonograph or radio is much preferred to the present enjoyed in the less quantifiable form of listening or dancing. It is in this manner that Puritan values perdure, maintaining the cultural continuity that canonical works of art are always at least partially involved in sustaining. Anglo-American modernism thus has a very complicated relationship to the cultural values reigning at the time of its emergence; it is both deeply invested in these values and openly critical of them. Anglo-American modernism, and especially the modernist novel, is not a hammer intent on smashing the Puritan ethos (despite its desire to imagine itself in this way) but a razor intent on cutting away the dead weight from this ethos in order to remold it into a shape appealing to post–First World War society. The modernist novel and the cultural position that it embodies are both repelled and attracted by Puritan values, and the same is true of their relationship to jazz, which they saw as both fascinating and terrifying. Ultimately though, the differences are much more significant than the similarities: the modernist novel wants to eviscerate rather than to subtly mold jazz, to cut its cloth to the shape of a society with which it is ultimately incommensurable, and at the same time to use jazz as part of its polemic against that which is ossified and obsolete in the Puritan ethos. The interplay of jazz and the modernist novel occurs in a transitional gap between a vanishing nineteenth-century Puritan ethos and an emerging twentieth-century Puritan ethos. Despite the role that jazz plays in this transition, the new configuration of Puritan values has no more suitable of a place in it for jazz, or for the African Americans whose attitude toward experience is embodied in it, than did the old one; the massive popularity of jazz in the 1920s did not prevent this decade from being a period of widespread lynching and other violence toward African Americans.[36] The modernist novel, and the new cultural configuration that it participated in bringing about, used jazz but did not embrace it or the rhythmic core of the music so antithetical to Puritan biases toward the object and toward a determinate futural orientation.

Despite the inherent tendencies of novelistic form, the novel in the hands of African American writers quite clearly had an entirely different impetus. As manifestations of, in Olly Wilson's phrase, "reinterpretation[s] of [the] American ideal as viewed through the prism of black experience," (90) the African American modernist novel is an attempt to use the form of the novel against racially repressive social forms. These attempts look to jazz not as a raw material but as a model, a model whose rhythmic and temporal implications are transposed into the novel in order to ventilate novelistic form and interrupt its developmental, progressive thrust. As the heirs to a novelistic and cultural tradition well aware that time is never objective and transcendental but is always, in a society structured by relations of domination and subordination, an imposition of a "social construct that marks the inequality between various social groups," African American modernists were attuned to jazz's performance of both a critique of objective time and a rival mode of temporal experience. The African American modernist novel listens to jazz not in order to keep alive an economy in which the present is sacrificed to the future but in order to fully confront the contradictions of the present as a way of making possible a future that is not merely a repetition of the past and its injustices.

The primary formal strategy of this confrontation is what James Snead calls "the cut." Snead defines "the cut" as an unexpected break or hiatus that brings about a "disturbance of expectations" in order to overtly insist on the repetitive nature of whatever form it occurs in (69). Although Snead begins his exposition of the cut with musical examples, he also points to instances of its use in literature, highlighting the picaresque as a form unashamed of utilizing the cut. The picaresque is a form with special importance for the African American literary tradition, and the use of certain aspects of picaresque form is a crucial part of the African American modernist novel. This is particularly true of James Weldon Johnson's *The Autobiography of an Ex-Colored Man*. According to Snead, the cut always skips "back to another beginning which we have already heard," and I now skip back to Johnson's novel in order to consider its use of the cut.

After the narrator of Johnson's novel is violently displaced from his position at the piano, we get a cut in the flow of the narrative that disturbs our expectations of what should necessarily come next. The description of events at the party is broken off and we are left with a number of unanswered questions: What happens after the German guest plays at the piano? Does the narrator play again? Do the narrator and the German guest speak?

This kind of break is not that unique in a novel but is usually followed and preceded by a set of maneuvers intended to incorporate it into the linear flow of the novel and transform it into a necessary event on the path to a goal reached at the end of the novel. This does not happen in Johnson's *Autobiography*; instead this cut is preceded and followed by a series of other cuts, establishing a narrative rhythm that depends more on disjuncture and dislocation than on continuity and necessity. The stringing together of these series of cuts highlights repetition by making the events that precipitate these cuts appear as different versions of the same event, namely, the narrator's jump from one path or occupation to the next when confronted by violence or coercion. This narrative rhythm makes the narrator's treatment at his patron's party into a repetition of other events that always seems to depend on race: his racial outing in a grade-school classroom, the shooting of a female admirer at the bar where he mastered ragtime, and the lynching that ends his career as a composer. These events are not subsumed into a tale that transforms them into meaningful steps on the path to the narrator's resting place at the end of the novel; they are instead left to stand freely in a repetitive series whose ultimate import is that "the separation between the cultures was perhaps all along not one of nature, but one of force" (Snead 75).

2

Music, Race, and Sublimation

Ragtime and Symphonic Time in
The Autobiography of an Ex-Colored Man

James Weldon Johnson's *The Autobiography of an Ex-Colored Man* is the tale of a man "stirred by an unselfish desire to voice all the sorrows, the hopes and ambitions, of the American Negro, in classic musical form" (147–48). Awakened from what he might call his "ragtime slumber" ("wasting my time and abusing my talent" [142]) by the intervention of his patron's German guest, Johnson's nameless narrator strikes out on his own to gather material from "the people," out of which he will compose a symphony that will both win him renown and "help those [he] considered [his] people" (147).[1] Had the narrator's symphony ever been completed, it would have been the type of work that J. A. Rogers might have pointed to as evidence in support of his statement that "jazz has a great future. It is rapidly being sublimated" (221). The dream of lifting and diverting jazz, ragtime, and other African American musical forms "into nobler channels" was not unique to Rogers and Johnson's narrator but was also shared by many intellectuals of the period, both black and white. In his *Nation* article of 1928 titled "Beauty Instead of Ashes," Alain Locke sees the "full promise" of African American music as lying in the future production of "sublimated and precious things," in which what he calls "the folk temperament" will scarcely be recognizable (423–24).[2] W. E. B. Du Bois's attachment to a similar version of Schillerian aesthetics is well known, and we saw the sublimating gaze of white musicians like Serge Koussevitsky and Paul Whiteman in chapter 1.[3]

The passion shared by Locke, Rogers, Koussevitsky, and Johnson's narrator for folding African American musical content into symphonic form betrays the extent to which their thinking is shaped by one of the key philosophemes of

American civilization's dream of itself, a philosopheme named in Roger's assertion that jazz is "rapidly being sublimated." Johnson's novel shows the logic of sublimation at work in the literary field, the musical field, and the social field. His play with ragtime, classical music, and the form of autobiography and the novel is an extended interrogation of the pernicious and violent effects of sublimation as a guiding metaphor of American life. Johnson contrasts society's investment in the movements of sublimation with the powers of another, more repetitive rhythm of understanding the world. This other rhythm is exemplified in the ragtime that Johnson's narrator learns to play in New York.[4]

Sublimation

Sublimation names the impossible but culturally valorized motion by which individuals, cultures, and nations build a future for themselves. Sublimation is at the center of early twentieth-century discourses of white superiority and black inferiority. The belief in culture and progress as processes of sublimation mapped an imagined movement toward higher and more refined stages onto beliefs that whiteness could be equated with a higher degree of intellectual prowess and blackness with a more bodily form of existence. James Weldon Johnson's novel is a sophisticated critique of sublimation and of the ways in which it is used to license racist violence and exclusion.

The motion and the future that emerge from sublimation depend upon the privileging of three interrelated conceptual operations: a model of truth based on a strict separation of thought and experience, the assumption that this truth is a timeless one valid for all future experience, and a suppression of materiality that legitimizes the distinction between thought and experience and is also the precondition for thinking of any truth as outside of time.

In his lectures on Kant's *Critique of Pure Reason*, Adorno sketches out the imbrication of the first two of these, referring to them collectively as the "residual theory of truth," a reductive method in which "everything that can be regarded as ephemeral, transitory, deceptive, and illusory is left to one side, so that what remains is supposed to be indispensable, absolutely secure, something I can hold permanently in my hands" (*Kant's Critique* 25). One can hear in Adorno's description the logic of sublimation: the movement by which "residual truth" is arrived at is an intellectual distillation in which experience is transmuted into thought by boiling off the inessential and the impure. The truth that results from this process is then conceived of as having a timeless quality that gives it an ease of applicability "to all future eventualities." The assumption here is that all possible forms of experience have at their core the same immutable and unchanging truths and thus while the process of arriving at truth takes place *in* time, the truth that arises out of it is not affected or shaped *by* time. Truth's emergence from experience is imagined as a process that ends when truth has been completely discerned and as a process that thus never need be repeated. We see this in Kant's statement that "though our knowledge begins with experience, it does not follow that it arises out of experience" (qtd. in Adorno, *Kant's Critique* 25). Time is treated by Kant in essentially the same way, acknowledged as a necessary condition of knowledge but seen as a kind of flaw that truly authoritative truth should seek to overcome. Time serves to separate truth from experience, and once this process is accomplished time becomes the motion by which new objects and experiences are fitted into already existing conditions of thought. In other words, time, in its avoidance of the genuinely new or unexpected, becomes timeless.

This conception of time and this denigration of experience are Kant's, but the importance of them for Adorno, as for me, stems from their role as the organizing principles of the form of modernity and exchange society existing at the beginning of the twentieth century. Adorno writes that "this strange idea of the truth as something lasting and enduring somehow always appears where urban exchange ideas have developed" (*Kant's Critique* 26). For him, the residual and timeless theory of truth that is distilled out of experience is, "in economic terms, . . . the profit that remains after deducting all the costs of production" (*Kant's Critique* 25). The timeless truth of Kant and of exchange society is modeled on the commodities that capitalism produces, and the aversion to the new is a function of exchange thinking's inability to imagine the emergence of anything that has not been paid for by the "proper" form of intellectual or economic labor.[5]

Exchange society mobilizes all the resources at its disposal to ensure that the future is profitable and that this profit is distributed in a way that doesn't threaten the intellectual, material, or social conditions of its existence. Thus any temporal movement that doesn't confirm existing categories of thought is suppressed out of a fear of profitless activity.

The key stratagem for minimizing the possibility of profitless activity is the separation of manual labor from intellectual labor, a conceptual operation based on the analogy that compares social processes to the chemical process of sublimation. The profit deriving from manual labor flows away from the bodies responsible for this labor to the "higher" realm of those who practice intellectual labor. Following the analogy of sublimation, this flow is figured as natural, and the realm of intellectual labor is figured as both self-sustaining and free from any manual labor. What sustains this analogy is the negation of materiality, both in the disavowal of the link between intellectual labor and the extraction of profit from the manual labor that makes it possible and in the disavowal of the fact that intellectual labor is also manual labor. The cultural logic of sublimation is at base a logic that operates by transforming the impossibility of an escape from materiality into the desirability and possibility of mastering materiality in order to move beyond it.

From beginning to end, from the narrator's proclamation that he is "playing with fire" (3) to his self-sacrifice "on the altar of duty," (204) Johnson's text is concerned with operations of sublimation. This is clearest in the narrator's description of the artistic process: "nothing great or enduring, especially in music, has ever sprung full-fledged and unprecedented from the brain of any master; the best that he gives to the world he gathers from the hearts of the people, and runs it through the alembic of his genius" (*Autobiography* 100). Here, Johnson lays bare the metaphor of sublimation. When he names the alembic we see the comparative operation lining up the processes of cultural production with chemical processes. An alembic is a heat-resistant laboratory vessel in which solid material is refined or transformed into gas. Like the chemical process with which it is compared, the creative process that the narrator describes here is a purification, one in which raw folk materials are refined into a more ethereal, and less material, finished product.

Ultimately incomplete, the narrator's creative project, fitting African American musical content into classical form, is the textual figure for the aesthetics of sublimation, but the problematic of sublimation and its relationship to a calculable, progressive form of time saturates the entire text. This chapter foregrounds two scenes from this saturated field in its attempt to track Johnson's play with the theme of sublimation. These two scenes frame the narrator's commitment to his symphonic project. The one that occurs first in the novel is a scene in which the narrator plays privately for his patron. The narrator plays ragtime, and the patron sits in mute, unmoving solitude. The other scene occurs after the narrator has made the switch from ragtime performance to classical composition. While gathering materials for his symphony, the narrator witnesses a lynching. Both scenes *expose* the material underpinnings of the widespread social desire for the narrator's symphonic project. The first scene is a figure for the insatiable commercial thirst for jazz and ragtime, while the second is a material literalization of sublimation; both are moments when naked power (whether economic or more overtly violent) displays its investment in operations of sublimation.

Lynching

The Autobiography of an Ex-Colored Man is a text whose central concern is the imbrication of aesthetics and violence. This can be seen in the violent displacement of the narrator from his piano bench, but it is even more powerfully figured in the way that the text organizes itself around the central event of a fiery lynching. During the narrator's trip to the South to collect musical material, he finds himself following a stream of excited (white) individuals in order to find out where they are going. He soon finds that the event generating so much excitement is a lynching. The narrator is stunned and unable to remove himself from the scene of the crime; he witnesses the gruesome event from beginning to end.

Although this lynching occurs fairly close to the end of the novel, its centrality is confirmed by the fact that it marks the passage of the narrator from "colored man" to "ex-colored man." His witnessing of the lynching is the event that leads him to forsake his ambitions of "voicing all the joys and sorrows, the hopes and ambitions, of the American Negro, in classic musical form" (*Autobiography* 48), to renounce the realm of art for the realm of money. In addition to ending the narrator's artistic ambitions, the barbarity of this incident spurs the narrator into a consideration of aesthetics and the violence of "Southern whites." According to the narrator, the ability of Southern whites to burn a man alive, reducing him to a pile of "blackened bones" and "charred fragments," (187) is a function of their inability to sublimate; they gratify their "old, underlying instincts and passions" (189) through lynching rather than through the more "civilized" means of reading a book or going to the theater.

In these musings on lynching, Johnson's narrator replaces the homogeneity of *the* white race by a division between Northern and Southern whites that figures each as a separate "people." In making this division, Johnson argues that race is tied to specific modes of aesthetic experience. Southern whites are judged as incompletely civilized because, unlike "an ordinary peace-loving citizen," they are not satisfied to "sit by a fire and read with enjoyment of the bloody deeds of pirates and the fierce brutality of Vikings" (*Autobiography* 189). In the narrator's view the gulf between the aesthetic sublimation and lynching is an absolute one. That the distinction between the two practices is a sharp one is undeniable, but a consideration of the etymology and multiple valences of the term "sublimation" shows that there is at least some common ground between the two. "Sublimation" is not just an aesthetic term but is also a term used in psychology and chemistry. In chemistry, sublimation is the transformation of a body from a solid state to a gaseous state. Although incomplete in its leaving behind of "blackened bones" and "charred fragment[s]," this is the process used in burning the lynching victim alive, transforming much of his flesh into the acrid smoke that strikes the narrator's nostrils.

In the musings of the narrator as well as in widespread cultural understanding, sublimation is a process that turns from the corporeal to the spiritual. Following the logic of the chemical process, sublimation turns people away from bodily gratification toward less bodily and more refined intellectual or spiritual satisfaction. In the narrator's example this is to substitute reading about brutality for practicing brutality. This process is tied to the forward and upward motion of civilization, a motion that replaces brute sensuality with the disinterested rationality on which Western civilization is supposedly built.

In her analysis of the logic of lynching in American culture, Robyn Wiegman illuminates the way in which the mechanisms for defining and reinforcing white supremacist power depend on both the hierarchy of values implicit in, and the motion of, sublimation. Lynching is a staging of white power (both illusory and real) that figures the black victim as absolute and hyperbolic corporeality in order to provide the background of difference against which white disembodiment is imagined. The killing and mutilation of the black victim emphasizes his bodily powerlessness and the powerful but "civilized" and disembodied nature of white power over his body.

Wiegman characterizes this ritual as a necessary effect of a constitution of the American citizen as "a disembodied entity, bound not to physical delineations but to national ones" (94). The equation implicit in this constitution of citizenship is that the maximum of freedom and power accrues to those with the least physicality, an equation based on the illusion that the path to power and wealth is traveled by renouncing or sublimating one's particularity and physicality. This equation of disembodiment with the privileges of citizenship legitimates the hierarchical structure of society by imagining the top positions in this hierarchy as being occupied by those who have successfully traveled the path to disembodiment and by inviting those lower in the hierarchy to think of themselves as on a path of renunciation and sacrifice, which will eventually lead them up the ladder of sublimation.

As Wiegman illustrates, the stability of this vision of society was shaken by emancipation, an event that swelled the ranks of citizens and strained the plausibility of the myth of white disembodiment. With black enfranchisement, the path to disembodiment and privilege became a very crowded one, and the hidden basis of the narrative of sublimation and renunciation became disturbingly visible. The fact that disembodiment was an imagined, and thus comparative, state rather than a real or absolute one became increasingly hard to ignore. Disembodiment is a metaphor that can only be sustained by recourse to a difference against which it is defined, a difference represented in the American imagination primarily by African Americans. With emancipation the sharp distinction between white citizens on the path to disembodiment and privilege and African Americans mired in corporeality lost some of its definitional power. Lynching is an attempt to reestablish this distinction, a ritual performance that strives to reinforce what Wiegman refers to as "the conflation of white male disembodiment and socio-symbolic power" (90).

Lynching attempts to sharply distinguish between mind and body and to map this distinction on to the distinction between the racial categories white and black. In *Blackness and Value* Lindon Barrett shows the key role that conceptions of time play in this mapping and its valorization of white over black and of immateriality over materiality. Barrett characterizes the role of time as follows: "in the United States those who bear white skin are understood in relation to spacelessness in time, significance, animation, the divine, whereas those who do not are understood in relation to timelessness in space, bestiality, culpability, obdurate materiality" (111). Here Barrett exposes the logic by which materiality and temporality are opposed to each other and by which the disembodiment tropologically connected to whiteness is made into a prerequisite of participation in the temporal progression that leads to wealth and privilege in the future. Blackness, corporeality, and timelessness are bound together in a configuration that is opposed to whiteness, disembodiment, and temporal progression. This ideological configuration depends upon an avoidance of the truth that space and time, as well as body and mind, are inseparable. The configuration of race enforced by the logic of lynching and of sublimation is one that suppresses materiality and time, for any time that can license the belief in the possibility of a "spacelessnesss in time" is an absurd distortion of time's dependence on space, a distortion as absurd as any notion of personhood that can imagine an individual as a manifestation of disembodied rationality. Just as we encounter no ghostly bodiless individuals, we never confront a time free from a complicated imbrication with space.

The impossibility of totally detaching mind from body, and, to a lesser extent, time from space, is something that inevitably confronts each individual. The occlusion of this impossibility is performed through the trope of mastery. American culture uses the notion of mastery to naturalize and obscure the impossible separations that license its existence. Thus, the form in which the obviousness of sublimation and disembodiment occurs to the individual subject is not "I have left my body behind and now reside entirely in my mind" but rather "I have a body, but it is mastered by my mind."

This is a familiar logic that reaches at least as far back as Descartes. Its counterpart in the distinction between time and space is equally pervasive but less well known. The intellectual operation of separating time from space is given its canonical form in Hegel's *Encyclopedia*.

For Hegel, time detaches itself from space by negating it, and, moreover, time is itself nothing but this action of negating space: "Negativity, thus posited for itself, is Time" (Derrida 43). Here time masters space in a negation that preserves as well as destroys, for in Hegelian dialectics (as in the cultural logic that follows from it) negation is a process that retains what it negates in order to lift it into a "higher" sphere. Time subsumes space, taking it into itself as part of a teleological forward movement. The detachment of time from space inaugurates the dialectical progress that Hegel describes as a movement upward through higher forms of consciousness and higher stages of civilization. That Hegel places the cultural and aesthetic forms of dark-skinned Africans at the abject beginning of this process (a beginning described as *outside* of dialectics and of history) underscores the fact that dialectical negation is one of the tools by which racial hierarchy is created and maintained. Time is at the very heart of the hierarchical thrust of dialectical progress, for, as Hegel's definition of it as negativity "posited for itself" indicates, time itself is dialectical negation. In his reading of the Hegelian construction of time, Derrida states that the "negativity in the structure of Aufhebung already was time" (Derrida 42). "Aufhebung" is the German word that Hegel uses to describe a dialectical negation that both suppresses and preserves. This term has been translated as sublation, supersession, and subsumption. Whichever translation is used, it is clear that the logic and dynamics of the Aufhebung are the same as the logic and dynamics of the sublimation involved both in the lynching that James Weldon Johnson's narrator witnesses and in the aesthetic alternative (reading about violence) that the narrator opposes to lynching.

Both manifestations participate in the illusory possibility of absolute mastery: lynching in its attempt to regain the mastery of the slave-holding past and aesthetic sublimation in its positing of self-mastery. Here the distinction between narrator and author is important, for while the narrator of the *Autobiography* is heavily invested in the opposition between lynching and aesthetics, the fact that the passage following the description of the lynching contains an implicit critique of aestheticizing vision suggests Johnson's (and the novel's) divergence from the opinions of the narrator. When it is suggested that "from a certain point of view," that is, an aestheticizing or "romantic frame of mind," the Southern whites responsible for the lynching look both picturesque and admirably chivalrous, as well as brave and just, the distinction that the narrator posits begins to seem less than absolute. The narrative's troubling of the narrator's distinction lets us see the ties between the violence and the aesthetics that the narrator wants to see as separate realms and begins to put us in the vicinity of the truth at which Johnson's narrative is aimed.

The divergence between the narrator's view and the way the narrative undercuts this view suggests that Johnson's novel is after a more extensive causal explanation of lynching, something more like Wiegman's analysis. For her, lynching is motivated not by the undercivilization of certain components of the American population but by the drive for mastery around which American civilization (both North and South) is constructed. Wiegman characterizes this motivation as follows: "The extremity of punishment in the lynching and castration scenario thus provided the necessary illusion of returning to the lost moment of slavery's totalized mastery—a moment never actually 'full,' though yearned for, indeed frantically sought after, through the disciplinarity of mob violence" (100).

In this account, an abstracted time and an abstracted space reinforce each other in a concerted effort to purge materiality and to reassert what Wiegman refers to as "a definitional authority over social space" (95). The impetus behind this ritual purging is the desire of a narrowly construed societal self-interest to imagine the rugged topography of the racialized landscape as a smooth nonconflictual social space through which ideas, persons, or goods can move without resistance. Such a conception of social space depends upon a progressive, nonrepetitive time that suppresses materiality by consigning it to the past as something that has been mastered and left behind in the process of sublimation. The presence of independent, nondeferential black subjects violates this conception by serving as a symptomatic indication that the slave-holding past was not a space of totalized mastery but a source of the mobile, unmasterable "blackness" that the lynching narrative figures as "incontrovertible chaos."

The purging of the unmastered past and the suppression of corporeality that coalesce in lynching's ritual of mastery are operations whose impossibility ensure that lynching will be repeated over and over again in a series that belies the very myth of sublimation and mastery it is intended to reinforce. As Wiegman notes, lynching's self-contradictory nature demands that it be "repeatedly staged" (89). The repetition of lynching troubles the separation of mind from body, and time from space, on which the hierarchies of racial privilege are based by suggesting that the mastery of one over the other is not permanent but is permanently in danger of dissolving. When disembodiment becomes an act that needs to be repeated it becomes a position potentially available to all subjects as an act whose successful completion in the past is no guarantee for its successful repetition. Thus, repetition is a source of persistent anxiety, an anxiety that haunts sublimation as well as the Hegelian notion of time that underwrites it. Hegel's definition of time as both the engine of upward dialectical and cultural progress and as "negativity . . . posited for itself" embodies a contradiction as intractable as that of lynching. Since time has no positive essence, it is slavishly dependent on the space from which it emerges and to which it must consistently and repetitively return in order to exist at all. Any consistent forward or upward thrust must be based on a suppression or occlusion of the insistent repetition that betrays the contradictory aporia of subjectivity based on sublimation. For Wiegman, this aporia is a "significatory lack," lynching's response to which she outlines in the following statement: "In choosing death and accompanying it with the most extreme practices of corporeal abuse, whiteness enhanced its own significatory lack, filling the absence of meaning that defined it with the fully corporeal presence of a hated, feared, and now conquered blackness" (100).

The theorization of lynching as response to a significatory lack brings us back to Johnson and the narrator's comparison of lynching and aesthetics, for aesthetic forms, like lynching, are primarily responses to significatory lacks. As Lukács asserts in *Theory of the Novel*, all aesthetic forms are "profound confirmation[s] of the existence of a dissonance" (72). Lynching, Johnson's novel, the narrator's ragtime, and the narrator's aborted symphony are all responses to the significatory lack engendered by the racialized nexus of subjectivity and privilege from which they emerge. For Lukács, the novel's response sets it apart from that of other forms of literature, insofar as the novel incorporates this lack or dissonance into its very form rather than striving to banish it. This makes the novel a privileged site for investigating the vicissitudes of the interaction between form and society. In Lukács's account the dissonance of the novel is the discrepancy between transcendental and empirical subjectivity, the impossibility of empirical, particular subjectivity ever corresponding with its transcendental ideal. The passage that the protagonist carves through the novel is its attempt to free itself from the stain of embodied particularity and to accede to the free realm of transcendent possibility, an attempt that shares with lynching the drive toward an idealized disembodiment. Here the problematics of racial relations and novelistic form are roughly isomorphic, an isomorphism that Johnson exploits in his novel of passing. Johnson's narrator passes for an "ordinary white man," and Johnson's novel, in its 1912 incarnation, passes for an autobiography.[6] By linking the two forms of passing, Johnson insists on the imbrication of the social, with its attendant violence, and the aesthetic. He argues, against his narrator, that aesthetic sublimation is not a surefire antidote to the "barbaric" sublimation involved in burning a man alive but is at least partially complicit in such barbarism.

Autobiography

That Johnson makes his argument about the connection between aesthetic sublimation and racial violence in the form of a spurious autobiography is telling, for autobiography is a genre that both exposes the underpinnings of the form of subjectivity dominant in any particular period and a form in which the operation of sublimation and the schematization of time are most evident. These two aspects of autobiography depend upon the fact that in it, there are two subjects, or more precisely, two "I"s: the narrating "I" and the narrated "I." The burden of autobiographical form is to shape these two "I"s into a coherent whole, to make them coincide in a nonreciprocal relationship that privileges the narrating I over the narrated I by objectifying and mastering the empirical past. Paul de Man describes this striving for coincidence as an attempted "alignment between the two subjects," a process "in which they determine each other by mutual reflective substitution" ("Autobiography" 70). This is the goal of autobiography, but as de Man points out, this goal is ultimately unobtainable. The narrating I and the narrated I can never settle into a stable relationship with each other because the time that has transformed the actions and experiences of the narrated I into past material available to the narrating I never stops. It works just as incessantly on the narrating I, and if the two are ever to coincide, time must come to an absolute stop. This is the only way to keep the I as narrating subject from slipping into the I as narrated object.

This distinction between the narrating I and the narrated I is closely linked to Lukács's distinction between the transcendental and the empirical self and to broader cultural understandings of the distinction between the present and the past and the mind and the body. The movement of time problematizes these cultural distinctions in the same way it destabilizes the separation between the two "I"s of autobiography

Autobiography works to posit its authorial subject-object as a distinct individual with a distinct past that it is linked to as owner to possession, but it cannot entirely escape the destabilizing movement of time. In de Man's words, autobiographical form "demonstrates in a striking way the impossibility of closure and of totalization" ("Autobiography" 71). Autobiography always begins in a time of writing that is subsequent to the time of the narrated events that constitute it, and thus tries to shelter its subject from the destabilizing power of time. Because the text inevitably has its own time, this maneuver never proves entirely successful. As a result, it is traditionally augmented by the authority of the proper name stamped on most autobiographies.

Autobiography resorts to the authority of the proper name, an authority borrowed from outside the text, to arrest the destabilizing slide of the "I" and its threatened problematization of the text and the identity that the text constitutes. For de Man, the moment of this arrest is the moment when "the specular pair has been replaced by the signature of a single subject no longer folded back upon itself in mirror-like self-understanding" ("Autobiography" 72). The social force of the signature seals off the autobiographical text, giving it a legal authority authorized by society rather than the by the tropological workings of the text itself. As de Man writes, "the name on the title page is not the proper name of a subject capable of self-knowledge and understanding, but the signature that gives the contract legal, though by no means epistemological authority" ("Autobiography" 71).[7] The conventions of autobiographical form serve to promote a self-understanding compatible with a society that presents itself as contractually based, much more than they serve to probe the limits and depths of subjective experience or understanding. Both through the presentation of an objectified past entirely at the disposal of the autobiographical present and through the privileging of an identity modeled on a legal subject capable of buying and selling goods and services, autobiography constructs the fiction of a subject sealed off from the vicissitudes of time and the repetitive imbrication of the different "I"s on which it is built, and consequently it is in full control of its own experience. This is a subject based on sublimation and mastery as much as the subject (but not the object) of lynching but in an entirely different way.

The subject of autobiography masters the past and the self through writing, and works to create a subject free from any dialectical or unpredictable relationship to otherness. At the same time, the subject of autobiography announces its ability to participate in the privileges of disembodiment by retreating from the realm of bodily interaction into the realm of textuality, a realm traditionally associated with disembodied rationality. In contrast, the lynching subject demonstrates self-mastery through the power to eliminate what it sees as unruly materiality from social space, purging a block to the conception of this space as nonconflictual and thus ultimately irrelevant to the sublimated subject's progress forward in time. Unlike autobiography, it is a ritual that requires the participation of another body, even if this body is present only to be destroyed.

Despite these differences, what is important to recognize here is how both operations of self-constitution depend crucially on the suppression of bodily materiality and on the suppression of the movement of time itself. Lynching and autobiography respond to a significatory lack by attempting to imagine a fleeting moment as a permanent one with no need for repetition. Despite its constant repetition, the act of lynching is designed to disguise and compensate for the fact that the bodily conditions of experience can never be left behind. In a similar way, the specific shape of autobiography, from narrative conventions to the name on the title page, struggles to cling to the coincidence of the narrating and narrated I that exists only in the moment of writing or speaking. Only such an arrest of time can prop up the instability of a subject dependant on the specular play of "I"s that otherwise would slide into each other in a movement incompatible with the fiction of autobiographical self-containment.

De Man's assertion that the identity created in autobiography is always a contractual one points to the way in which the suppression of time and repetition in lynching and autobiography work to underwrite possessive individualism, a conceptual system in which the subject is seen as the possessor of himself and of his capacity to labor. It is crucial for the legitimacy of this system that the subject be seen as master of himself, for otherwise the economic arrangements of society look less like contractual arrangements entered into freely and rationally and more like naked exploitation. It is also important that the sublimating self-mastery of the subject be conceived of as a completed rather than recurring act; otherwise, economic arrangements look like something in need of constant reexamination and renegotiation.

In leaving his narrator without a name, and his first publication of the *Autobiography* without a named author, Johnson works to destabilize these fictions of self-mastery and their attendant suppression of repetition. Johnson's play with autobiographical form is part of his critique of sublimation and of the narrative forms of identity based on it. This critique also works by way of Johnson's manipulation of another literary form, one more candidly engaged with the vicissitudes of time and repetition: the picaresque.

In *Literature as System* Claudio Guillén describes the picaro as an individual who is involved in a "tangle, . . . an economic and social predicament of the most immediate and pressing nature" (77). The picaro is almost always both impoverished and orphaned, a combination that insures that the picaresque is a genre of movement, adventure, and travel. The fact that the picaro is constantly in motion and constitutively cut off from the aid of virtually any social support network shows the extent to which the picaresque is a form in which the experience of the subject is sharply impacted by the material conditions through which the subject moves. The impetus of picaresque form is toward an exposition of subjectivity markedly different than that of the novel; in the picaresque, materiality is never surmounted and is at least as much of a force in steering the course of the picaresque subject as the picaro's cogitations are.

In the picaresque we get a model of subjectivity always in the process of being constituted, always being shaped and reshaped by the friction of its movement through social space. Johnson uses the picaresque movement of his narrator to give us a subject both aware of its fetters to social space and aware of the possibilities for negotiating this space without totally succumbing to it. This is a subject neither absolutely detached from nor absolutely determined by its surroundings. Johnson uses the picaresque to display the impossibility of the absolute detachment that sublimation posits; the narrator's movement is not one in which he masters each scene and leaves it behind, but is a movement characterized by flight and compulsion. The lynching that ends the narrator's dream of symphonic glory is merely the most dramatic of a series of incidents in which the narrator is the victim of compelling forces. The death of his mother, the theft of his tuition money, the closing of the cigar factory, all put the narrator in motion as an object subject to the vicissitudes of material forces larger than himself. This lack of mastery and self-possession is important, because if the narrator moves from scene to scene without mastering them, it is entirely possible that he will be forced back into the same scene in a return that is not the completion of any circle but is the kind of unsubsumed repetition so threatening to sublimation, progress, and the constitution of meaningful narrative. The picaresque posits the possibility of a repetitive motion that goes backward and sideways as well as forward. In the schema that the narrator presents of his life, the narrator's developmental and spatial motion repeatedly demonstrates the separation between motion and telos.[8]

The possibility of unsubsumed repetition manifests itself in the conclusion of the novel in New York, the only locale that the narrator visits twice. Returning to the scene of his success as a pianist, the narrator finds himself no better off than in his first visit. Without a job, without any contacts or marketable skills (at least not any skills that would not mark him as a member of "a people that could with impunity be treated worse than animals" [191]), the narrator begins again, repeating his earlier attempt to carve out a space for himself in the city. His second residence in the city gives him much greater financial success. With his post-lynching decision to "change [his] name, raise a moustache, and let the world take [him] for what it would" (190), the narrator turns himself into a proper Puritan subject dedicated to working and saving. That this self-shaping is conceived of as an operation of sublimation is clear when the narrator writes, "I denied myself as much as possible in order to swell my savings" (195). When he takes up his life as an ex-colored man, the narrative he uses to describe himself is a novelistic one: the story of a successful, sublimating subject who moves forward by burning off the impurities of his past and renouncing race, ragtime, and the picaresque movement of his previous life.

This is the condition and the space from which the narrative is written, the narrator's identity as a presumably white New York businessman. Despite the promised freedom of subjectivity based on sublimation, the opening pages of the narrative reveal a constraint quite unusual in the autobiography, namely, the narrator's inability to produce his name. His success has only been achieved through a circumventing of racial categories, an operation that has left him unable to give his autobiographical assay the element that defines it, the signature of its author. The wound of incompletion that this leaves on the text is testament to the fact that sublimation is not just a move forward that leaves inessential dross behind, but is a process that requires a sacrifice of the past and of that part of oneself that does not fit into the hierarchy of reigning social values. This reveals that sublimation is essentially self-sacrifice, a binding of oneself to social norms that is not detachment but is merely another socially sanctioned form of constraining attachment. The imposition of the narrator's sublimating and novelistic success in New York on top of the picaresque rhythms of his previous life exposes the constraint and repetition involved in such success and dramatizes the truth that "everyone who practices renunciation gives away more of his life than is given back to him" (Adorno and Horkheimer 55). The despair that the narrator expresses at the end of the *Autobiography* is in perfect agreement.

In New York, the narrator imagines his life as a white businessman as a break from everything that had preceded it. However, the break in the novel and in the narrator's life brought about by his witnessing of a lynching is not a clean one; the Benjamin Franklin–like narrative of renunciation and accumulation that replaces the episodic narrative of travel does not stand on its own as it should if the notions of progress and civilization embodied in it are genuine. For despite the narrator's pride in his frugal habits, his comments make it clear that the main cause of his financial success is his ability to speak Spanish, a skill picked up in the narrator's days in the cigar factory: "My knowledge of Spanish was, of course, the principal cause of my good luck; . . . it placed me where the other clerks were practically put out of competition with me" (195). The narrator's success as an "ordinary white man" is ultimately predicated upon an accident from his presublimating days. The accumulation of economic and social capital that accrues to the narrator in New York exposes the falsity of the connection between race and the ability to practice renunciation and of the belief that this kind of renunciation is sufficient for the creation of economic wealth. The ascent of the narrator through the economic and social strata of New York is dependent on an event prior to and outside of the story of sublimation and renunciation that should explain this ascent, as all such ascents are. Before the beginning of all such narratives of sublimation there is another pattern that creates the possibility of the ascension to privilege that then gets written as sublimation. The narrator's allegedly sublimating success is predicated on a skill from the period when his life moved to the rhythms of the picaresque, and in Johnson's juxtaposition of the narrator's life as a colored and ex-colored man he gives us an imposition of a novelistic pattern of sublimating success on top of a repetitive, picaresque pattern.

Although the narrator's ability to shed his earlier identity and assume another one is threatening to an economic system predicated upon the financial responsibility of a subject able to sign its name to contracts, the shape of the subjectivity that the narrator assumes after the lynching is a model of desirable capitalist comportment. Acting in a manner that goes against the grain of all his previous experience, the narrator adopts a time-sensibility that posits a fixed relationship between the present and the future, a time-sensibility that lets him use a calculation of present activity as the index of future conditions. In adopting the expectations of the white business and social world that he moves in, the narrator adopts a sense of time that subordinates the present to the future and totally neglects the past. This transformation shows the narrator retroactively adopting the values of the patron for whom he used to work.

The Patron

Much of the narrator's behavior in New York reflects the values and ideas that he absorbed from the patron when he accompanied the patron to Europe. The lynchers enact the physical violence that drives the narrator to pass for white, but the patron exposes the narrator to the conceptual violence implicit in the complex of ideas about race, time, music, and sublimation that shape the narrator's movement toward whiteness. What the patron most impresses upon the narrator are his ideas about the irrelevance of the past, about the free, detached circulation of art, and about the sublimating movement of time.

Like the narrator as he is reincarnated in New York, the patron shows a pronounced indifference to the past. This indifference to the past manifests itself in the patron's scorn for the narrator's planned return to America, a return that he refers to as "this idea of making a Negro out of yourself" (145). The patron sees the narrator's artistic plans as an endorsement of the racial division of American society, a division that he has as much disdain for as the narrator. To the patron, race is something that one assumes rather than something one is born into; he finds it ludicrous that the narrator's past might be behind his desire to work with "Negro themes" and can see this desire as nothing more than a free and irrational choice, based as it is on a seemingly unnecessary exposure of the narrator to prejudice and violence. Unlike Johnson, the patron cannot see that divisions based on race are both irrationally arbitrary *and* productive of a cultural heritage that has a different value or weight for individuals of different races. He is unable to understand that the race of the narrator is not just a function of decisions and categories in the present but is produced by the weight of the past on the present, both the past of the narrator and the past of the people who have produced the "Negro themes" that the narrator is so eager to get his hands on.

Concomitant with the patron's blindness to the past is his theory of art, a theory perhaps best understood as a "free market" theory of art. In his continuing attempts to dissuade the narrator from his intended course of action, the patron argues that "music is a universal art; anybody's music belongs to everybody; you can't limit it to race or country" (144). When the patron speaks, he speaks the language of capital; art is attached only to those who can appreciate and pay for its value. Herderian nationalism and racial expression are as meaningless to him as the narrator's plan to "make a Negro" out of himself. The universality of art that the patron espouses envisions an art unattached to and untainted by the conditions of its making, free to circulate beyond the bounds of race and nation. In this construction art bears none of the responsibility to community that is so important to both Johnson and his narrator. We should recognize here the conditions of the circulation of jazz that characterized its propagation in the period bookended by the two release dates of Johnson's novel, as well as the conditions of the narrator's presence in Europe. The narrator's detachment from the Harlem ragtime scene makes him liable to the financial arrangement that binds him to the patron and allows him to circulate throughout Europe. His very situation is an exemplification of his patron's theory of art, an exemplification that the unbinding from responsibility to race or nation is a binding to the dictates of capital. In his passage through the capitals of European culture, the narrator serves as a kind of living phonograph subject to commands of performance at any time of day or night and prohibited by the conditions of his contract with the patron from performing for anyone besides the patron and his guests. What the patron imagines as a "universality" of art is the replacement of one set of constraints for another, the severing of the ties to the past that the demands of racial and national identity constitute allowing for the "free" contractual agreement predicated on the patron's ability to continue to pay for the narrator's complete allegiance.

Although the patron is ultimately unable to convince the narrator to drop his plan to return to America, the nature of the narrator's rebuttals show that he has partially adopted the patron's logic of detached self-interest. The patron's argument has such a strong impact on the narrator that he extends his deliberations for a couple of weeks, and when he finally makes his final decision he writes that he "settled the question on purely selfish grounds, in accordance with my millionaire's philosophy" (147). He puts his concluding argument to himself in the following form: "I argued that music offered me a better future than anything else I had any knowledge of, and, in opposition to my friend's opinion, that I should have greater chances of attracting attention as a colored composer than as a white one" (147). The narrator's inability to dispel the patron's logic leaves the patron's voice ringing in his head and indicates the extent to which his admiration for his millionaire "friend" continues to influence his thinking even after he has left him. This influence on him is so strong that the narrator's reaction to the lynching he witnesses is virtually predetermined by it. Moreover, the patron's effect on him is present even before the lynching in the very shape of the narrator's musical project. In his intention to "voice all the joys and sorrows, the hopes and ambitions, of the American Negro, in classic musical form," (148) the narrator perpetuates the patron's philosophy and hierarchy of values as much as he will in his later life as "an ordinarily successful white man" (211). For although the narrator spends quite a bit of time weighing the wisdom of his plan to return to the states and compose a symphony out of Negro themes, he never reflects on the actual shape that his artistic project (making ragtime into classical music) will take. The extent of the thought used to settle on this particular project is summed up in his exclamation (which comes across him "like a flash"): "It can be done, why can't I do it?" (142). The project that the narrator plans to undertake is inspired in him by nothing other than his treatment at the hands of his patron's German guest. As in the lynching that ends his symphonic ambitions, the motivating force here is shame, shame at being the purveyor of a music that could so easily be dismissed. The narrator's decision to abandon ragtime for classical music is a defensive choice designed to remove him from a situation in which his position at the piano is subject to such violent usurpation. As such, it is essentially a coerced decision, no different than the other decisions that articulate the different episodes of his life and of his narrative except for the fact that here the mode of activity undertaken in the episode that follows this decision is less distinct from what had preceded it and more determined by the forces from which he flees. In other words, despite his physical break with the patron, his return to America finds him engaged in a project that treats the music that he sees as material for his symphony in a manner remarkably similar to the way in which his patron had treated him and his music.

The narrator's stance can be seen in the following passage: "I gloated over the immense amount of material I had to work with, not only modern rag-time, but also the old slave-songs—material which no one had yet touched" (142–43). In looking forward to his trip to the American South to gather material for his project, the narrator sees the music that he will encounter as a form of raw material remarkable as much for its being untouched by other hands as for any intrinsic musical character. At another point, the narrator describes the musical richness of a "big meeting" (a kind of religious camp meeting) as "a mine of material" (173). The use of a mining metaphor here is a telling indication of the narrator's adoption of what I have described as the patron's free market theory of art. The narrator imagines his trip to the South as a mining expedition in which he aims his headlamp at the obscure backwaters of small Southern communities in search of the most valuable veins of musical ore to chisel out of their surroundings. After removal from the context in which they are originally found, it is clear that these musical "nuggets" will be taken far from their original settings, for the narrator repeatedly expresses his urgent desire to "get to some place where I might settle down and work" (182). It is clear that he finds the environs in which the music that he takes as his inspiration is formed as no fit place for the kind of artistic construction that he has in mind. He imagines a solitary workshop in which he can run his newly acquired material through "the alembic" of his genius, distilling and purifying it into a form fit for expression in classic musical form.

What is most striking about the narrator's actions in gathering material for his symphony is the way in which he attempts to transform collective expression into individual expression. The music that the narrator describes being inspired by is so intimately linked to the situation in which it is performed that it is hard to imagine exactly what the narrator takes away from it in his notebooks. The two figures that the narrator is most impressed by, the preacher John Brown and the hymn leader Singing Johnson, are most remarkable for their improvisational skills and their ability to judge the perfect moment for the employment of any musical or rhetorical effect. Singing Johnson's impressiveness lies in his unfailing knowledge of "just what hymn to sing and when to sing it" (178) as well as of the appropriate key for each congregation, while John Brown's brilliance is a result of "an imagination so free and daring" that, when combined with his "intuition of a born theatrical manager," (175) allows him to employ his knowledge of oratory to tailor his sermon to the exact shape most guaranteed to fit the needs of each congregation. Brown's powers convince the narrator that "eloquence consists more in the manner of saying than what is said" (176). All in all, the narrator's description of the performances that he witnesses in the South emphasizes their improvisational flexibility and responsive suppleness, elements that seem unlikely to be captured in the narrator's notebook of "themes and melodies" (173). The narrator's approach appears likely to founder on the same fundamental mistake as that made by the bespectacled German guest when responding to ragtime: mishearing the essence of music in substantive rather than relational terms.[9] What the narrator puts into his notebooks are just those aspects of music that fit into the notation and conceptual scheme of Western classical music, while what is left out are all the elements that contribute to the power and beauty of performances such as Singing Johnson's, all that makes up what the narrator refers to as "that elusive undertone, the note in music which is not heard with the ears" (182).

In short the narrator has committed himself to a course that directly contravenes the distinctive genius of the music described in his narrative, both through his insistence on transforming collective musical practices into a work attributable to an individual creator (that is, with a signature—unlike the novel itself) and in the resultant fixing of improvisational, contextual practices in a rigid system of notation meant to guarantee the music's unvarying repeatability in whatever context it might ultimately find itself. The choice of form has decided this course in advance; what the narrator's confrontation with the patron's

German guest has left him with is an unthinking commitment to what he calls "classic musical form," a symphonic form given its canonical shape in the early nineteenth-century period of heroic bourgeois individualism and still saddled with the rhythms and logic of this conception of subjectivity.[10] Despite the narrator's disagreement with his patron over his plan to return to America, the musical project that the narrator's sojourn in Germany has left him with ensures that the aesthetic and social values of the patron accompany the narrator in his journey through the South. What is at the heart of these values and of the musical form in which the narrator is committed to working is the intense desire to "blot out" time.

The seemingly impossible goal of "blotting out," "bridging over," or "escaping" time is what the narrator tells us the patron is after in his marathon late-night listening sessions. Summoning up the narrator "during the early hours of the morning" and putting his powers of endurance to the test by making him labor at the piano for three or four unbroken hours at a time, the patron makes the narrator "his chief means of disposing of the thing which seemed to sum up all in life that he dreaded—time" (143). The idiosyncrasy of the patron's rather irregular expectations of when and for how long the narrator should play for him is matched by his idiosyncratic response to the music. For this response is more of a nonresponse than anything else. The response of the guests at the first occasion on which the patron had the narrator play is characteristic of the way in which virtually everyone in the text responds to the narrator's performance of the music "that demanded physical response"; they are astonished and surprised and end up "involuntarily and unconsciously" doing "an impromptu cakewalk." The patron, on the other hand, takes the music as a kind of soporific "drug," sitting grimly and mutely, and "making scarcely a motion except to light a fresh cigarette" (121). The patron is deaf to the demands that the music makes and refuses to yield to its bodily imperatives, choosing instead to hear in it a confirmation of his power to command and a possible escape from the time that will eventually destroy this power.

The patron listens to ragtime to hear what cannot possibly be there. In the same way, Americans gripped by primitivist visions looked toward Harlem and to African Americans for a kind of primal savagery that was also definitely not there.[11] This mishearing and misrecognition are licensed by a denial of coevalness that makes the patron and the devotees of primitivism into judges rather than participants. Imagining themselves as more sublimated and thus more highly evolved, the patron and the primitivist reception of jazz hear in the music a stage of existence that they (as either individuals or members of the white race) have passed through and thus contain. In this mode of thinking the ability of the rational part of the self to judge and master other "less rational" parts of the self is the basis for individuals conferring upon themselves the ability and the right to judge and master musics and cultures structured around a logic unfamiliar to these individuals. This is why the patron sits as motionless as a statue in the face of "music that demanded physical response"; to respond bodily to ragtime would be to threaten the basis of the patron's carefully crafted subject position and the sense of mastery that goes with it, a position and mastery dependant upon a subtle disavowal of the ground on which they rest.[12] This disavowal is the basis of the relationship between the patron and the narrator, and is reminiscent of a similar relationship in Hegel's *Phenomenology of Spirit*; Hegel's description of the dialectics of the master-slave relationship gives us the model for the patron's method of attempting to simultaneously enjoy and renounce ragtime. In Hegel's master-servant dialectic the master poses as a disembodied desire by assigning all of his bodily tasks to the servant and then forgetting or disavowing his relationship to the servant, severing his connection to a tie that impedes the master's ascension into the realm of the ideal. Judith Butler describes this relationship as one in which the master says to the servant (without actually saying it): "You be my body for me, but do not let me know that the body you are is my body" (35). This disavowal is a staging of bodilessness through the act of projection, a disavowal that we see in the blasé, detached posture of the patron sitting listening to ragtime. To see this is to see in the patron's position a dependence on a dramatic staging of bodilessness not unlike that of the lynchers whom the narrator will later encounter. Despite the sharp distinction that the narrator's emotional attachment to the patron leads him to suggest, the patron and the lynchers both are dedicated to an ideology of sublimation and mastery that makes necessary the projection of their corporeality onto the narrator or onto those of "his" race. This projection is necessarily accompanied by a disavowing assumption of difference that posits a gulf between the bodily corporeal object of projection and the subjects intent on disavowing their own corporeality through such projection. In keeping with his universalism, the patron's disavowal appears not to depend overtly on race ("I found that he was a man entirely free from prejudice" [145]), but, like lynching, it does depend upon the assumption of a progressive, nonrepetitive time and the figuring of the past as an instrumentalized and mastered raw material. The patron avoids bodily response to the ragtime he listens to both because such a response looks like a return to an unsublimated past in which his body responds to impulses outside of his own control and because to let his body move to the vibrations emanating from the piano would put him in the same time as the narrator, threatening to abolish the gulf separating patron from artist, to reverse the relationship between the two, and to bring the patron's mastery and disavowal of his dependence on his servant crashing down. If the patron were to dance to the narrator's ragtime, whether "involuntarily and unconsciously" or not, the assumption of the kind of timeless temporality that allows the patron to imagine himself as a free, powerful, and self-determining subject exposes itself to the risk of disarticulation and dissolution. The patron's subjectivity and temporality are those that Adorno and Horkheimer describe as depending on "the three-part schema of time" in which the past is instrumentalized and the future is rendered calculable and predictable. We should see in the narrator's adamantine immobility the self-restraint that Odysseus exhibits when he has himself bound to the mast in order not to respond to the lure of the Siren's enchanting tales of Odysseus's past. The patron's binding of himself to the mast of blasé renunciation serves the goal of preventing full participation in the music surrounding him by dropping a conceptual veil over a past that threatens to undo his mastery. For Adorno and Horkheimer's Odysseus, the past is threatening because it exerts a magnetic attraction luring him into a pattern of mythic repetition. For the patron, any non-instrumentalized past is threatening because of the possibility that such a past might throw him face to face with not only his own corporeality but with the subordinated corporeality of other disavowed "servants" on which his mastery in the present depends. His mastery has been bought and paid for, but to open the present to the unruly power of the past is to call into question the validity of the coin in which this purchase was made. The patron's power to command the narrator to play for him in the middle of the night is a financial power based on the extraction of value from the labor power of bodies subjected to the control of the patron's capital in the past. The petrified, locked-up labor of these workers from behind the veil of the past is the patron's power over the narrator in the present. Thus, what the narrator really is face to face with in the late night sessions, and what fills him with "a sort of unearthly terror" (121), is the power of capital, an essentially inhuman force: "He seemed to be some grim, but, but relentless tyrant, possessing over me a supernatural power which he used to drive me on mercilessly to exhaustion" (121). That the patron's power and mastery have their source in the flow of capital derived from exploited labor explains his desire to obliterate time. The curtain that the detemporalization of time throws over the past obscures this exploitation by refiguring the past as both noncoercive and having little relevance to the present.

The detemporalization of time that the patron clings to in his stubborn refusal to heed the music's incitement of motion is an avoidance of a particular form of the future as well as a barrier separating the present from the past. Beholden to the values of calculability and predictability, the future that the patron listens for should sound like a subtle variation of the past, a further step on a developmental line drawn from the past through the present and into the future. To hear this in ragtime requires an immensely powerful imaginative apparatus, one capable of distorting or effacing the supple unsecured future that peeks from between the music's aliquant ripples and cascades of sound. Approaching ragtime without the epistemological focus of the patron and with the weight of his cultural baggage quite differently distributed, the narrator describes it as a music of "surprise" and "the unexpected": "the intricate rhythms in which the accents fell in the most unexpected places"; "a sort of pleasant surprise at the accomplishment of the feat" (99).[13]

The narrator's responsiveness to ragtime allows him to hear the music as a dislocation and interruption of the developmental time that the patron strains to hear in it. Antithetical as this music is to the patron's mode of imagining subjectivity and temporality, it is somewhat surprising that he is drawn to it at all. His attraction is a symptom of the extent to which time is a problem for him, a problem pressing enough to give him the desire to escape from it and to lead him eventually to escape it "by leaping into eternity" (143), that is, by taking his own life. Time is problematic for the narrator because the repetition that he is at such great pains to avoid or disavow is at the same time an indispensable component of his existence. The narrator frequently refers to the patron as his "millionaire friend," and his wealth is the attribute that most defines him. This wealth was extracted from the labor time of those laboring for him in the past and thus is, in Jacques Attali's terms, a "stockpiling of time." According to Attali, it is repetition that makes such stockpiling possible: "We have seen that the first repetition of all was that of the instrument of exchange in the form of money. A precondition for representation, money contains exchange-time, summarizes, and abstracts it; it transforms the concrete, lived time of negotiation and compromise into a supposedly stable sign of equivalence" (101).

Money stamps the sign of the same on different situations, defining all varieties of interpersonal exchanges as only quantitatively different and thus making each exchange yield different quantities of the same abstraction, money itself. Depending on the exchange logic of money, as the patron does, puts one in the position of receiving every situation as a repetition of the process in which exchange-time is extracted from use-time. This logic attenuates the force of anything new ("surprise" or the "unexpected") by measuring it in terms of the relations of exchange existing in the past and fostering a nondialectical relationship to any new object, in which this object is owned or mastered by a nonresponsive and unchanging subject.

This is the situation of the patron and of his relationship to ragtime; his life is an attempt to escape from the ennui of the repeated event, but his subservience to the logic of exchange renders him unable to break out of this logic and to fully experience anything new or unique. Dead to the "surprise" and "unexpected" contained in ragtime, the patron is a figure for a particular version of hopelessness. In his attempt to dissuade the narrator from returning to America, he argues that "evil is a force, and, like the physical and chemical forces, we cannot annihilate it" (146). Collective action, political struggle, and any attempt to change or ameliorate injustice are considered by the patron to be futile because of their deluded belief in a future qualitatively different from the present.[14] For him, the only proper response to the world is an individual cultivation of a detached aesthetic appreciation of novelty and the exotic. The narrator is locked into his temporal dilemma by the fact that his privilege is based on a disavowal of the possibility of change.

In his use of the narrator and his music to stage a ritual confirming his own bodilessness, the patron shares with the lynchers a dependence on disavowal and a desperately felt need to assert "definitional authority" over both the past and the social space of the present. What distinguishes the patron's ritual from the lynchers, apart from the crucial difference in the level of physical violence in it, is the valence of the future in it. The future is much more problematic for the patron than it is for the lynchers, a function of the different shape that the process of sublimation has in their respective imaginations. For the lynchers, sublimation is a process not yet fully completed, a process that has not yet yielded the power and freedom that it is supposed to deliver. The rage manifested in lynching is a rage at the fact that sublimation has somehow not worked properly. Whether this blocked sublimation is felt as a cruel trick or as an inability within the self, lynching directs all rage and frustration at a racialized body bearing sole responsibility for sublimation's inability to deliver. It does so in order to restore, at least temporarily, faith in the ideal future that sublimation promises.

For the patron, on the other hand, sublimation is a process all too well completed. It figures for him as the process that has led him to his present position of power and privilege, a position imagined as the end point of this process, beyond which stretches an endless and timeless expanse. Relief from the dreariness of this expanse is what the patron seeks in diversions like the narrator's ragtime. The lack of enjoyment that the narrator derives from this ragtime, the result of its provenance in a place imagined as behind and below the patron's point of sublimation achieved, stems from the patron's inability to conceive anything more desirable than his current position. He fears that time might undo his privilege, passing him by and putting him in a situation that forces him to admit some responsibility or subordination to something outside of or beyond himself. His position is, thus, one characterized both by an intense desire for the new and an equally intense aversion to what the new might bring. We have seen how the narrator's description of the patron attributes to him the power of capital, and we see here in the patron's paradoxical reaction to the newness embodied in ragtime, and, indeed, to the future in general, a paradox, or antagonism, of capitalist society itself. This antagonism is described by Terry Eagleton as capitalist society's need to "combine some solid anchorage in the world with ceaseless transformation" (130–31). A society like the one we see in Johnson's novel "draws," in Eagleton's words, "for its self-ordering upon a dynamism which it simultaneously denies" (129). This is the vampirism of a relatively rigid ruling hierarchy that seizes upon the fluidity and vitality of other forms in order to refresh the power of an order so invested in the stable, predictable, and enduring that it is by itself unable to engender anything but an increasingly attenuated repetition of the same.[15] This is to suggest that what we see in the midnight encounters between the adamantine patron and the put-upon but obedient narrator is not just an isolated master-slave struggle but a confrontation of the power of capital that drives the industry responsible for much of the marketing and dissemination of jazz and ragtime with the very music that is both an object of this industry's operations and an object embodying a logic incommensurable with these operations. The (il)logic of this encounter is the (il)logic of using ragtime to attempt to "blot out" or "escape from" time, an (il)logic and mishearing that depends upon disavowal and the imagined separations of sublimating developmental time.

Classic Musical Form

In listening to ragtime in this way, the patron expects from it those things that Adorno tells us the symphony delivers, a suspension or compression of time that sustains his sense of selfhood by delivering him from the threat of repetition and consecrating a nonreflexive unidirectional experience of time. The pairing of Adorno and the patron is not a gratuitous one, for, despite their divergent attitudes toward jazz, both come to the music expecting it to deliver the same kinds of experience as music from the European classical tradition. Their experience with the masterworks of the European tradition (for clearly, the novel's constant characterization of the patron as intensely cultivated implies such a familiarity) makes them familiar with the way the symphony, in Adorno's words, "suspends time-consciousness, contracts time, and in doing so annihilates the contingencies of the listener's private experience" ("Radio Symphony" 117). Adorno's exposition of the way the symphony works to blot out or suppress time tells us much about Johnson's juxtaposition of ragtime and classical music. Johnson gives us the move from ragtime to classical music as part of the narrator's movement toward whiteness, and Adorno's analysis shows us the investment of classical form in promoting the fictions of disembodiment and temporal transcendence upon which whiteness depends.

According to Adorno, the symphony suspends time-consciousness and ab-stracts the listener from the particularities of their own experience.[16] It does so by virtue of its "particular intensity and concentration," a function of the fact that "a truly symphonic movement contains nothing fortuitous"; in it "every ele-ment is ultimately traceable to very small basic elements" ("Radio Symphony" 116). What we see here is a link between the totalizing integration that makes a work into a monolithic whole by banning everything not fully subordinated to the overall form of the work and the suspension or abolition of time. Time is abolished because in this construction there is no friction between different parts of the work or between any of the parts of the work and the form that contains these parts.[17] What the listener hears in the succession of these fric-tionless parts is a parade of necessary moments to which she or he is asked to merely nod in assent. The listener's private experience is set aside in what is es-sentially a ritualized celebration of universality purged of all contingency, par-ticularity, or conflict.[18] The abolition of time and particularity enacted in the symphony depends, ultimately, on a manipulation of volume that can only be described as the presentation of a force that is both overwhelming and undiffer-entiatedly ideal at the same time. Adorno describes this in the following terms: "The power of a symphony to 'absorb' its parts into the organized whole, de-pends, in part, upon the sound volume" ("Radio Symphony" 118). According to Adorno, to achieve the proper symphonic experience, and concomitant sup-pression of time, the range of volume presented to the listener must vary not only from soft to loud (from piano to forte) but from "Nothing to All" ("Radio Symphony" 123). Expressing as it does a vastness beyond that which any indi-vidual can imagine themselves producing, the massed sound of the symphony delivers the listener into a sublime transcendent space overwhelming enough to separate those who enter it from their private experience.

What Adorno describes here is the aesthetic analog to Michael Hanchard's central insight in "Afro-Modernity: Temporality, Politics, and the African Di-aspora": that time is determined by power and by power differentials. We have seen that Hanchard, following Fabian, explicitly links time to the relations of power and the mechanisms that distribute power unequally within any par-ticular society, alerting us to "the distinct temporal modalities that relations of dominance and subordination produce" (253). Hanchard is speaking specifi-cally of racial time, as am I, but the implication of his critique is that all time is a function of force and power, an implication that, when combined with Zora Neale Hurston's dictum that "discord is more natural than accord" (305), leads us to expect that time will necessarily be replete with surges, ebbs, lapses, and eddies. To expect otherwise is to fall prey to the idealistic illusion that time is transcendental and thus motionless in its total detachment from any tangible object that might move "through," "with," or "in" time, all metaphors obscuring the fact that time is an abstraction determined by, as well as determining, movement. Time is secondary as well as primary, a truth testified to by the fact that Kant's designation of time as an a priori category depends itself on a deadened temporal metaphor ("a priori," "the first") that borrows from the language of temporal cause and effect to arrive at a nontransient firstness, a curious first thing that never happened and will never pass (R. Smith 20–21). Primarily a technique of social coordination, time, when detached from social experience, reduces itself to the same sterile principle of self-consistency that threatens to engulf a rationality conceived of as the mere satisfaction "of certain axioms of formal coherence" (Aglietta 14). A clock is valued not because it tells us anything about the outside world (as a clock that beats more slowly when it is damp outside might) but because it is consistent with itself, methodically beating out the same interval that it beat out yesterday and will beat out tomorrow. Faulkner's assertion that "time is dead as long as it is being checked off by little wheels" (82) is part of a nostalgic romanticization of the past, but it is correct about the inadequacy of a mechanical time imagined as independent of the society that produces it.

Thinking of time as detached and regular may be a kind of illusion, but it is an illusion whose pervasiveness accurately references the overwhelming forces that go into producing it. A time that surges and ebbs is the function of a give and take between different configurations of force, but a time that is both transcendental and absolutely regular can be engendered only by a concentration of force so overwhelming that any individual force that confronts it is rendered virtually inconsequential. The pervasiveness of a time that presents itself as a nonconflictual ticking off of abstractly equivalent intervals is brought about by the ability of society to marshal and organize force, both ideological and physical, in such a way that the individual subject is at every turn confronted with an array of forces incommensurably greater than what it can imagine itself generating. This is why the abolition of time that the symphony strives to deliver is dependent on the ability to generate a range of volume far exceeding that which the individual can possibly produce. The sound volume of the symphony surrounds and engulfs the listener, removing him from a position in which any response other than awed submission is possible and drawing him into an imaginary and bodiless "symphonic space" free from contingency and the friction of contesting forces. The symphony asserts the opposite of Hurston's dictum that "discord is more natural than accord" by presenting a puissant auditory vision of force naturalized as necessity and by inviting the listener to set aside her individual experience in order to join in the timeless but forward march of symphonic progression.

It should not be forgotten that the range of volume presented in symphonic performance depends upon extra-aesthetic arrangements as well as aesthetic ones, for the symphony orchestra is one of the most capital-intensive aesthetic apparatuses ever assembled. To deliver the massive range of volume described by Adorno, upward of sixty-five intensively trained musicians are necessary. These musicians must be not only individually trained but collectively drilled in the kind of precise coordination demanded by symphonic aesthetics. Both individual and collective training are necessary to purge any individual idiosyncrasies of expression, intonation, or phrasing. The rigorous discipline that makes the uniform sound texture of classical music possible depends on a sublimating process that transforms the difference of the bodies that produce these sounds—differences in size, shape, and motion of lips, tongues, wrists, and fingers—into a sameness of sound that allows for a coordination of individual sounds in an undifferentiated mass. The amount of time this process takes, both on the individual level of repetitive practice and training and on the group level of rehearsal and large-scale coordination, gives some idea of the expense involved in producing a symphonic performance. Combining this with the costs of instruments, scores, and performance and rehearsal halls shows the intensity of capital concentrated in each individual symphonic performance. A massing of economic forces engenders the massive sound of symphonic performance; this is a social investment in a vision of social space that is as nonconflictual, frictionless, and abstract as the aesthetic space created in symphonic performance.

Removing the listener from any real relation to the musicians in front of him and to his fellow listeners on either side of him, the engulfing power of massed symphonic sound has an abstracting effect that transposes individuals into an abstract, idealized timelessness by severing any link between the movement of time and their own experience. It wields force in an effort to make time appear as a natural rather than a social force. The symphony performs this operation in the fairly abstract realm of aesthetic experience, but it mirrors the workings of the very same operation in the concrete realm of social experience and the ordering of civic space. Perhaps the most telling example of this is the institution of standard time that took place in the period just before that of Johnson's novel, an event that Stephen Kern calls "the most momentous development in the history of uniform, public time since the invention of the mechanical clock in the fourteenth century" (11). Established by the railroad companies, the elimination of the roughly eighty different local times in the United States involved a disruption of commonsense experience evident in the baptism of the day on which it took place (Nov. 18, 1883) as "the day of two noons." At midday the clocks in the eastern part of each time zone were set back, necessitating an unprecedented repetition that could only be performed with the aid of an overwhelming economic and ideological justification powerful enough to make any objection to such a counterintuitive and revolutionary operation appear unreasonable. The definitional power involved in this temporal interruption and institution is not to be underestimated, implementing as it does a shift in orientation away from the observable position of the sun in the sky and toward the abstract boundaries of an arbitrarily created time "zone" created out of nothing. The motivation behind the creation of standard railway time is primarily economic, an end to the confusion that complicated the railways' operation and generation of profits, but it is also part of larger trends (scientific, military, political, and so on) militating for uniform time as necessary to avert the kinds of conflicts and disputes over time that might endanger the efficient operation of all aspects of society.

What is important to see here is the way a concern with minimizing chaos and disorder is the impetus for removing responsibility for the construction (and maintenance) of time from the realm of intersubjective interaction by assigning concern with the functioning or measuring of time to institutions larger than and largely unresponsive to the individual. Such institutions, like the sound structures of symphonic performance, derive their power from agglutinations of capital, and like the dynamics of symphonic form, they manipulate time in order to remove the friction between the individual and the structures they move in and to attenuate or obliterate the relevance of the past to the present and the future.

This is obvious in the creation of a standard railway time that wipes away a traditional time reckoning in one stroke, but it is also a crucial function of the way that symphonic form deploys time and force. "Creation ex nihilo," is how Adorno labels this power of the symphony to posit its own beginning as a necessary one capable of detaching itself from anything that precedes it, a power that is also operative in the novel. As we have seen, the time-suspension that the symphony performs works through the intense unity of its movements, movements that aim at constructing every one of its elements out of a few basic melodic or harmonic cells, portraying its forward progress as a kind of Aristotelian natural growth in which the symphony moves toward a realization of a telos that it has within it from the very beginning. Adorno describes this as a process in which "structurally, one hears the first bar of a Beethoven symphony only at the very moment when one hears the last bar" ("Radio Symphony" 116). What is dominant here is an insistent proleptic impetus that suspends fulfillment until the very end of the work by creating an abstracted symphonic space where connections of the present to any moment before the beginning of the work or to the listener's own conditions are suppressed. Adorno's connection of this proleptic suspension to the mustering of overwhelming symphonic force lets us see that the process of suspension is a deception, a sleight of hand dependent on the masking power of symphonic volume. Adorno even goes so far as to refer to this as "the drug tendency" ("Radio Symphony" 120) of music, a characterization that should recall Johnson's narrator's assertion that the patron "seemed to take [ragtime] as a drug" (131). The kind of drug in question here is clearly an amnesiac, for the symphony's presentation of its beginning as a creation ex nihilo fosters the illusion that detachment from the past, the basis of the forms of mastery that Johnson is engaged in critiquing, is not only possible but de rigeur, an achieved and existent part of the subjective and social landscape.

The symphony that the narrator leaves his patron to compose is not a repudiation of the patron's ideas about art, society, race, or time. It is instead the formal embodiment of the patron's outlook. That the narrator has become intensely attached to this form, and remains so even after the termination of his physical proximity to his patron, speaks of the power of the patron's ideology. The narrator leaves the patron to pursue an end quite foreign to the patron, the use of art in the service of racial uplift, but he leaves him intent on using means eminently compatible with the patron's outlook, a symphonic form predicated upon the possibility of detaching the present and the future from the past. This ideology of detachment is at the heart of all the various strains that constitute the novel's concern with mastery and sublimation. The belief in a possible detachment of, or at least sharp separation between, mind and body is a crucial support for fictions of both sublimation and the racialization of corporeality. The power of abstraction fostered by symphonic form and embodied in a residual theory of truth revolves around the detachment of knowledge from experience. Just as crucially, the legitimacy of the patron's mastery and the white supremacist beliefs of the lynchers depends on the violent detachment of the present from the past. I have described this detachment as a conceptual veil or barrier, but Michael Hanchard's description of it as the imposition of "tabula rasa" is more pointed in its explicit equation of detachment with violence. Hanchard writes, "tabula rasa, therefore was an act of metaphysical violence, erasing historical narratives that acknowledged the roles of prior actors and agents in history" (250). The aesthetic ideology that the narrator takes with him into the South is based on creating a space for individual creation (or self-creation) by erasing or effacing the already existent narratives that belie the integrity of the individual in their depiction of this individual's dependence on, and immersion in, a dense weave of social relations. The positing of a blank slate turns the present of a self-possessed individual into a pivot that removes or detaches him from a social time and space constituted by messy interactions with others long enough to transform these interactions into mastered and unidirectional ties. In terms of Johnson's narrator's experience in the American South, this pivot is the narrator's notebook, an instrument that turns the call-and-response of the revival meeting into inert patterns of musical notation to be utilized by the narrator only later, a prefiguring of the yellowing scraps of manuscript with which the novel concludes. The call-and-response of a shared social space vibrant with the tangible vibrations of sound felt as much as heard survive in the narrator's notebook as raw material stored and ready for the time when the narrator moves on to compose his symphony. This delay and this separation of aesthetic creation into two detached stages, the collecting of material and the composing of a symphony out of this material, is the mark of the narrator's acquiescence to a regime of sublimation and detached mastery. To have undertaken the shaping of his composition (and, even more radically, the performance of this composition) in the midst of the realm where call-and-response is dominant would have been to let the narrator's composition ring out as another response and another call in a potentially endless pattern of repetition with no ultimate origin.[19] The possibility of situating the narrator's efforts in this way is forestalled, however, by his adherence to the conceptions of individuality, temporality, and creation instilled in him by his experience in Europe, a replication of his patron's mute nonresponse to his ragtime. Relying on an impulse to detach himself from his immediate experience, the narrator eschews the dynamics of the music he hears in the South in favor of the musical logic that the patron's German guest had so forcefully and rudely thrust upon him. The narrator conceives of composition as an exclusively intellectual activity and thus follows a plan that shelters his thought processes from the experience that contributes to this thought.

Unlike the narrator, Johnson's novel is quite critical of detaching individual creation from the social matrix out of which it inevitably emerges; Johnson works to undo belief in tabula rasa and in detachment of the present from the past. He does so by foregrounding the link between force and abstract timelessness that undergirds the ideology of sublimation and that symphonic form's creation ex nihilo presents as aesthetic sublimity.[20] Johnson makes this link apparent in the two most overt displays of violence in the novel, the lynching and the shooting of a white woman in the club where the narrator learns to play ragtime. In both of these instances, the narrator experiences a suspension of time-consciousness, but one much less pleasant and much more crudely engendered than that experienced by a listener in a concert hall. In his description of the lynching that he witnesses, the narrator writes that "it was over before I realized that time had elapsed" (187). In his account of the jealousy-inspired shooting of "the widow" at "the Club," the same removal from any consciousness of time's passage is apparent: the narrator's flight is a nondescript blur that leads him to write "how long and far I walked I cannot tell" (124). In both cases the spectacle of violence removes the narrator from his usual sense of time and transforms him into a mindless and mute victimized object, a metaphorical leaf blown by the wind of violent force itself.

In these scenes showing experiences of timelessness brought on by unexpected and unsanctioned eruptions of violent force, Johnson dispels the myth of timelessness as the medium of free, self-determining individuals. The narrator is never more bound by the fetters of physical causality than when he mindlessly flees from the club or when his stupefied horror prevents him from turning away from the lynching. These scenes take the grid of the narrator's planned symphony and use it to plot the narrator's real-life experience; in this transposition from the aesthetic register to the everyday, the pleasure that symphonic form yields becomes a very unpleasurable terror. Johnson literalizes the aesthetics of symphonic sublimation and shows that the pleasure the symphony promises to deliver centers on the presentation of an alluring but impossible trajectory.[21] Alluring because it is the trajectory of ascension into the sphere of absolute and unlimited power; impossible because the protagonist of this ascension is never an individual—the sublimating movement narrated by the symphony is the movement of power enshrining itself, a movement that does not bring individuals with it. In Johnson's novel two figures, the patron and the narrator, attempt to make this sublimating movement their own: one ends up committing suicide and one ends up languishing in despair and regret, lamenting the "sacrifice" of his musical talent. The sublimating trajectory of power's endorsement of itself takes no one into a realm of absolute power, but it does deposit individuals on different levels of the not absolute but still very real hierarchy of power that governs American society. This assignment of power and privilege is very much dependent on race, as can be seen in the fact that the narrator becomes financially successful only when he decides to live "as a white man." The promise of sublimation is false for both the narrator and the patron, a falseness that says much about the configurations of American society.

The powerful allure of sublimation does not leave the narrator even at the end of the novel, for his closing lamentation focuses on the end of his symphonic ambitions and does not touch on his abandonment of the music that gave him his greatest success and promised the greatest career, namely, ragtime. The narrator has been so successfully interpellated that even when he realizes the course of his life has taken an ignominious turn, he looks back only on the single event of the lynching that led him to renounce his symphony and his race. Thinking of the narrative of his life as a kind of creation ex nihilo, a creation in which his position at the end of the novel flows from one definite cause detached from anything that precedes it, the narrator forgets that the autobiography he writes is shaped by a pair of violent events rather than a single such event. Like the beginning of standard time out of the day of two noons, his singular fate starts with a repetition. The importance of the lynching in determining the narrator's end is clear, but the determining power of the shooting at the club is of at least equal importance. The two events share the power of detachment as well as narrative-shaping power; both show the ability of force to literally detach the narrator from his past by inspiring flight.

Again, Johnson shows a literalization of the patron's (and ultimately, the narrator's) ideology of aesthetic sublimation by turning the detachment that is valorized in this ideology into realities quite impossible to valorize. The barbarity of the shooting and the lynching are decisive points in the narrator's tale. The first one removes him from a rich ragtime culture and puts him in contact both with the idea of making ragtime classic and with the patron's ideas about art; the second hastens the end of his immersion in the musical culture of the South.[22] These two violent events frame the period of the narrator's turn from ragtime to classical music and lay the groundwork for the narrator's sudden decision to undertake a life as a white real estate speculator. In between these two events are sandwiched the German guest's displacement of the narrator from his piano bench and the narrator's debate with the patron over his future course of action, determinants of the narrator's ultimate course that are less barbaric but no less decisive or powerful. The first set of events is physically violent, and the second is rhetorically coercive; the two sets should be seen in concert, as signs of the complementarity of physical and ideological force and of the patron and the lynchers. It is this complex of forces that Johnson takes aim at in his novel. I have used the dynamics of the narrator's planned symphony to explicate this complex and Johnson's critique of it, but the dynamics of the novel have their own connection to this complex.

Johnson's novel shares with the symphony that its narrator sets out to write a proleptic and prefigurative impetus. This impetus is clearly evident in the first sentence of the novel: "I know that in writing the following pages I am divulging the great secret of my life." The first declaration of the novel immediately shifts the reader's attention forward in expectation of the revelation of "a great secret," a proleptic shift compounded by the second paragraph's use of the future tense to promise the completion of the narrator's psychological disclosure in the book's "last paragraph." In pointing beyond itself and promising a totalizing synthesis at the end of the novel, Johnson's beginning lays bare a tendency of all novelistic form, what Paul de Man describes as the tendency in novels for the beginning to contain "everything essential that the end will confirm" (*Romanticism* 19). The novel's prospective prefiguring of its own end has two main effects. First of all, by tying the beginning firmly to the end, it adds weight to the novel's self-presentation as a firmly unified string of necessary events. Second, it creates an atmosphere in which the self-positing power of the novel's narrating consciousness can be taken as the self-determining autonomy of a transcendental subject. This tendency betrays the novel's complicity in the illusion of a subject in full command of his own experiences and, ultimately, of his own goal. What happens in the proleptic first moment is a separation of a literary self from an empirical self disavowed by this literary self. The literary self that is separated in this moment has a knowledge of its own destiny that no empirical self can ever possess and thus is the precondition for the distinctive temporality engendered by the novel. At work here is the literary equivalent of symphonic creation ex nihilo, with all the same attendant links to detachment, mastery, sublimation, and deception. Deception because the sublimating work of separating a transcendental or non-empirical consciousness from an empirical one is supposed to be a gradual process that occurs over time rather than as the result of the instant and illicit act characteristic of novelistic beginnings. The prolepsis of novelistic beginning aids this deception by directing attention toward the novel's completion and by figuring the positing of a separate literary self as a process always underway but never traceable to any concrete origin. The temporality engendered by this proleptic positing creates a situation in which, in de Man's words, "the fiction is all present and all future, but has no past since, unlike empirical existence, it has a self-determined source prior to which it has neither existence nor memory" (*Romanticism* 21). The tendency of novelistic beginnings is to figure themselves as distinct from the non-novelistic moments that precede them.

The success of the novel's proleptic gambit creates a bit of a problem, for if a novel is to constitute itself as a progress (or a regress) it needs a past against which to measure itself. The novel gives itself a self-determining origin, but this origin is unfixed and is without the kind of inertia that might justify a unidirectional or sublimating movement into the future. Like the beginnings of symphonies, the beginnings of novels have an unwarranted and slightly scandalous quality that novels usually work to hide. The novel does this by using its power to create temporal syntheses and reversals in the service of a retrospectively reasonable and comprehensible past that can appear as a condition of "always-already-progressing," (Eagleton 120) a sourceless and eternal motion as "motus quo" (Perry Anderson 47). The difficulty of achieving such a past effect highlights the delicacy required of beginnings and endings in forms that aspire to closed-off organic totality. To achieve their characteristic effects, the novel and the symphony require endpoints capable of lifting these forms out of their empirical and social contexts while at the same time capable of presenting themselves as evanescent revolving doors that present no barrier to the timeless flow of progressive, sublimating temporality.

Even the most cursory glance at the play of verb tenses and doubled first-person pronouns in evidence on the first page of the *Autobiography* reveals the delicacy of its opening. Simple present, present progressive, the subjunctive, and future tense all make their appearance before the phrase "I was born" marks the settling into the past tense mode characteristic of autobiography. The complex delicacy of the tensed play that precedes the autobiographical narrating of the past is a game that plays with the conventions of novelistic beginning, a serious game that enacts the expected apparatus of proleptic expectation and separation of a literary from an empirical self in order to expose this apparatus and its complicity with a regime of racial hierarchy.[23] Johnson does this by combining prolepsis with a movement that lifts the veil from the normally self-obscuring apparatus of beginning by going through its operations with a step-by-step baldness. The opening delineates its own mechanisms in order to undercut them.

This process begins in the first paragraph, which consists of three sentences each starting with a first-person present tense declaration: "I know," "I feel," "I know." In these declarations, a present tense literary consciousness emerges and announces its role as the constitutive focal point of the entire text. They initiate the movement of the text but do not participate in it, exempting themselves from the time of the narrative in order to shepherd the text along the path staked out for it in advance. Following the dictates of the reductive model of truth, this consciousness owes its existence to the experience that it describes, but it holds itself apart from this experience by figuring it as a movement that ends with the constitution of its own literary consciousness. Thus, the repeated atemporal expressions of knowledge ("I know that," "I know that") occur from a position that is the same at the beginning of the novel as it is at the end. Withdrawn from the flow of time that will drive the progress of the empirical self immersed in the narrative, the literary self detaches itself from the empirical self in order to portray a self-mastery that follows the mind-body division of sublimation. This is all in accordance with de Man's description of how novelistic beginnings function, as well as with the desire of autobiographical form to stabilize the volatile subject-object imbrication that characterizes autobiography, but the statement sandwiched between the twinned "I know"s, "I feel," is a bit of a problem for this schema. "I feel" is a statement hard to attribute to a literary or transcendental self. It speaks of a complicity of knowledge and flesh even when it is used, as it is in Johnson's opening paragraph, as a metaphor for a form of intellectual intuition. The presence of this present tense admission of empirical pollution undoes the establishment of a detached literary subject that Johnson mimics, especially since it too is repeated. In the third sentence of the opening paragraph, the repeated "I know" that starts the sentence is followed by a repetition of "I feel" that is not subordinated to "I know" but is linked to it by the coordinating conjunction "and." The repetition of the statement "I feel" on the same present tense level as "I know" troubles the clean separation of a pure literary self from an empirical self of the narrative but does not disturb the proleptic time scheme of the novel. This is a disturbance that does not occur until the second paragraph of Johnson's novel, a one-sentence paragraph starting in the present tense but ending in the simple future tense, laying out in advance the entire path of the novel and encapsulating in one stroke the two time dimensions juggled by the mechanisms of novelistic form: "And too, I suffer a vague feeling of unsatisfaction, of regret, and of almost remorse, from which I am seeking relief, and of which I shall speak in the last paragraph of this account" (3).

Between the present tense and the future tense, the preposition "from" marks a detour into a very pregnant instance of the present progressive: by marking the "vague feeling of unsatisfaction" and "regret" that he suffers from in the present tense as something "from which [he is] *seeking* relief," the narrator registers the inability of the progressive time of the novel to deliver satisfaction, even in its own terms. The phrase "from which I am seeking relief" combines a present progressive tense with a verb ("seeking") pointed toward the future and an object ("relief") suggesting cessation. This mixture betrays an imbrication of temporalities that sweeps the present tense position of the literary consciousness into the time of the narrative it is supposed to control. Unlike the combination of present tense with present progressive that occurs in the three sentences of the first paragraph, here the present progressive is not subordinated to the present tense, an indication that the literary consciousness of the narrator has not succeeded in separating itself from the empirical consciousness narrated in the novel. The lack of separation is evident in the choice of a present tense verb ("suffer") as well as in this verb's relation to the present progressive phrase that it fails to subordinate or master; even in the active voice the verb "to suffer" betrays the objecthood of the writing or speaking subject by speaking of the impact of outside forces on it. The narrator suffers, and what he suffers from is an inability to detach himself from the corporeal and the past, an inability to properly sublimate.

This is made most clear in that part of the text that the second paragraph proleptically points toward: "the last paragraph of this account" (3). The opening of the novel promises to speak of the "vague feeling of unsatisfaction" that the narrator suffers from in the last paragraph of the novel, and it does but only after the beginning of the last paragraph first speaks of satisfaction: "My love for my children makes me glad that I am what I am and keeps me from desiring to be otherwise" (211). Here we see the satisfaction that sublimation and novelistic progress should deliver: a contentment at the self-sufficiency of "I am what I am" and "relief" from the restless desire that makes one dissatisfied with the present. The happy deliverance from the discontents of time is belied by what follows: "and yet, when I sometimes open a little box in which I still keep my fast yellowing manuscripts, the only tangible remnants of a vanished dream, a dead ambition, a sacrificed talent, *I cannot repress* the thought that after all, I have chosen the lesser part, that I have sold my birthright for a mess of pottage" (211). This is what the ex-colored man suffers from, intermittent failures to maintain the repression on which his present tense contentment and self-sufficency rest. Intermittent because this description is given to us in the iterative, a form that alludes to repetition by "narrating one time what happened n times" (Genette 116). Even though it is narrated only once, the event that occurs every time the box of manuscripts is opened is a repetitive disruption of the narrator's self-sufficiency, a syncopated rhythm in which unmastered returnings belie his ability to detach himself from the past. The narrator's inability to fully sublimate his past experience shows that the progress traced in the novel has not succeeded in removing him from the demands of corporeality, and that he is just as liable to violent blows and impositions of timelessness as he was in the past. What happens "every time" the narrator opens his box of manuscripts is that the past grips him with a force that defies mastery. In these recurring moments an alternative time-consciousness emerges, a sense that the past travels with us and is inextricably bound up with the present. The forward movement of time is not halted, for even hazy reveries can be measured by the clock, but it is swung, given a vibrational charge indicating the material underside of its role as abstract principle or objective measurement.

Johnson's manipulation of the link between the opening and the closing of the novel mimics the proleptic and aestheticizing operations of novelistic beginnings and endings in order to expose and deform them. Johnson gives us an ending that repeats the beginning in its refusal to obey a schema of sublimation based on the possibility of a clean separation between literary and empirical consciousness and, ultimately, between mind and body. In doing so, Johnson upsets the mechanism by which corporeal embodiment is equated with blackness. The repetitive imbrication of mind and body, subject and object, and literary and empirical consciousness makes untenable any schema that assigns corporeal embodiment exclusively to particular types of subjects or that denies the impact of corporeality on consciousness.

What conception of race, then, does Johnson's novel leave us with? The oblique and elliptical way that the narrator approaches any statement of racial identity makes it difficult to establish exactly what race is for the narrator, but it is clear that it is not a biological determinant. Although he does not conceive of racial identity in the way the patron does, as a kind of freely made choice, the narrator's belief that he has "sold [his] birthright for a mess of pottage" is not a lament over detachment from a naturally given racial essence (211). Instead, like Esau, he regrets having sold something that should not be sold. The narrator sees his error as succumbing to the allure of financial success and allowing the power of money to dissolve the ties that bind him to anything outside of himself, his children, and his white wife. In "selling his birthright," he redefines his complex relationship to his social environment and his past as a simple and limited relationship. He does this by making himself as deaf to the claims the past makes upon his present as the patron was to the call of his music. Race, then, is figured as the mode in which an individual lives his responsiveness to the calls of the past and the claims of his social environment.

As an ex-colored man, the narrator allows certain calls directed at him to go without a response, the result of his seduction by a conception of social space as uniform, homogeneous, and nonconflictual. Donald Lowe descries this mode of conceptualizing space as characteristic of a bourgeois society placing "a premium on objective reason" (55). According to Lowe, bourgeois society "reduce[s] the intersubjectivity of the world, as well as the reflexivity of embodied life" by locating "the conscious calculation of actions in an impersonal space, where all nonobjective considerations would be discounted" (55). This is the space of sublimated subjects interacting as unfettered buyers and sellers free from coercive restrictions. It is also the space of the traditional symphonic concert hall, a space in which sound separates rather than unites listeners by presenting them with precisely refined tones requiring no response.

In the last section of *The Autobiography of an Ex-Colored Man* the narrator imagines himself as inhabiting such a space, but in the preceding sections of the novel the narrator is a victim of this imagined objective social space. By narrating the violence that life as "a Colored Man" makes the narrator susceptible to, Johnson shows that the goal of acceding to equal participation in this kind of imagined social space is a problematic one for the narrator because this space is created by the violent suppression and exclusion of black bodies. Like the symphony, the novel, and autobiography, objective social space is a form created by an abstracting detachment from embodied experience and by the imposition of inside-outside boundaries that expel bodily otherness. In writing of the complicity of "the forceful and the formal," Lindon Barrett describes the institution of such forms as a process in which "value is violence, then it is form" (33). The violent episodes around which Johnson's narrative revolves are figures for the violence that institutes social or aesthetic forms and their attendant temporalities. Form is violent because it expels Others and otherness, but as Barrett points out, it is also violent in its "forcible disruption of Otherwise established forms," forms that follow a logic and a rhythm different than that of dominant society. Keeping this in mind, one sees that the form of white bourgeois subjectivity that the narrator accedes to at the end of the novel is predicated upon an effacement of alternative imaginings of social space as well as the disqualification of racial otherness.

Rag Time and Ragtime Space

Johnson draws attention to this kind of effacement in his contrasting of the objective social space of the white New York business world and the patron's salons and dinner parties with scenes in which space and the interactions that take place in it are configured according to an entirely different logic. Foremost among these scenes are "the Club" and "the meeting." These two locations are remarkable for the powerful configurations of sound that take place in them, and, indeed, the narrative presents the sounds flowing out of the club before it gives any visual or objective description of it: "we heard mingled sounds of music and laughter, the clink of glasses, and the pop of bottles." These are all sounds indicating openings, decantings, or outpourings—the dynamic emptying out of containers and bodies. The plangent resonance of the club and of the meeting is what distinguishes them from the objective social space that seduces the narrator. The fiction of objective social space posits subjects with distinct and inviolable boundaries, but in the Club sound and its effervescent shaping threatens these boundaries. Sound threatens the fiction of objective social space, for sound always creates a material link between its creator and its hearer. When one strikes a piano key or enunciates a syllable by letting one's glottis vibrate, an oscillating wave is created that strikes not only the ears but the entire bodily surface of all subjects within the sound's range.[24] The physical properties of sound require exposure and even a certain amount of risk; looking through a window or across a velvet rope in the Cotton Club lets one imagine oneself as a detached observer or judge, but to hear someone or something one has to open the window and let the sound into one's "own" space.[25] It is the disrespect of sound for personal and social boundaries that makes the control of music an essential task for societies interested in perpetuating themselves. This is clear in Plato's assertion that "the modes of music are never disturbed without unsettling of the most fundamental political and social conventions"; it is equally clear in the vehement denunciations that accompanied the spread of jazz and ragtime in the 1910s and 1920s.[26]

The difference in acceptability of ragtime and the symphony is the difference between divergent treatments of the materiality of sound, the symphony striving to rationalize and constrain the materiality of sound in keeping with the dictates of objective social space, and ragtime reveling in the expansive but unruly possibilities of such sonic materiality. In its engagement with the materiality of sound, ragtime announces itself as what Barrett calls "an Otherwise produced form" and as a form linked to a conception and experience of space not governed by a sublimating suppression of materiality. It is this kind of space that Johnson shows us in his depiction of the club and the meeting, spaces richly resonant with a continual and repetitive wash of oscillating sound. This is the space of the call-and-response of Singing Johnson and his unnamed respondents as well as the space of the call-and-response structure of the ragtime that animates the club. The foregrounding of sound in the space of call-and-response, a space that one might call "ragtime space," means that this space has a different time as well as a different relationship to sound. For, as Fabian writes, "it is the sensuous nature of language, its being an activity of concrete organisms and the embodiment of consciousness in a material medium—sound—which makes language an eminently temporal phenomenon" (163). The materiality of language, as of music, "is based on articulation, on frequencies, pitch, tempo, all of which are realized in the dimension of time" (Fabian 163). Ragtime space is the suppressed condition of objective social space, just as the materially engendered temporality of call-and-response is the suppressed condition of the progressive, developmental time of sublimation. In ragtime space, detachment and disavowal are impossible.

Ragtime is a music that "demand[s] physical response," and in ragtime space every linguistic, gestural, or musical call also demands some form of response. Ragtime space leaves the materiality of every call—every word or note—unveiled, and the naked materiality of communication strikes the recipients who inhabit this space, marking them as both objects immersed in waves of sound and subjects compelled to respond to this sound, even if this response is the willed feigning of nonresponse. Responsiveness defines the subject in ragtime space, where the question of how one responds to the calls that strike one displaces any question of absolute freedom or determined slavery. Between a sublimating freedom untainted by the past and a stultifying mechanical repetition of unchanging biological fate, ragtime space and the syncopated time that organizes it gives the subject enmeshed in it a ragged motion in which a never ending succession of calls deliver the possibility, but not the assurance, of fortuitous change. Like the narrator in his susceptibility to intermittent waves of unrepressed memory, the ragtime subject responds to calls from the past, both because sound's propagation is a process that takes time to reach the subject and because music, as Attali puts it, "is also past time to be produced, heard and exchanged" (9).

For the narrator and for the subject that dances its response to the repetitive calls of ragtime, the shape of identity is determined by responsiveness to cultural memory. For as Samuel A. Floyd Jr. tells us, ragtime and jazz are forms of cultural memory, repositories of "meanings that comprise the subjective knowledge of a people, its immanent thoughts, its structures and its practices, [which] become conscious and culturally objective in practice and perception" (*Power of Black Music* 8). This is what the ragtime subject and Johnson's narrator respond to, objective manifestations of cultural memory that ring out in the compelling sound of ragtime. The past that troubles the narrator at the end of the novel is not just his own but that of what he calls his "mother's people" (210). His life as "an ordinarily successful white man" is shaken by the calls of cultural memory and the call(s) of race, the response to which he cannot totally avoid. The narrator's situation at the close of the novel and the resonance of ragtime throughout the novel figure race as a form of responsiveness, or responsibility, to cultural memory. This is not to suggest that race is given here as choice, for the essential character of the call of cultural memory is that it, like ragtime, "demands" response. The narrator is no less raced because of the way that he has chosen to respond to these calls; Johnson shows us the narrator's race trembling within him as the impossibility of transforming the past into inert matter. The resonance of this scene is in its depiction not of a failed sublimation but of sublimation as objectively false in its injustice to the past. Thomas Huhn characterizes this injustice as follows: "What is unjust about sublimation is its valorizing of suffering, and by extension, repression" (292). Huhn reminds us that sublimation attempts to transcend suffering by fixing it in an economy of profit and loss that transforms the investment of those who suffer into a profit accruing to those who thrive. When we recall that the narrator's past includes the witnessing of a lynching, the impropriety of figuring the past as a set of necessary steps to a fortuitous future is shockingly clear. Johnson's text interrupts this succession by juxtaposing it with a repetitive, syncopated time that rings out from the ragtime space and ragtime temporality woven into it. Alongside of his critique of a developmental time that flees from the past, Johnson models a call-response time that figures every present as in dialogue with a succession of past presents. This ragtime does not transcend the past but clings to in a nontranscendence that hopes to make room for the past in a future that swung repetition might eventually break free from the stranglehold of a present hostile to the possibility of an-other time and an-other present and future.

In his portrayal of ragtime, Johnson attempts to substitute the swing and pulsing oscillation of a resonant, relational social space and time for the swing of black bodies from trees.

3
"Carolina Shout" and the Rhythms of Rent-Party Performance

Matter is not spread out in space and indifferent to time; it does not remain totally constant and totally inert in a uniform duration. Nor indeed does it live there like something that wears away and is displaced. It is not just sensitive to rhythms but it exists, in the fullest sense of the term, on the level of rhythm.

—Gaston Bachelard, *The Dialectic of Duration*

The dances they did at the Jungles Casino were wild and comical—the more pose and the more breaks the better. These Charleston people and the other southerners had just come to New York. They were country people and they felt homesick. When they got tired of two-steps and schottisches (which they danced with a lot of spieling), they'd yell: "Let's go back home!" . . . or "Now put us in the alley!" I did my "Mule Walk" or "Gut Stomp" for these country dances.

Breakdown music was the best for such sets, the more solid and groovy the better. They'd dance, hollering and screaming until they were cooked. The dances ran from fifteen to thirty minutes, but they kept up all night until their shoes wore out—most of them after a heavy day's work on the docks.

—James P. Johnson, *Runnin' Wild*

The gap between the anonymous publication of *The Autobiography of an Ex-Colored Man* in 1912 and its reprint in 1927 with Johnson's name on the title page fostered intense speculation about the identity of the work's author and of its narrator. In his real autobiography (*Along This Way*), Johnson tells of meeting someone who actually claimed to be this mysterious author in Johnson's presence. While this act might be read as the kind of usurpation that musicians like Johnson's narrator were often subject to, it could also be seen as an example of the kind of playful participation in the work that its anonymous status invited.

In his anonymous publication of the novel, Johnson challenges conventional notions of authorship. This chapter takes up the challenge, and suggests that Johnson's novel is a coauthored work, a work that participates in the collective and antiphonal effervescence characterizing the ragtime and dancing taking place at The Club. At The Club, Johnson's narrator learns to play ragtime; he does so by appropriating the musical configurations of others and incorporating them into his own style. In his writing, Johnson himself takes up some of these same musical energies and incorporates them into his novel. This suggests that one of the important coauthors of the *Autobiography* is another Johnson, the virtuoso New York pianist James P. Johnson. James P. Johnson's improvisational skills mark him as a better likeness for the anonymous narrator than is James Weldon Johnson himself. His music has the same ability to surprise and to demand response that James Weldon Johnson gives to his narrator's music. In James P. Johnson's ragtime and stride performance, we can hear the alternative construction of temporality that the *Autobiography* works to incorporate into its form.

James P. Johnson is an intriguing figure in the history of jazz and in the history of the intellectual scene in interwar New York. He is perhaps best known as the composer of the "Charleston" (although a tiny percentage of those who can identify the Charleston can identify Johnson), the strains of which have become a clichéd figure for a shallowly understood "Jazz Age,"[1] but his musical accomplishments are remarkably diverse, including as they do important works in both jazz and classical music, as well as in musicals and even opera, and in ensembles ranging in size from solo piano to soloist with symphony. His productivity can be seen in the partial catalog of his works that he made in a 1930 letter to James Weldon Johnson asking for help in securing a Guggenheim fellowship: "I have in Manuscript a 'Symphonic Suite' on St. Louis Blues—2 symphonies, a Piano Concerto & other compositions for major symphony orchestra also piano pieces." The best known of Johnson's classical works is the piece "Yamekraw," orchestrated by William Grant Still and performed at Carnegie Hall in 1927. Johnson's classical output is impressive, but he was even more prolific in the field of jazz, cutting over 170 records and piano rolls, including at least five different versions of "Carolina Shout." The sheer number of his recordings gives some sense of his influence, but the accounts of contemporary musicians are even more telling. Duke Ellington, whose piano style was heavily influenced by Johnson's playing, has this to say about him: "James, for me, was more than the beginning. He went right up to the top" (94). Like Fats Waller and Count Basie, Ellington learned Johnson's 1921 recording of "Carolina Shout" note for note (Ellington, *Music* 34). Through Waller and Ellington (as well as through his own recordings and performances) James P. Johnson's performance practice has had an impact on virtually every pianist who has ever played jazz. The appeal that his playing had for musicians like Waller and Ellington is due at least partially to the way that he was able to synthesize an emerging blues style with the established compositional practices of ragtime, stride, and New York jazz, and in doing so to add a new level of fluidity, elasticity, and improvisational élan to an already compelling musical form.

Johnson's music also had a powerful effect on those outside of his field. In a letter dated January 24, 1937, Langston Hughes writes to Johnson, "I have long known and admired your work," expressing an admiration that eventually led Hughes to collaborate with Johnson on the 1940 opera/musical, *The Organizer*. Hughes was not alone in his admiration, for Johnson's work was well known to all the important figures of the Harlem Renaissance.

In fact, if the Harlem Renaissance is understood as more than a strictly literary movement, then James P. Johnson appears as an important part of it. If the Renaissance is understood more broadly, as an intense becoming urban and equally intense intellectual and aesthetic reflection on the status of African Americans in a society largely indifferent or antagonistic to their existence, then the power and sophistication of James P. Johnson's works mark him as a key, or even central, figure in this movement. His collaboration with Hughes in 1940 has been credited, but there is a way in which Johnson, like other jazz musicians of the period, is an uncredited collaborator in all the aesthetic productions of the Harlem Renaissance.

Of all of James P. Johnson's music, it is his 1918 composition "Carolina Shout" and his 1921 recording of it that most hauntingly animate James Weldon Johnson's *The Autobiography of an Ex-Colored Man*. Its treatment of time and of the rhythm of the relationship between work and world resonate throughout James Weldon Johnson's novel.

One might say that the 1921 recording of "Carolina Shout" lasts three minutes and nineteen seconds. This would tell you something about the recording but would miss most of what is important about its relationship to time. Near the end of "All the Things You Might Be by Now If Sigmund Freud's Wife Was Your Mother" (an essay that takes its title from a Charles Mingus composition), Hortense Spillers suggests the complexity of the relationship between jazz and time when she writes that "it would take a good long time to learn to hear it [Mingus' music] well" (141). How long can it take to hear, or to listen to, something that always takes up the same span of measured clock time? (Surely Spillers is not suggesting slowing down the recording or playing it backward to *really* hear it.) The vicissitudes of time and performance at work here demonstrate the ultimate inadequacy of counting ticks on a clock or measures in a composition, despite the necessity of this counting.

In counting up the 174 bars and ten sixteen-bar sections of "Carolina Shout," the one truth that reveals itself is the heavy dependence of James P. Johnson's performance on repetition. Like many jazz pieces, "Carolina Shout" is constructed out of a few basic building blocks. In this case four sixteen-bar sections are put together to make up the performance, three of which are repeated at least twice. Except for the introduction and coda of the piece, every part of "Carolina Shout" measurable by a clock or metronome is a repetition of one of these four sections. In addition to this repetition of the piece's basic building blocks, there is also repetition within these sixteen-bar sections. For example, the first sixteen-bar section starts off with a four-bar pattern that is repeated three times. Repetition inheres both within and without the basic building blocks of the composition, making it a rhythmic arrangement of a field of repetition as pervasive as that engendered by any clock.

Critics have consistently noted Johnson's foregrounding of rhythm above all else. In *The New Grove Dictionary of Jazz*, Willa Rouder places Johnson's "rhythmicization of his musical ideas" at the core of Johnson's performance practice. Gunther Schuller agrees, writing that, "With his strong, striding left hand, Johnson focused his attention on the rhythmicization of melodic ideas, often suppressing the later element to the point of extinction" (217). The emphasis on rhythm in Johnson's music, and especially in "Carolina Shout,"[2] betrays an intense involvement with the problematics of time and subjectivity at work in James Weldon Johnson's text. The bold rhythmic power coursing through performances like "Carolina Shout" is the mark of a temporal logic that allows James P. Johnson's music to function in a social realm governed by an abstract, sublimating time without succumbing to its dictates.

"Carolina Shout" refutes both the possibility and the desirability of sublimation and its attendant temporality. Its repetitive structure traces a movement that couples virtuosic adaptation to dominant time structures with an improvisation on the imbrication of thought and bodily experience that keeps alive other temporal possibilities. When James P. Johnson strikes the piano keys in a way that maintains the trajectory of forward motion characteristic of the piece[3] and simultaneously pushes and pulls on the beat (as in measures 29 and 30) to reveal its latent vibrational affinities, he demonstrates a mastery of time that embraces the interrelatedness of mind and body, and of space and time. This is a mastery unlike that imagined by the reigning imperatives of American culture, a mastery that has no dependence on the detachment that drives sublimation and subtends racial hierarchies. In its repetitive return to the same melodic and rhythmic patterns, Johnson's "Carolina Shout" leaves nothing behind but unfolds itself as a rhythmic structure allowing the return of any of its previous sections. The possible and actual return of previous sections of the piece belies any belief in the possibility of fully mastering and moving beyond the past, for all the performance's past sections are also possible futures. When these sections return (as we see at 2:19, a repetition with variation of what occurs at 1:04) and Johnson improvises a new way of traversing the same musical terrain (Ellington: "it seemed as though you never heard the same note twice" [*Music* 94]),[4] he performs the mastery of nonmastery, an employment of an unmatched mastery of the keyboard, of time, and of improvisation in service of the recognition that the past and the body are never fully mastered. His performance revels in the material, not as the manifestation of some brute mindlessness but as the site for all innovation and all improvisation that doesn't merely deliver the expected and the already known.

Driven by the belief that a repeated pass through any of the sections of the composition might yield a difference missed on the first time through, Johnson's performance refuses to renounce the sections that have already passed by. "Carolina Shout" insists that the present is always insuperably attached to both the future and the past, and that repetition, if handled properly, is more likely to open onto a future possibility than onto a regressive past. The plangent ring of struck keys and the syncopated rhythms that cut across bar lines are the aural mark of what Paul Allen Anderson calls "an aesthetic of tonal impurity" (55), an aesthetic interested in convergence, fluidity, mixing, and relationality, and which is blithely indifferent to schemas imposing divisions between mind and body, and between present and past.

This eschewal of detachment and division has a profound effect upon the way "Carolina Shout" constructs its audience. Themselves the product of the imbrication of performer and audience, the clangorous declamations of "Carolina Shout" pull from and give back to the audience that James P. Johnson played for with such great frequency. Starting around 1913, Johnson performed in "The Jungles," the black section of Hell's Kitchen. His audience there was made up largely of laborers from the South who danced much of the night to Johnson's solo piano. The dancing style of this audience had a sharp impact on Johnson; he improvised and composed rhythmic figures and cadences to suit the dancers that he played for. Responsive to the shouts and dance steps of the Carolina Island dockworkers who made up much of his audience at the Jungles Casino, James P. Johnson incorporated these elements into his piece in a way that makes "Carolina Shout" emerge less as a work forged in the "alembic" of some genius's imagination and more as a recombination and continuation of already existing dynamics.[5] Hearing "Carolina Shout" for the first time, much of James P. Johnson's audience heard an improvised version of what was already familiar—a reconfiguring of parts of their own Southern experience in Johnson's virtuoso manipulation of sound and rhythm.

The provenance of "Carolina Shout" is thus not traceable to one discrete subject but emerges from the space of performance, a space in between and containing both performer and dancers. The call-and-response structure of "Carolina Shout" (most clearly heard in the eight bars starting at 1:05, measures 53–60) mimics the call-and-response structure of the interplay between Johnson and his audience. This form of antiphony, however, departs from a model that figures call and response as versions of cause and effect in which the two elements can always be distinguished from each other as the products of discrete individuals with their own delimited space.[6] For we should hear in "Carolina Shout" the strong imbrication and motile reversibility of call and response. This is evident in the transmutations that occur in the treatment of the repeated section approximately two minutes and thirty-six seconds into the recording of 1921 (measures 112–19). Here the established pattern of repetition is interrupted and intensified by a substitution of the call motive for the motive that had served as a response up to this point in the performance. The result is a call-call section that hastens repetition by excising the section interposing itself between repeated calls. In its smashing of these two sections together, this call-call pattern completely removes the already heavily attenuated distinction between call and response, and between performer and dancing or listening respondent. It is as if the energy and propulsive flow created by the opening two-plus minutes of the performance has launched "Carolina Shout," its performer, and respondents into a space free from distinction, a space in which call and response merge into a collective shout that celebrates the flow of subject into object, and of present into both past and future.

Despite its intensity, this is not a moment of transcendence, for the trajectory of rhythm and sound created out of pianistic virtuosity and danced responsiveness does not aim at any spatial or temporal beyond. The strict adherence to temporal regularity is never abandoned, and an eight-bar Call-Response section follows close on the heels of this interruption of call following call. Nonetheless, the polyphonic merging that characterizes this call-call section is not unique in "Carolina Shout," for it is merely the dramatization of an impulse that runs throughout the performance. This impulse is what Samuel A. Floyd Jr. is after when, in his analysis of a Jelly Roll Morton performance from the same period (1926), he excises the "and" from "call-and-response" and defines "Call-Response" as the master trope of jazz's treatment of time and rhythm. Floyd's conceptual intervention points to the imbrication and interchangeability of call and response by pointing out the way that every call and every response are links in an inexorable and unending chain of antecedent and consequent responses and calls, even if they occur at the beginning or end of a piece. Calls are responses to previous responses, and responses become calls to which subsequent calls respond. In such a pattern, no musical figure can claim priority as origin, a point Floyd emphasizes when he describes Morton's "Black Bottom Stomp," and by implication all music from this same tradition, as "fraught with funded meanings from the Afro-American music tradition" ("Ring Shout" 409). All calls, all starting points, refer back to some earlier performance, and in the jazz tradition that "Carolina Shout" is a part of they do so by troping on this antecedent in a way that highlights their status as repetition and response.[7]

The pattern of substitutive exchange and reversibility at work here also applies to the relationship between performer and listener, for as Floyd notes, in the musical tradition built on the trope of Call-Response there is a pronounced "tendency to make performances occasion in which the audience participates." This is true enough in the sense that Floyd intends in his description of comments such as "Oh yeah," "Say it," "He's cookin'," and "That's bad," comments that become "extensions, elaborations, and refinements" of the performance, but it is even more exaggerated when the response from the audience includes dancing ("Ring Shout" 403). According to the great tenor Lester Young dancers could actually become part of the musical performance: "I have a lot of fun playing for dancers because I like to dance too. *The rhythm of the dancers comes back to you when you're playing*" (Malone, "Jazz Music" 287). The response a musician gets from a dancing audience (such as the one Johnson played for at the Jungles Casino) is not just a series of interjections but a participatory intervention in the very rhythm of the performance. The influence of the waves of sound and motion emanating from a dancing audience upon the performance of a piece like "Carolina Shout" is an extreme example of the erosion of the priority of the performer, an erosion brought about by the tendency of the dancers' reactions to become determinants of what will come next in the performance, as well as responses to what has just occurred. This dialogic motion makes the performer on the piano bench a focal point rather than an origin of the sound and energy resonating in the space that he shares with the audience. James P. Johnson's improvised variations are a response both to the sound coming from the piano and to the sound coming from the audience, a reflection of the fact that he is just as much in between performed sound and audience as are the dancers. This is the situation and the motion of Call-Response, not a back and forth between discrete subjects but a coeval Call-Response rhythm in which listeners, dancers, and performers collaborate in revising and refiguring their shared time and space.

It is important that the performance of and around "Carolina Shout" is a revising and refiguring, for a foregrounded repetition is an essential organizational principle of the piece and of an ethos assuming that the ritual of its performance and of its danced reception will soon be reenacted, on the next night, in the next club or room. In its embrace of repetition, the interaction of organized sound and social subjects that is "Carolina Shout" clings to what it is given, in a renunciation of any transcendence that would move away from its constitutive temporal and social conditions. In place of transcendence, "Carolina Shout" limns a strategy of reaggregating otherwise, a strategy of shaking, or shouting down, the coercive facticity of such conditions in order to make them vibrate with previously unheard or unthought possibilities.[8] To a strictly objective gaze, spaces like "The Club" in James Weldon Johnson's *Autobiography* or "The Jungles Casino" where James P. Johnson performed offer little suggesting value or potential; but when subjected to the roving unhoused rhythms of "Carolina Shout" these spaces are reaggregated otherwise, in a configuration in which the similarity of motion between legs and arms sculpting the same space, or the felt affinity between the sequence of struck keys and executed steps, might be more significant than the bodily integrity of individuals or distinctions between performers and respondents.

Performed in the right way and to the right audience, "Carolina Shout" rearranges expectation and relationality, exerting the kind of gravitational pull that both warps established lines of similitude and compels participation in its troping on time. The two tendencies are interdependent: reaggregating participation and imaginative redefinition play themselves out in an elliptical departure from the circle of the unchanging that neither is capable of on its own.

The capability of "Carolina Shout" to "demand response" is, thus, of crucial importance.[9] But what is it, exactly, in the music that demands response? The two elements that most reliably engender response are error and incompleteness. The assuredness of Johnson's playing and the nature of the response it arouses make it clear that it is not error that elicits a response to "Carolina Shout" but incompleteness. This is not to say that "Carolina Shout" is a deficient work, but that it adheres to an aesthetic of incompleteness, and that it takes as its subject the incompleteness of time and of the "now" that an objective, linear version of it presents. Time is incomplete because it contains the ontological instability of the past and the future. Hegel characterizes this incompleteness and instability as follows: "The present is, only because the past is not: the being of the now has the determination of non-being, and the not-being of its being is the future; *the present is this negative unity*" (*Philosophy of Nature* 235).

The present is cloven by its relation to the past and the future, relations that mark the present as consisting of both being and not-being. Every present is an unstable mixture, a negative rather than a positive unity, and is thus characterized by a radical instability.[10] Hegel refers to this instability as the "absolute disquietude" (*unruhe*) of the moment and sees it as the impetus behind the forward drive of the dialectic. In his characterization of time as an unstable mixture of being and not-being, Hegel sounds like the revolutionary that Marcuse claims he once was,[11] but the openness of this moment is soon closed down in various ways (through reference to infinity, and through what Adorno calls a "logicizing of time"),[12] ways that allow a movement into place, motion, and matter that leaves the disquietude of the moment behind. Despite this eventual suppression of the openness and incompleteness of the moment, Hegel's rigor in this section of the *Encyclopedia* leads him to formulate (if only briefly) the radical instability of both time and the moment, and in doing so to open a crack in the system of idealism through which one can see that time has none of the independence of an abstract "negativity . . . posited for itself," but is dependent on the particular way that the actions of individuals and communities negate the past and the present.[13]

In her assertion that "discord is more natural than accord," Zora Neale Hurston shows that she is more capable than Hegel of thinking and moving in "the absolute disquietude of the moment" (305). Hurston asserts the primacy of discord in her consideration of African American aesthetics, a consideration that sees a stylized performance of incompleteness as essential to the power of most African American forms to compel response. Focusing on dance as a way of limning a characteristic of all "Negro art," Hurston describes it as "dynamic suggestion."[14] In the following passage, Hurston describes dynamic suggestion as the way the "Negro dancer" uses a play with incompleteness to create a powerful telling effect in his or her audience: "No matter . . . how violent it may appear to the beholder, every posture gives the impression that the dancer will do much more . . . But the spectator adds the picture of ferocious assault, hears the drums [and finds himself] participating in the performance itself—carrying out the suggestions of the performer" (302).

The power of this kind of performance resides in what is left unexpressed and in the ability of the performer to trope or signify on incompleteness. In this troping, the dynamics of the performance are turned toward the spectator, eliciting from him a response that continues the trajectory ("keeping time with the music") begun by the performer. "Carolina Shout" performs the same transfer of energy and expansion of the realm of performance with its troping on the incompleteness of time itself.[15] The insistent adventurousness, forward motion, and rhythmic tension of "Carolina Shout" stem from its performance of "dynamic suggestion." The force with which this suggestiveness strikes the listener reminds us that dynamics are, first of all, "the interplay of forces" (Aglietta). The forceful, rhythmic interplay of James P. Johnson's right and left hands suggests to those within its reach both that they move their bodies into the dynamic stream of time and that they heed the "interplay of forces" living in the time to which they move their bodies on a daily basis. This is to say that the performance of time and rhythm exemplified in "Carolina Shout" is both a dynamic suggestion of time's incompleteness and a suggestive pointing to the dynamics that shape time. In its establishment of a dynamic relationship between the various subjects struck by its sound, "Carolina Shout" improvises on and through the possibilities inherent in the fact that the basis of time is the relation between individuals.

Obeying what Kimberly Benston calls "an insistently revisionary impulse" (115) (an impulse that he identifies as the hallmark of black modernism), the rhythm of "Carolina Shout" moves and shapes itself in the opening created by the realization that the shaping of time is always a reshaping of time, a response both to "the absolute disquietude of the moment" and to previously established modes of responding to this disquietude. In doing so, it performs time so that one can feel vibrating in it the dead labor and unrealized potential sedimented in all received time structures, as well as the uncertainty of an open relation to the future that precedes both hope and fear.

One of the most pronounced marks of James P. Johnson's occupation with the absolute disquietude of the moment and the aliquant inseparability of past, present, and future that it engenders is the rhythmic suspension that first occurs in the thirty-seventh bar of "Carolina Shout" (0:45 into the recording) and that reoccurs throughout it. In these sections of "Carolina Shout" it feels as if the rug has been pulled out from beneath one's feet and that the solid momentum of the performance's opening has entered a vertiginous zone that inverts one's relationship to both sound and time. The musicologist Gunther Schuller describes these sections as measures in which "ternary patterns [are] superimposed on the basic 4/4 beat," a superimposition that works "to "loosen up the vertical structure and to free it from the unremitting binary phase division" (218). In the terminology of the pianists themselves, this is usually referred to as the utilization of a "broken bass"; its effect in this performance of "Carolina Shout" is to establish, in the space of one four-beat bar, a counter-rhythm that interrupts the existing pattern of rhythmic momentum in order to heighten the tension of an already audacious rhythmic stance by highlighting the precariousness of this stance and its labile tendencies. The unexpected break provided by this measure cultivates a form of corporeal skepticism in the subjects attuned to its resonance and possible recurrence, a preparedness for future breaks or lapses that distinguishes the most flexible dancers from those wedded to a rigid expectation of the same and that is the sign of an ability to feel the presence of the future within the present.

In the sharp lurch created by the displacement of strong and weak beats one feels the vertigo of a chasm opening up before one's feet, the joyful shock that the solid time of existence is shot through with incompleteness. This shock of dislocation makes tangible the insight that time should always bear the label "under construction." Listening to the way this dislocation reoccurs in "Carolina Shout," one feels compelled to move one's body to something in time that does not yet exist, to dance the potentiality of a rhythmic translation of incompleteness (or ontological insufficiency) into bodily motion. This moment of suspension opens the horizon of the future within the vicissitudes of the present moment. Something of the intensity with which this opening strikes the listener is captured by Hurston when she writes of a performance in which the listener "finds himself keeping time with the music and tensing himself for the struggle" (302).

Hurston describes a performance that orients the listener toward action, much as Johnson's performance does. In fact, the form of "Carolina Shout" organizes itself around the felt obviousness of Houston Baker's assertion that "form must be conceived of as a mode of action" (17). James P. Johnson's conception of composition as an extension of performance practice embeds the logic and motion of the situations of performance in the form of his piece. These situations both enable and are enabled by "Carolina Shout," a kind of Call-Response interaction revealed by the relationship between Johnson's compositions and the rent parties at which he frequently performed these compositions.

In his study of James P. Johnson's career, Scott Brown describes the rent party as "a form of mass cultural expression, the initial essence of which derived from the physical and cultural displacement of a people" (165). A crucial part of Johnson's experience as a performer, the rent party was a mixed form whose dynamics and raison d'être lie somewhere between those of the cabaret and those of the extended family gathering. A social gathering whose economic rationale is clearly stated in its title, the rent party is a creative response to the financial demands of a property-holding system that enriches the real estate speculators and landlords responsible for Harlem's inordinately high rents.[16] Promising food, drink, and social and sexual interaction as well as dancing, the whole enterprise revolved around the piano player. A good pianist was the sine qua non of a successful rent party, the financial and recreational success often depending directly on the quality and reputation of the pianist engaged.

There was a clear, if unofficial, hierarchy among the pianists who played at rent parties, and from the late 1910s until the mid-1930s, James P. Johnson was at the top of it. His booking agent, Lippy Boyette, would sometimes arrange for Johnson to play as many as three parties in the same night, which would require "starting in the afternoon and continuing through late the next day" (Brown 168). Pianists were well rewarded for playing at rent parties—in cash, food, drink and social prestige—but in Johnson's passion for playing at such gatherings there is something that exceeds desire for remuneration. Throughout James P. Johnson's career, he exhibited an almost demonic desire to perform and improvise, a desire that led him to seek both as many places to play as possible and to play as many different choruses and variations as possible of "Carolina Shout" or of any of his other pieces. Both his life and his performance practice organized themselves around this desire to repeat, this passionate search for the new combination, the unheard resonance lurking in any performance situation—be it rent party, cabaret, or recording session—and any piece or section of a piece. The intensity of this passion is demonstrated in an anecdote that the pianist Joe Turner tells of Johnson's involvement in rent parties and other informal jam sessions:

> James P. loved competition. Jam sessions he loved, and for this reason he would go home rather late. We would have our jam session until two or three the next afternoon. He was then living on Long Island, and his wife would come all the way to Harlem, and she would go from street to street until she heard the piano. And she would recognize his style, and then she would go up to the apartment to get him out of there and take him home. He was not the kind of fellow who would look around for women or anything. He just loved to play the piano. (Brown 221)

James P. Johnson, in his performance practice, as well as in his life, could quite literally conceive of no end to the repetitive reconfigurations of the different strains of his compositions, or to the resonant social spaces in which these strains were performed. There is a homology between Johnson's desire to experience the sound of his performance in as many spaces as possible and his desire to play the different repeated strains of his compositions in as many different ways as possible. Both desires betray an almost erotic attachment to repeated sections and repeated performance as opportunities for new configurations of the self and new patterns of fingers striking keys, keys striking strings, and vibrations striking those in the shared social space of the performance.

What we hear in "Carolina Shout" is the realization of Houston Baker's injunction that "form should be conceived from the point of view of action." The form of "Carolina Shout" is a pianistic manifestation of the mode of action of its performer and respondents, a mode of action and of aesthetic creation that combines a mobility not untethered from context with a responsiveness to particular contexts not divorced from an impetus to move beyond them. James P. Johnson's conception of composition as coextensive with performance practice embeds the logic and motion of performance, as well as the social context of performance, in the very form of the piece. This recalls Adorno's assertions that one can actually hear feudal patronage in Bach's music, and the bourgeois concert hall in Beethoven's.[17] What is different in "Carolina Shout" is that the social practice sedimented in it is not kept in an inert form but functions as an incitement to further elaborations of this practice. Unlike the music that Jacques Attali describes as functioning "to make people believe in [the] existence and universal value [of order], in its impossibility outside of exchange" (57), Johnson's music serves to incite non-transcendent transformation by compelling listeners to move out of their current positions and to explore the new configurations of subjectivity that bodily mimesis of pianistic shouts offers.

The way this incitement to transformation addresses its audience is markedly different from the way classical music or other forms of legitimating music address their audience. The legitimating music that Attali describes asks the audience to believe in an order whose power lies outside of themselves, and to take pleasure in the position assigned to them by this configuration of power. As a result, the audience invoked by this form of music is necessarily a striated one, carved up by the classes and functions necessary for the function of the social order that produces both audience and music. The audience called into being by "Carolina Shout" is quite different. It is a polymorphic, fissile mass; its components are driven by the call of a rhythmic injunction to feel the possibilities latent in their position and in their selves. Interpellated simultaneously at the molecular, individual, and collective level, members of this audience move to create their own collective order and to compete both with Johnson's riffs and variations and with those of the dancers on either side of them.

Behind this invocation of an audience that improvises its own principles of organization is a treatment of form that struggles consistently against a formalist tendency to close work off from world and to posit form as coextensive with "the constitutive capacity of the mind to impose structure on the world of sense experience" (Jay 148). In Johnson's improvisation, composition, and performance, work and world are propelled into an interaction as intensely complicated as the interplay between Johnson's left and right hands.

The link between Johnson's music and the world of the rent party is not merely incidental, for situations like the rent party structure the music's field of possibilities.[18] The insuperable filiative bond between the two can be seen in Duke Ellington's account of how James P. Johnson's agent, Lippy Boyette, was able to use Johnson's presence to conjure a rent party out of thin air: "Lippy would walk up to any man's house at any time of night. He'd ring the doorbell. Finally somebody would wake up and holler out the window about who was it making all the disturbance. Lippy would answer, 'It's Lippy, and James P. is here with me.' These magic words opened anybody's door, and we would sit and play all night long" (qtd. in Jansen, 76). What is remarkable here is that the possibility of a Johnson performance can actually engender a rent party, can summon it into being in the absence of any preparatory apparatus. The sound of Johnson at the piano is enough because a composition like "Carolina Shout" has taken into itself the force of the social ritual that is the rent party and thus can serve as the germ around which a new enactment of the ritual can be formed.

From the opening introduction to the closing coda, "Carolina Shout" gives to the ear prepared to hear it intimations of a time-space fusion untethered to the imperatives of substitutability and exchange structuring the world outside of Johnson's performance. Heard properly, it whispers the possibility of another time and another space: a rhythmic (rag)time divorced from dreary mechanical repetition, and an expansive rent party freed from the imperatives and injustices of rent.

Unfortunately, "Carolina Shout" is not immune to mishearing. In fact, as many critics (Levine, Baraka, Spillers, Moten, and others) have noted, a particularly persistent form of mishearing has been (and continues to be) the condition for the acceptance of jazz among the majority of American listeners. James Weldon Johnson gives us a powerful illustration of this in the patron's attempt to use the music to "blot out time." According to James Baldwin, what allows listeners like the patron to mishear the music is a form of "protective sentimentality." He writes, "It is only in his music, which Americans are able to admire because a protective sentimentality limits their understanding of it, that the Negro in America has been able to tell his story" ("Many Thousands" 24). The "protective sentimentality" that Baldwin describes is a habit of consciousness built out of "a suspect reliance on suspect and badly digested formulae" that fails "to convey any sense of Negro life as a continuing and complex group reality" ("Many Thousands" 36, 39). To hear "Carolina Shout" without hearing in it refigurings of time, sociality, and subjectivity is to rely on a "protective sentimentality" that functions by detaching heard notes from the dynamic and temporal lines that connect these notes to the social and relational matrices out of which they arise and to which they address themselves as elaborative, improvised revisions.

This mode of hearing is a "protective" mishearing because it not only imaginatively severs the link between the music and its social context, but it also promotes an illusory separation between the music and its listeners. Separated from the trajectory of the music's motion, the detached listener dampens its extramusical implications by standing in an ossified present that enables the listener to imagine himself only as a judge of the music's worth, and which allows enjoyment of only those musical elements fully consonant with the listener's previously established self-conception. The tendency of this form of listening (or of mishearing) is to understand as an object what is really a "cultural transaction between human beings and organized sound" (Floyd, "Ring Shout" 405).

What this means is that one does not really *understand* the music unless one moves with it, standing under its mobilizing waves of sound with a willingness to don the mantle of improvisational becoming and rhythmic challenge that it proffers to those open to its call.

To hear "Carolina Shout" in this way is to hear a significant, and significantly under-heard, aspect of the context out of which works like James Weldon Johnson's *The Autobiography of An Ex-Colored Man* emerge. However, "Carolina Shout" is much more than a musical artifact of a past age; it is an aural argument against the kind of monumentalizing history to which it and most of jazz have been subjected. This monumentalizing tendency is a version of what Du Bois calls "irreverence towards time," an irreverence that results in an inability to hear (or see) the incomplete or unfinished nature of all cultural artifacts. Moving with the argument of "Carolina Shout" lets one hear the movement of works like it and *The Autobiography of an Ex-Colored Man* toward each other and toward our present as improvisations on the unfinished project of shaping a culture with both room and time for the interplay of knowledge and pleasure embodied in James P. Johnson's performance. "Carolina Shout" tropes on the incompleteness of itself and of time, and in doing so it pushes for a repetitive response that hears the yet-to-be realized temporality sounding in the music and in the latent vibrations of our historical and social setting.

4

Forms of Repetition and Jazz Sociality in *The Great Gatsby*

> And so we beat on, boats against the current.
> —F. Scott Fitzgerald, *The Great Gatsby*

> Beat is an entity of relation.
> —James Snead, "Repetition as a Figure of Black Culture"

It has become a truism of Fitzgerald criticism that *The Great Gatsby* is a novel about time.[1] An even more banal commonplace is that Fitzgerald is *the* novelist of the Jazz Age. What has been much less remarked is the fact that Fitzgerald's writings, fiction and nonfiction, are about as far from a celebration of the Jazz Age as possible. For Fitzgerald, the Jazz Age was a period of wasted energy, dissipation, and puerile frivolity, a period whose essentially meaningless nature is summed up, for him, by the pervasive repetition of the phrase "Yes, we have no bananas" ("Echoes" 22). This view pervades all of Fitzgerald's writings; a particularly telling formulation of it occurs in his essay "Echoes of the Jazz Age." In this essay Fitzgerald sums up the 1920s by saying, "it was all borrowed time anyway" (21). In this statement, Fitzgerald's views of the jazz age and his preoccupation with time come together, indicating the extent to which his judgments of American culture depend on his ideas about how time does, or should, unfold itself.

Although Fitzgerald's engagement with any music that could meaningfully be referred to as "jazz" was in many ways quite shallow, his dismissal of the decade in which this music first came to a dazzling fruition and first captured the imagination of most of the world (as well as the decade in which Langston Hughes, Nella Larsen, and James Weldon Johnson published some of their most important works) speaks of his attachment to a conception of time and progress that jazz calls into question. To say this is to suggest that the preoccupation with time that characterizes *The Great Gatsby* marks the novel as a working out of the same questions of temporality and the proper shape of society operative in James Weldon Johnson's engagement with jazz.

The Great Gatsby argues for the propriety of a particular model of development, and shapes itself as response to, and critique of, departures from this model. Its treatment of Gatsby, Tom, Daisy, and other major and minor characters works to catalog and diagnose mistaken notions about the proper rhythm of individual and cultural development. The most salient of these notions is James Gatz's infamous confusion about time ("Can't repeat the past? . . . "), a confusion that stems from his overvaluation of and unyielding fixation on a magical moment from his youth, and the object that his imagination has metonymically attached to this moment: Daisy Buchanan. Gatsby's downfall is figured as the consequence of this stubborn attachment to a lost moment of youth, a situation that is not unique to *The Great Gatsby*. Each of Fitzgerald's novels features a figure like Gatsby, a character whose inability to relinquish the past inevitably wounds or kills him. The pathos invested in Dick Diver's failure to successfully pull off a water-skiing trick his aging body is no longer capable of (*Tender Is the Night*), in Monroe Stahr's romance with a woman who resembles his late wife (*The Last Tycoon*), and in Anthony Patch's puerile insistence on his right to the privileged leisure of his youth (*The Beautiful and Damned*) are signs of Fitzgerald's enduring fascination with the question of how one deals with a moment of prepossessing intensity that lies in one's past. Although the answer to this question is almost always a tragic one (as with Gatsby's perforated body in the pool), the power of his writing lies in his ability to grant full power to the attraction of the past at the same time that he catalogs the dire effects of the past's siren song. Fitzgerald is primarily a lyricist of vanished moments from the past.

The figures who most suffer from overinvestment of the past in Fitzgerald's work are predominantly figures from the other side of the class divide that so obsessed Fitzgerald. It is not insignificant that Dick Diver, Jay Gatsby, and Monroe Stahr are all interlopers in the rarefied upper class atmosphere that the Buchanans, the Warrens, and Cecelia Brady take for granted. The passage of time and the possibility, or propriety, of movement between different social spheres are inextricably bound up with each other in Fitzgerald's thought. This can be seen in his essay, "Echoes of the Jazz Age," a judgment of the 1920s whose conclusion, "it was all borrowed time anyway," rests on the belief that the failing of the decade is in essence a failure of the standard of taste: "I remember a fat Jewess, inlaid with diamonds, who sat behind us at the Russian ballet and said as the curtain rose, 'Thad's luffly, dey ought to baint a bicture of it.' This was low comedy, but it was evident that money and power were falling into the hands of people in comparison with whom the leader of a village Soviet would be a gold-mine of judgment and culture" (21). This is the ur-scene of Fitzgerald's

Jazz Age, a scene in which an aesthetic response meant to strike us as obviously inappropriate is intended to demonstrate the failing of an age "that eventually overreached itself less through lack of morals than through lack of taste" (15).

Fitzgerald's figuring of an age in which the matching of aesthetic or social situations with individuals unequipped to properly respond to them as "borrowed time" stems from his belief that a society unable to prevent such mismatches from occurring is not only impoverished and distasteful but literally unsustainable. The belief he shares with Nick Carraway, that "a sense of the fundamental decencies is parceled out unequally at birth" (6), leads him to see the movement of individuals in orbits to which they do not "belong" as a necessarily temporary aberration.[2] The fact that in Fitzgerald's illustration of this situation the source of "vulgar" or "class-less" response is Jewish is not incidental, for Fitzgerald's literary and social imagination assumes a link between race and taste.

These are the themes *The Great Gatsby* concerns itself with: the dangerous lure of a vanished past, a rising tide of demotic vulgarity, and the rhythms of culture and time that link the two together. *The Great Gatsby* uses the figure of Jay Gatsby as a vehicle for a meditation on time that mobilizes all the resources of modernist narration to repudiate both the naïve forward-looking optimism of Gatsby and the cynical static detachment of the Buchanans in favor of the aesthetic recuperation of time that the novel itself performs. The novel works to purge its form of the dissonance between different temporalities, but it ultimately fails to fully detach itself from the forms of repetition working to restructure American culture.

Repetition and Rivalry

The conflict at the heart of *The Great Gatsby* is the rivalry between Jay Gatsby and Tom Buchanan, a rivalry that is also a clash between two modes of temporality. Fitzgerald associates each character with a specific social rhythm and a specific region of the country. Gatsby represents a hasty acquisitiveness associated with the Midwest (or sometimes just "the West"), while Tom represents a cynical detachment that is associated with the East and hostile to any temporal movement that delivers anything but a static repetition of his own social and economic privilege. Gatsby honestly but mistakenly embraces a traditional notion of progressive acquisitiveness; Tom manifests a cynically knowing disbelief in this notion.

Each character betrays an anxiety about the movement of time and about repetition itself. Each of them wants to use repetition to move beyond or escape the most unsettling powers of repetition. Gatsby wants to repeat the past;

he embraces repetition as a tool with which to seize his enchanted object: Daisy. Tom wants to repeat the present; he embraces the protocols of a social world that endlessly repeats the privilege and power of his wealth and whiteness. He is uneasy, however, with his sense that repetition tends to move beyond society's present arrangement.

Neither character is interested in repetition for itself, and neither one embraces the movements of repetition that James Snead links to improvisation and change. In the contrast between Gatsby's hurried Midwestern pacing and the cynical, detached repetition of Tom, the narrative presents us with two distinct temporalities, and the two alternatives are meant to be exhaustive. The melancholy pathos with which *The Great Gatsby* ends depends upon the exclusiveness of these two temporal models and of their both turning out to be bankrupt.

The rhapsodic admiration of Gatsby's "extraordinary gift for hope" (6) that Nick expresses before beginning his narrative is a heavily qualified one (both by Nick's expressions of scorn [6] and by Gatsby's fate), an expression of the fact that Gatsby's hyperbolic version of Midwestern anticipatory acquisitiveness is meant to be seen as a foreclosed possibility, an end as dead as Gatsby himself. Even clearer is the inadequacy of the cynical detachment associated with Tom, for Fitzgerald's narrative asks us to read it as a symptom of the "vast carelessness" and cynicism that characterize Daisy and Tom (188). These are the blunted alternatives on which the operation of the text depends, a sharp distinction between the hasty, grasping, forward motion of Gatsby and the Midwest and the Buchanans' cynical and static detachment. These two temporal stances are portrayed as if they are the only possible modes of treating time, but the conclusion that Nick Carraway's narrative wrings from them does not account for a different aspect of temporality not only present in his tale but crucial to the functioning of the novelistic form in which it is presented. For the form of Gatsby's belief in "the green light" and "orgastic future" is not only an accelerated version of the form of futural orientation that the text figures as "Midwestern"; it is an intensification of this mode of temporality to the point at which it undergoes a qualitative shift and enters into the realm of repetition. When Gatsby expresses his belief that the past is as attainable as the future, plainly evident are both the novelty of his position and the tortuous new shape of a temporality that had previously underwritten notions of progress, and of forms of forward and upward motion as diverse as Manifest Destiny, "rugged individualism," and sublimation. The vulgar grasping of James Gatz/Jay Gatsby, despite his emergence from outside the circle of named, stable houses that Nick Carraway describes, is not the absolute other of a proper "Midwestern" notion of progress and forward motion but is the extension and intensification of this logic to the point where it begins to fold back in on itself.[3]

The name of this logic is commodification, a persistent strain in American life well before Benjamin Franklin equated time with money.[4] As Ross Posnock notes in his article "'A New World. Material Without Being Real': Fitzgerald's Critique of Capitalism in *The Great Gatsby*," the shape of Gatsby's vision of Daisy and of himself is structured by Gatsby's belief in the essential fungibility of persons and things, a belief in abstract equivalence powerfully deluded enough to think that the past, as well as the present and the future, is an appropriable object. At the moment that Gatsby first kisses Daisy, he is "overwhelmingly aware of the youth and mystery that wealth imprisons and preserves, of the freshness of many clothes and of Daisy, gleaming like silver" (157). The metonymic linking of Daisy to money and wealth is a conceit unfailingly maintained throughout the novel; even Nick, who consistently strives to differentiate himself from Gatsby, participates in upholding this commodifying equation.

Both Gatsby and Nick, and indeed all the characters in the novel, move and think to the rhythm of money, a rhythm focusing attention on the blunt immediacy of objects as objects and dulling awareness of the participation, investment, incorporation, and embodiment of subjects in, with, and as objects. Gatsby is an object of narrative desire for Nick, Daisy is an object for Gatsby, and everybody is an object for Tom Buchanan. This objectification of the world of experience has a profound effect on the movement of time itself. As Georg Lukács writes, objectification leads to a situation in which "time sheds its qualitative, variable, flowing nature; it freezes into an exactly delimited, quantifiable continuum filled with quantifiable 'things'" (*History* 90). Reification of time reinforces the requirement "that . . . society should learn to satisfy all its needs in terms of commodity exchange" (91).

Gatsby satisfies his need to "recover . . . some idea of himself" (117) by treating the past as a commodity to be purchased, as an "abstract, exactly measurable, physical space" just as amenable to the power of money as the property that Gatsby's house sits on (Lukács, *History* 90). In doing so, Gatsby is both a good and a bad capitalist: in his inability to imagine anything standing outside of the circuits of exchange established by capital he sees the world as capital requires, but in the freezing of the movement of time wrapped up in his romantic fixation on Daisy, Gatsby disregards the way that capital always exempts itself from the law it establishes. Capital is both a commodity (when incarnated as money) and the condition of possibility of all commodities. As a result, capital both reifies time and requires a temporal motion incompatible with this reification. As any reader of *Capital* knows, the passage from money to commodity (M–C) is not in itself satisfactory but must inevitably lead beyond itself in a temporal motion that knows no end.[5] Capital is the shark of the social world, an entity for which the end of motion is the end of existence. Gatsby falls prey to capital's ideology of itself in his belief that there is an ultimate object at the end of cycles of exchange. For him, this object is Daisy, and in his complacent satisfaction with her he freezes the movement of capital, a mistake that ultimately leads to his extinction. Gatsby is duped by the lure of commodity exchange, which holds out the promise of leading to something beyond itself but which inevitably remains within the repetitive grooves of its own self-valorizing and self-perpetuating motion. When Gatsby's body is found in the pool, it mimes this motion, revolving slowly and "tracing . . . a thin red circle in the water" (170). Gatsby overinvests himself in an object (Daisy), and his violation of the unrelenting motion of capital results in his being transformed into a lifeless object himself. Gatsby's fascination with Daisy and with the social world she represents blinds him to the necessary duplicity of the capital that shapes this social world. Gatsby wants to repeat the uniqueness of his romance with Daisy but believes that the repetitions that came after his first meeting with Daisy and that will inevitably come after his second meeting can be arrested or banished. He sees capital's ability to procure but not its dependence on an endlessly repetitive rhythm of investment and disinvestment.

In "Repetition as a Figure of Black Culture," James Snead writes that each culture's treatment of repetition is precipitated by "the discrepancy between our personal growth—the very model of linear development—and the physical plane upon which life unfolds, characterized by general recursiveness and repetition" (59). The dilemmas engendered by this discrepancy are the contradictions that *The Great Gatsby* sets out to resolve.[6] In his reflections on the fate of Gatsby with which the novel concludes, Nick describes an experience intended to condense all the significance of Gatsby's tale, the "transitory enchanted moment" when European explorers first encountered the island of Manhattan. For Nick (and for Fitzgerald) this is a moment when the island "flowered . . . for Dutch sailors' eyes," and they found themselves "face to face for the last time in history with something commensurate to [man's] capacity for wonder" (189).[7] The experience described here is one in which the space for development, the arena for human action that Snead describes as "the physical plane upon which life unfolds," is seen as boundless and inexhaustible rather than "characterized by general recursiveness and repetition." The power of this passage lies in the intensity of the nostalgia it embodies for a moment ("the last time in history") untroubled by the need to repeat, a moment in which the path of the individual encounters no obstacles to its development but is allowed to follow, like Gatsby, its own Platonic conception of itself. Nick's mixture of repulsion from[8] and attraction to Gatsby revolves around Gatsby's embodiment of a restless, futural orientation upon which America was founded but felt by Nick to be increasingly out of step with the time in which he and Gatsby live.

Unlike Snead or the jazz musicians who exemplify the embrace of repetition he describes, neither Nick nor Fitzgerald has made peace with the idea "that the world is not inexhaustible in its combinations, nor life in its various guises" (59). Their ideal, even if conceived of as lost, is the profoundly undialectical situation in which an individual subject faces an objective world amenable to his will and unresistant to his imaginative or physical construction of it. The paradoxes of this ideal's existence in the midst of a world that is unremittently social, as well as ultimately finite, expose themselves in the descriptions of an object central to the rivalries and exchanges of the text, namely, Daisy's voice. The source of a magnetic charisma irresistible to all who hear it, this voice is both given a very specific content ("money") and an immunity from time and decay ("inexhaustible charm"). This combination is possible only in an object seen from the outside, with a romanticizing vision that mistakes the allure that an object emits for its determinate configurations of possibility. To see something in this way is to see it with the "wonder" that characterizes Gatsby's way of seeing the world. This kind of wonder endows its object with unlimited possibilities, making it free from any entanglement with the past that might limit its suitability for the beholder. This wonder describes both the Dutch sailors' vision of a continent new to them and Gatsby's vision of Daisy. The two visions are twinned both by language—the island "flower[s]" for the sailors, while Daisy "blossom[s] . . . like a flower" for Gatsby—and by the way that each combines a sharp newness with a fixity that determines the subsequent trajectory of those experiencing these visions.

Just like the explorers in their wonder at stumbling upon a realm they believe to be infinitely open,[9] Gatsby sees in Daisy the allure of a realm limitless enough to accommodate his monstrously ambitious dreams, the realm of privilege encompassed in the aura of a "'nice' girl" like Daisy: "She was the first 'nice' girl he had ever known . . . There was a ripe mystery about [her house], a hint of bedrooms upstairs more beautiful and cool than other bedrooms, of gay and radiant activities taking place through its corridors and of romances that were not musty and laid away in lavender but fresh and redolent of this year's shining motor cars and of dances whose flowers were scarcely withered" (155–56).

This passage shows that Gatsby's fascination with Daisy is engendered more by the mystery and promise that surround Daisy than by Daisy herself. What excites Gatsby's desire is Daisy's embodiment of perpetual ripeness, a ripeness seemingly capable of delivering an endless and endlessly fascinating stream of objects and experiences. As with the link between Daisy's voice and money, the use of "this year's shining motor cars" to describe this allure is revelatory of the extent to which Gatsby's pursuit of Daisy (the pursuit that drives the entire text) is motivated by his total adoption of the patterns of commodity production and consumption. Gatsby's "greatness" resides in his belief that he can possess the green light and the future, as well as in his lack of the cynicism that characterizes the society he aspires to join. This "greatness" is a function of his unqualified belief in the ideology of the class that produces Daisy and her mysterious allure. Unlike the inhabitants of this structure, who use a cynical detachment to hold themselves apart from both the mystifying allure that Gatsby falls prey to and from time itself, Gatsby thinks he can have both "this year's shining motor car" and the very newness that makes it shine. His position on the outside of the social world that he idealizes keeps the impossibility of this hidden from him; his "wonder" at the voice seen as both "deathless" and "full of money" blinds him to the fact that this voice is the one attribute of Daisy immune to his motivating desire, the desire of possession. The tension between the fixity of what can be possessed and the unlimited possibility that can adhere only to what has not yet been, or can never be, possessed is the source of both the cynicism of those raised to see possession as natural (Daisy, Tom, Jordan) and the idealism of those, like Gatsby, who strive to realize the promise of possession.[10] That this promise can only be sustained from the outside shows that it is an optical projection of the time and logic of possession rather than a realizable attribute of it.

Time, Possession, Exclusion

Tom and Gatsby pursue different temporal strategies for possessing Daisy, but both recognize that their struggle over her is a struggle over the power granted to those allowed to inhabit the top echelon of the American social structure. They both desire to possess not only the "inexhaustible charm" of Daisy's money-filled voice but also the freight of value and possibility that her voice is made to bear.

Tom Buchanan wins the battle over Daisy, and the way he wins is determined by the logic of possession. The necessity of Gatsby's death and the inevitability of Tom's survival are functions of the way in which this logic governs the plot's unfolding. The logic of possession determines the relation of Tom to Daisy, of Gatsby to Daisy, and, ultimately, of Nick to Gatsby; this determination has everything to do with questions of time. In a section of *Minima Moralia* entitled "Morality and Temporal Sequence," Adorno suggests that in a situation like Daisy's, a situation that requires a choice between lovers, the real source of conflict is not any mixed emotional state but "the phenomenon of prior engagement." According to Adorno, in rivalries like Tom and Gatsby's, "abstract temporal sequence plays in reality the part one would like to ascribe to the hierarchy of feelings" (78). The fact that "who came first" is a factor in decisions that are at least partly emotional betrays the extent to which possession, which is (or should be) a relationship between a person and a thing, insinuates itself into relationships between people. For to give weight to priority is to concede a link between it and exclusivity. The question of who came first only matters if their priority is translated into the power to exclude others and to forbid other relationships. This is, of course, a property relation, one whose demands of exclusivity explain Gatsby's insistence that Daisy disavow any previous love of Tom (116).[11] Gatsby and Tom both relate to Daisy as a possession, and the result is that neither can tolerate any claim that another might have to her affection, even if it lies in the past.[12] By making her into a possession they have introduced a heightened anxiety into their relationship to her, for, in the words of Adorno, every possession "is experienced in relation to its possible non-being" (79). In short, they fear her slipping away from them because "the desire to possess reflects time as a fear of losing." Once Daisy is transformed into a possession and the relationship to her is given the fixity and exclusivity of ownership, the future can only be a threat. To neutralize this threat, time is made into an abstract and irreversible temporal sequence in which the second, third, fourth, or nth possibility cannot in any way challenge the unassailable position of what comes first.

It is clear that Tom and Gatsby both act in accordance with the assumptions of abstract temporal sequence and "the exclusive character of what comes first," but it is less clear which one of them actually does come first. Gatsby met, wooed, and kissed Daisy first, but Tom was the first (and last) to enter into a binding matrimonial contract with her. The novel conveys the sense that, in some ways, Gatsby's relationship with Daisy is not entirely legitimate. Even Nick, who represents himself as a partisan of Gatsby, writes that Gatsby "had no real right to touch her [Daisy's] hand" (156). In question here is the constitution of firstness. That this is a question at all betrays the fact that any claim to priority (or simultaneity, or any position deriving from "abstract temporal sequence") is dependent on perspective, or, in other words, is a function of what Johannes Fabian calls "received time-space fusions" ("Of Dogs Alive" 189).[13]

In "Of Dogs Alive, Birds Dead, and Time to Tell a Story," Fabian details the way that what counts as "here" and "now" (as well as "there" and "then") are always based upon the way "shared time and space are fused into identities we call community, society, civilization and history" (189). "Here" and "now," and the assignations of identity and difference that depend on them, are not givens but are constructs of expectation. The shared time implied in nowness is more than physical synchronicity; it is a relationality based on assumptions about the event that the now is attached to. Communal expectations of what will take place in any event are usually strong enough to figure actions that don't conform to these expectations as the future or past (usually the past, as in primitivism) of some other event and thus outside the "here" and "now" of the event in question. The conservatism of these habitual ways of treating identity and difference,[14] and of thinking community, are readily apparent, based as they are upon a stubborn unwillingness to revise expectations regarding any event, and upon a preference for breaking off identity, "in the sense of identification with another," and replacing it with otherness.

This form of conservatism leads Nick to believe that Gatsby "had no real right to touch [Daisy's] hand" back in Louisville in 1917. The event in question is courtship, a ritual intended to secure the future of society by attaching desirable women (and their financial resources) to eligible men. Daisy is certainly desirable, but Gatsby lacks eligibility because of his poverty. Gatsby is an "illegitimate" suitor because he extracts an emotional commitment from Daisy that binds her to an uncertain financial future. Because Gatsby doesn't play the game by the rules—because he doesn't conform to the expectations that govern the event of courtship—his claim to priority is nullified. He is cast outside the community whose "here" and "now" are shaped by assumptions about the proper forms of courtship and marriage, and thus is seen as never having been "there" at all. Gatsby does not properly repeat the previously established courtship ritual, and thus is figured as either too early (before he had acquired a sufficient fortune) or too late (after the shape of the courtship event had been firmly established) to count as the "first" claimant to Daisy's affections.

The power that excludes Gatsby, that declares him to be too late even when he gets there first, is the power of an established society to shape its own narrative, to control not only the present but the past and the future as well. As I have been suggesting, this power takes the shape in *The Great Gatsby* of substituting the past for the future. This is what Tom does when he confronts Gatsby in the suite at the Plaza hotel; he uses the power vested in him by his social position to construct a retrospective narrative that discredits Gatsby in order to untangle and extricate his narrative from Tom and Daisy's. Fearful of a future in which Daisy leaves him for Gatsby, Tom wields the past as a weapon. Attacking Gatsby on two fronts, he both substitutes a story of Gatsby as a "common swindler," bootlegger, and associate of Jews for Gatsby's story of himself as war hero and "Oxford man," and appeals to his past with Daisy as a bulwark against Gatsby's attempt to obliterate any history that puts Daisy with Tom rather than with him. In the second of these strategies, Tom leans on the claim to Daisy's affections given him by his bald priority, emphasizing events too concrete to be susceptible to Gatsby's attempt to replace Tom's priority with his own: "Not that day I carried you down from the Punch Bowl to keep your shoes dry?" (139). In doing so, Tom is on fairly solid ground, ethically as well as practically, for he emphasizes the one legitimate argument in favor of his priority, namely, that disregarding this claim leads to the annulment of "a shared past life" and the deletion of experience itself (Adorno, *Minima Moralia* 78).

Although his retention of Daisy marks his rhetorical use of the past as a practical success, Tom's argument against Gatsby's bid for Daisy loses all ethical validity when he argues that his priority gives him a claim on Daisy's future as well as on her past. This extension of his claim into the future is the transformation of a legitimate argument for priority into an illegitimate argument for "the exclusive right of priority" (79). Such an argument is illegitimate not just because it defends the logic that transforms persons into possessions, but because it utilizes a logic of exclusivity and exclusion that legitimizes nativism and racial privilege. In Adorno's words, "there is an irresistible path" that leads from "the touching feeling" of a lover's anxiety lest he lose the love and tenderness that were never possessions to begin with "by way of the little boy's aversion for his younger brother and the fraternity-student's contempt for his 'fag,' to the immigration laws that exclude all non-Caucasians from Social-Democratic Austria, and right up to the Fascist eradication of the racial minority" (79).

The path from marital fidelity to racial genocide is quite a long one, but most of the connections it requires are graspable by the far-from-lightning-quick intellect of Tom Buchanan. In the following passage, Tom voices his concern over the perceived evaporation of the "priority of exclusivity" that he rightly sees as a threat to his privilege and power: "Nowadays people begin by sneering at family life and family institutions and next they'll throw everything overboard and have intermarriage between black and white" (137). This utterance echoes Tom's earlier declarations concerning race war, and we should hear the dependence of his ideas about race and the decline of civilization upon the power of both abstract temporal sequence and received time-space fusions.[15] Tom articulates, in all his ineloquent obtuseness, the closed temporal movement of the society that engenders figures like him and the immense powers of exclusion embodied in this movement. Combining adherence to an abstract temporal sequence that subordinates subsequence to priority with the time-space fusions of community that either recognize or refuse to recognize claims to priority, this movement shapes itself as an untroubled progression from predictable quality to predictable quality.

Following the logic of a naturalized chronology, this movement endows with inevitability the belief that after 4 must come 5 (and then 6, 7, "and so we beat on") and allows the appearance of anything else (another 4, a 2, a 3.4, a negative number, or fraction) to be ignored, suppressed, or configured either as an inconsequential survival from the past (primitivism) or a temporary aberration (the Jazz Age as "borrowed time"). Traced out here is the closed circuit of a limited temporal movement that functions through a rigorous policing of its borders and a reliance on the conceptual structure of possessive individualism.

As we saw in previous chapters, the time compatible with possessive individualism is a time invested in forestalling the rise of any newness incompatible with the prerogatives of exchange. It attempts to forestall newness by fostering an imagination and a narrative identity that makes all encounters into moments fitting into an already existing story, rather than into starting points for new stories or occasions for the restructuring and revising of already existing stories and identities.[16] This is a time that, in Fabian's terms, "substitutes categorically imposed otherness for experienced otherness" as a way of limiting the challenge of dialectical interaction ("Of Dogs Alive" 199). Possession limits the enjoyment and revisionary capacity of any situation by making the components of a situation into inert objects that are to be claimed by a subject but that can make no claim upon this subject. This one-way movement—a barrier to listening, understanding, or any genuinely erotic relationship—from subject to object does not let anything outside of the subject impact its rigid carapace of identity.

Jazz, Modish Negroes, and the Limousine

Gatsby constructs himself and his pursuit of Daisy according to the logic of possession and exclusivity, a logic intended to keep figures like him away from women like Daisy. A specific construction of and with time is used to write Gatsby out of Daisy's story, and a similar exclusionary strategy can be seen in the narrative treatment of a figure that condenses Tom's fear of blackness and Tom, Nick, and Gatsby's aversion to repetition: the limousine that passes Nick and Gatsby on their way into New York City. Nick and Gatsby are passing over Blackwell's Island on their way to lunch in the city when Nick sees something that strikes him as a fantastic and absurd spectacle. He sees a limousine pass by, "driven by a white chauffeur" and "in which sat three modish Negroes, two bucks and a girl" (73). The sight makes Nick laugh out loud. He takes the limousine's passing as a sign that the normal restrictions on possibility no longer apply, with the result that "Anything can happen now . . . anything at all" (73). The way that Nick (and Fitzgerald) attach significance to the "three modish Negroes" is a specific narrative strategy, a "construction with time" that Fabian counts as one of the two main strategies for suppressing actually experienced otherness. This strategy consists in construing events as omens, not only in retrospect but at the actual moment they occur. As the narrator of the novel, Nick is recounting this event retroactively, but the thoughts it inspires in him are given in a present tense emphasized by the presence of the word "now" ("Anything can happen now . . . "). Nick experiences the "three modish Negroes" as a portentous omen not only later but also at the very moment they come into his sight. In doing so, he performs a proleptic act that depends upon seeing a present event as part of the past. According to Fabian, "events acquire meaning as omens when we construct them as a past for narratives to build upon" ("Of Dogs Alive" 192). This is, of course, a traditional part of the way novels give themselves a cohesive shape, by conferring meaning upon past events through their being experienced later as fulfilled, "as giving to the end of the story a quality that we call meaningfullness" (Fabian, "Of Dogs Alive" 192). The significance of Nick's encounter with the three chauffeured African Americans is that he makes it into an omen not only as the novelist that he will later become but also as a participant in it. In reacting to blackness in the way that he does, Nick confirms Fabian's assertion that "in ominous experiences contemporaneous events are being related to the person who experiences them as essentially past" (192). This incident also begins to show us that Gatsby is not the only character confused about time, and that the distinction between Nick and Gatsby shares some of the weakness of the distinction between Nick the narrator and Nick the actor, as well as the distinction between Fitzgerald and Nick.

But to say this is to side with Nick in his assumption that the encounter on Blackwell's Island is significant solely for what it says about his (and Gatsby's) future. I would like to stay with the chauffeured limousine for a moment and reflect on what it means that its presence gets constructed as an omen, as well as on the other possibilities that it and its occupants might signify.[17]

In the narrative operation that makes the occupants of the limousine into a past present, the occupants' past is excised, a past that is not allowed to participate in the narrative Nick constructs. The particular circumstances that put the three African Americans in the back of the limousine and that will partially govern their ability or desire to ride in limousines in the future are treated as unnecessary complications to be ignored. This ignorance transforms the three figures into motionless props without their own specific trajectory. Lacking a past or a future, they cannot possibly be rivals to Nick or Gatsby. When Nick makes them into an omen, he suppresses the real significance that reflection upon their past and future might deliver. The possibility of questions like "where did they come from?," "where are they going?," and "where did they get the money for the limousine?" is foreclosed in the interest of maintaining the clean but tragic path that Nick makes of Gatsby's story. This means that the narrative functioning of the text is as invested in maintaining boundaries like "the indiscernible barbed wire" (155) that should keep James Gatz away from girls like Daisy as is Tom Buchanan. The conceptual barrier that makes the black occupants of the limousine into objects of ridicule occludes the possibility that Nick might take an interest in their stories and that this interest might affect the shape of Nick's actions or writing. Put simply, the occupants of the limousine have no time and thus present no challenge to the time that moves Gatsby and Nick inexorably toward the poetic ending that Nick makes of Gatsby's death and of his own return to the Midwest. The encounter with the limousine thus is not an encounter with another specific trajectory engendering its own specific future, a trajectory and future that might figure as possibilities for Nick or Gatsby, but functions as a symptom of unlimited possibility, a situation in which "anything can happen . . . anything at all" (73).

The resemblance of this with the treatment of "the fat Jewess" in "Echoes of the Jazz Age" is unmistakable. Just as the presence of the vocal Jewish patron at the theater is for Fitzgerald *anything but* an occasion to celebrate the democratization of culture, the unlimited possibility signified by the sight of African Americans in the back of a limousine is a thing to be lamented rather than praised. The valence of Nick's statement that "anything can happen" is suggestive of transportation into a world as devoid of the ground for meaningfulness and meaningful distinctions as a world in which the sun might capriciously refuse to rise. This is of a piece with the denial of any specificity or similarity of movement to the limousine occupants; their lack of any explanatory narrative lets them appear as symptoms of an irrational and unexplainable social chaos rather than as the harbingers of emerging modes of sociality and production constitutive of new, but not unlimited, possibilities of self-fashioning and meaningfulness. The received time-space fusions that ground Nick's position of narration are so firmly fixed that the specific possibilities operative for the limousine occupants are simply not imaginable for him except as part of a fantastic and absolutely formless social world. For Nick and Fitzgerald to be able to imagine the back of the limousine from the inside would entail a confrontation with the fact that the otherness seen in it is neither absolute nor formless but has its own specific form and history.

Put in these terms, the figuring of African Americans in a limousine as an omen of a vast entropic future, productive of only chaos and meaninglessness, is isomorphic with the reactions to jazz (both positive and negative) that imagined it as a libidinally charged formlessness rather than as a new and distinct form with its own methods and possibilities. If we pause to think about the forces that might have placed three black subjects in the back of a limousine, in either the 1922 of the narrative's setting or the 1924 of its production, then these two astigmatic assignations of significance come together, for the most likely milieu to have generated these subjects is the new market in jazz and popular culture. The utilization of performers from this market at Gatsby's parties is indicative of the opportunities for the accumulation of wealth outside of

Nick Carraway's participation in the bond market or Tom Buchanan's inheritance.[18] Given the rapid expansion of the market for "race music" (exemplified by the 75,000 copies of Mamie Smith's "Crazy Blues" sold in Harlem in one week[19]), is it not likely that the capital generated by this market is enabling the passage of the limousine that Nick finds so fantastic? Could not the salary of the white chauffeur and the hire or purchase of the limousine have their provenance in the market's investment in the popularity of the names and the performance styles of figures like Bessie Smith, Wilbur Sweatman, James P. Johnson, or Alberta Hunter? What Nick envisions as a remarkable incident might actually be the fairly regular passage of James P. Johnson, his protégé and constant companion Fats Waller, and Johnson's wife Lillie Mae (herself a former singer) from the Johnsons' Long Island home to the performance spaces of Manhattan. The "three modish Negroes" in the car could possibly be the music entrepreneur Perry Bradford shepherding Louis Armstrong and Bessie Smith back from one of their 1924 recording sessions. It is not even out of the realm of possibility that the occupants of the car could be the key figures of the short-lived Black Swan record label, the pianist and bandleader Fletcher Henderson and vocalist Ethel Waters accompanied by W. E. B. Du Bois, the label's administrative and financial director. The vibrant New York jazz scene has no shortage of figures who could be the referent for the limousine that Fitzgerald presents to us as an ominous portent. W. C. Handy, Eubie Blake, Willie Smith . . . all could possibly have passed by Fitzgerald's fictional automotive point of narration.

At stake in these possible coincidences of fictive characters and historical figures is the particular way in which Fitzgerald's imaginative use of the novel's setting participates in a vision that not only distorts its setting (as all narratives invariably do) but distorts it in a way that promotes the values of a particular class and repeats the intellectual maneuvers used to denigrate the values, aspirations, and rights of other classes, races, and groups.[20]

The list of historical figures who could possibly be in the limousine on the bridge serves to remind us of the real history of what Carraway and Fitzgerald see as emerging from a fantastically mysterious nowhere. (And here they are like Paul Whiteman in thinking that jazz "sprang into existence . . . from nowhere in particular" [Meltzer 117]) With these figures in mind, it is clear that the limousine cannot possibly be what Fitzgerald makes of it. The movement of the narrative necessitates that the limousine and the figures in it be taken as markers of a limitless (and hopelessly disordered) possibility, but narrated objects are never entirely tractable; the novel's attempt to create a strictly circumscribed narrative geography always depends on forces, conventions, and established significations from outside of their nominally closed borders. Thus the black figures that the narrative uses to advance its own ends have been placed

1. The pianist Eubie Blake and his car exemplify the energies passing by Nick and Gatsby on their trip into Manhattan.

in the back of a limousine not by any random force but by the real (and not absolutely limitless) forces involved in the production, reception, and marketing of jazz and other forms of African American music.

Beale Street Blues

These forces are not entirely outside of the novel. Their penetration of Fitzgerald's literary and cultural imagination is evident in the jazz at Gatsby's parties and in the "burst of jazz" (135) that accompanies the confrontation at the Plaza. In both cases, jazz is as vaguely fictional as possible, the better to serve as an inert prop. But there is one instance of jazz in which the historical context of its production is not so well effaced; namely, the performance of the "Beale Street Blues" that marks Daisy's detachment from Gatsby and subsequent availability to the flattering attention of Tom: "All night the saxophones wailed the hopeless comment of the 'Beale Street Blues' while a hundred pairs of golden and silver slippers shuffled the shining dust" (158).[21] "Beale Street Blues" is, of course, a composition by W. C. Handy, a bandleader, composer, and music publisher whose financial and artistic success makes him both an aesthetic rival to Fitzgerald and an example of the way that the fluidities of culture, class, and race that Fitzgerald found so disturbing could land a figure from outside the small circle of traditional privilege in a position of relative affluence and power. Handy is the type of figure who could be in the limousine passing Gatsby and Nick, a figure whose real background cannot show itself if the economy of *The Great Gatsby* is to function as it does. Distorting the significance of a figure like Handy in order to tell a tale of American culture awash in a tide of directionless, demotic possibilities, Fitzgerald performs a similar operation on Handy's composition by attempting to make it the "hopeless comment" that he needs to accompany Daisy's cynical transfer of desire from Gatsby to Tom.

To see how out of tune Fitzgerald and Carraway are with the vibrations set in motion by Handy's "Beale Street Blues," only a few words from Langston Hughes are necessary. Hughes, whose poetic ear was especially attuned to the blues, describes them as "sad songs, but with an undercurrent of hope and determination in them" ("Glory" 477). For Hughes, the blues arise from and narrate situations in which hope seems impossible, but their treatment of these situations is always an improvisatory lament that squeezes an impossible hope from the pleasure and pain involved in stating and lingering over these dire straits. In "Songs Called the Blues," Hughes makes it clear that "you don't have to understand the words to know the meaning of the Blues, or to feel their sadness, or to hope their hopes" (161). Thus, while the lyrics of "Beale Street Blues" partially support Fitzgerald's characterization of it as a "hopeless comment," the musical setting and performance of these lyrics endow them with a significatory resonance quite antithetical to hopelessness (and it is the wordless performance of saxophones that Fitzgerald describes as "hopeless"). Despite his insistence that the meaning of the blues is not coterminous with the denotative meaning of its lyrics, Hughes uses the lyrics to "Trouble in Mind" to illustrate the alchemy of hope and hopelessness characteristic of the blues:

Trouble in mind, I'm blue,
But I won't be blue always:
The sun's gonna shine
In my back door someday.

Hughes concludes "Songs Called the Blues" with "And for that sunshine, everybody waits" (161). The thesis is that, despite their immersion in present troubles, the blues are an instrument for keeping alive the possibility of future happiness.

Fitzgerald and Carraway have thus assigned "Beale Street Blues" a role and a meaning far removed from its actual significance. They have made of it an instrument of hopelessness and passive resignation, and of its repetitions the fungibility of one man for another, the soundtrack to Daisy's acceptance of Tom Buchanan's proposal. This misrepresentation is absolutely crucial for the shape of the plot and the shape of time that Fitzgerald wants to make the plot support. If Daisy were a blues woman, she might have waited for Gatsby. She would have heard in the "Beale Street Blues" an articulation of loss that does not consign the lost object to an absolutely irretrievable past and thus does not foreclose the possibility of its return. She would have learned from its treatment of repetition that what is behind one (in the past) may also be in front of one (in the future), no matter how impossible this may seem. This relationship between the future and the past is an example of what Angela Davis describes as the power of the blues to "construct seemingly antagonistic relationships as noncontradictory oppositions" (xv). Allowing a relationship between past and future neither as reductively simplistic as Fitzgerald's conception of it nor as deluded as Gatsby's, this power also lets subjects like Daisy fashion for themselves autonomous expressions of desire in a social landscape intent on fastening subjects to predetermined, and inevitably heterosexist, narratives of desire and fulfillment. Thus, to say that if Daisy were a blues woman she might have waited for Gatsby is not to suggest that the blues fosters adherence to a rigid "stand by your man" narrative but to point out that the rhythm of pieces like "Beale Street Blues" offer a matrix for self-shaping or active self-construction.[22] The waiting that Hughes shows us in the blues is not the passive waiting of Daisy, who "wanted her life shaped . . . by some force—of love, of money, of unquestionable practicality—that was close at hand" (159). It is an active waiting that constructs subjectivity as a vector stretching itself toward a desired future.

Daisy, however, is not a blues woman and, in the absence of her ability to hear the active temporal posture available to her in the blues, acts in accordance with the shape of time that Fitzgerald's novel constructs as inevitable and inescapable. *The Great Gatsby*, and indeed all of Fitzgerald's novels shape themselves according to a pattern in which the freshest, most uniquely powerful and intensely meaningful event or experience occurs in youth and the rest of life is a sliding away from this irrecoverable event.[23] This pattern applies to nations and races as well as individuals, a universality that allows Fitzgerald to figure Gatsby's fate as the fate of the reading community constructed by the novel, the fate of the famous "we" that concludes the novel: "So we beat on, boats against the current, borne back ceaselessly into the past" (189). Like Daisy, "we" are "borne back ceaselessly into the past" because the things we desire, according to Fitzgerald, are always behind us. Hope is delusional, because it leads us to look in the future for that which lies only in our memory, and to engage in what Fitzgerald elsewhere describes as "the foredoomed attempt to control one's destiny" ("Offshore" 26).[24] The renunciation of hope and the evacuation from the future of any fortuitous possibilities that this stance necessarily entails code the understanding of jazz given in the novel. The figuring of the sound emanating from Handy's "Beale Street Blues" as "hopeless comment" is not accidental or incidental; it is absolutely central to the temporal movement of the novel and to Fitzgerald's cynical dismissal of the demotic reconfigurations of culture in the 1920s. The Jazz Age is all "borrowed time" because it is an abandonment of the patterns of natural aging and adjustment that Fitzgerald is so invested in.

In his description of this period, nothing is more distasteful to him than the sight of people pursuing the pleasures of youth that do not properly belong to them.[25] The practice of dancing and drinking by a generation that should be settling down both fails to yield any real pleasure, and, more importantly, threatens the hierarchical underpinnings of society by postponing the assumption of the role of guardians of culture by those whose youth is behind them.[26] This amounts to a whole generation repeating the wrong thing. The revelers attempting to horn in on the pleasures of youth seem absurd to Fitzgerald because they are trying to repeat the patterns of a vanished youth rather than the patterns of preceding generations.[27] As James Snead notes, repetition is necessary for the maintenance of any culture; what Fitzgerald laments is the failure of the Jazz Age generation to perform a "repetition of apparent consensus and convention that provide[s] a sense of security, identification and rightness" (60).

Behind Fitzgerald's investment in a fixed pattern of aging as decline, and, in forms of repetition that support this pattern, is a social vision structured by a belief in an insuperable scarcity of the most important human goods. At the beginning of *The Great Gatsby*, Nick Carraway voices his commitment to the truth that "a sense of the fundamental human decencies is parceled out unequally at birth," and the same commitment is evident in the following passage from Fitzgerald's essay "Echoes of the Jazz Age": "things were getting thinner and thinner as the eternal necessary human values tried to spread over all that expansion" (22). The trouble with the Jazz Age is the same as the trouble with Gatz(sby)'s intrusion into the world of the Buchanans: there is simply not enough to go around. Here we again see the saturation of Fitzgerald's imaginative logic by the rules and logic of the marketplace. As in the bond market in which Carraway works, value is inseparable from scarcity.

In "Adjectives and the Work of Modernism in the Age of Celebrity," Aaron Jaffe shows a similar "ideology of scarcity" (8) operative in Anglo-American literary modernism. According to Jaffe, the modernist emphasis on economizing words and on thinning out the ranks of a crowded literary pantheon is indicative of a wholesale transfer of the system of value and "consummate veneration of scarce goods" from the economic to the literary realm (10). Fitzgerald's concern with the inflated reputation of writers and actors as well as businessmen and politicians betrays his participation in this "ideology of scarcity," and he extends the logic of this ideology into the realms of pleasure and of values. When the revelry of the Jazz Age is described as "a children's party taken over by the elders," the consequence for Fitzgerald is that "the children" are "puzzled and rather neglected," as if there were only so much fun to go around. Implicit here is the belief that scarcity inevitably governs the realm of enjoyment, making it something that can only be attained at the expense of someone else and rendering impossible any enjoyable party without a necessarily limited, exclusive, and well-enforced guest list. Now, the assumption that scarcity is an inescapable fact of the capitalist economy in which *The Great Gatsby* is situated is at least partially legitimate (although any Marxist would quickly point out that there are other forms of economic organization), but the belief that pleasure and enjoyment follow the same laws of scarcity is without even this shred of support. For it to be true, there would have to be a set of invisible regulations and restrictions at work in governing the rationing and circulation of pleasure. Fitzgerald's transfer of scarcity from the economic realm assumes the operation of a kind of Federal Reserve Board of pleasure and values, an institution that determines the size of the supply of pleasure available and assigns it a fixed temporal rate of depreciation and return. In a sense, this assumption is correct, because one of the tasks novels like *The Great Gatsby* perform is this kind of ideological regulation. *The Great Gatsby* uses the seductive pleasure of its reading to teach a calculus of affective profit and loss, and like lessons given in the trading of bonds, the proper role of the future and of temporal movement in calculation is an intrinsic part of this education.

The major operation of the text is to use the blunt force of scarcity to underwrite the transfer of affective investment from the future to the past. This is the reason for the overwhelming aura of nostalgia that permeates the novel; the past is given a weight that when combined with the belief that the future can be won only at the expense of the past requires that the cathexis of the future be withdrawn.[28] The zero-sum swap of the past for the future is an investment in nostalgia that attempts to persuade us that our future lies with Gatsby or Nick but not with the blackness in the back of the limousine that speeds past Gatsby and Nick.

Like Nick, Fitzgerald is nostalgic, and what he is nostalgic for is a past in which "money and power" were securely in the hands of those with the proper cultural values. For Fitzgerald, it is obvious that "money and power were falling into the hands of people in comparison with whom the leader of a village Soviet would be a gold-mine of judgment and culture" ("Echoes" 21). The use of the gold-mine metaphor is telling, for it marks the dependence of Fitzgerald's lament on the assumption that scarcity and hierarchy govern the realm of taste (and of pleasure) as well as the realm of wealth. Operative here (as we were with the role of sublimation in American culture) is the overgrown power of what is essentially a metaphor. Fitzgerald is saying that the value of pleasure and of taste is *like* the value of money (or of bonds). Now, pleasure may be fleeting and scarce, but its attainability cannot be calculated in the same way that the acquisition of grain, pork bellies, or heating oil is. Pleasure, as ultimately incalculable and unpredictable as it is, tends toward the stigmergic; that is, its acquisition, production, and use are transferable without loss, and its transference often increases the intensity or quantity of what is transferred. Like music, the florescences of pleasure depend on an interaction that can enrich all who take part in it.

Taste, even if narrowly construed as the reproduction of already established patterns of acquisition and appreciation, is also something that can be acquired without anyone else's loss. At stake here is not the scarcity of taste but the reliability of the link between taste and privilege. The weakening of the link between taste and wealth has to be seen as decline rather than as possibility, because to think otherwise would be to violate Fitzgerald's deep attachment to nostalgia and his sense that the most luminous possibilities always lie in the past. This is Fitzgerald's "construct of expectation," a construct that licenses his alignment of the hierarchies of pleasure and taste with the hierarchy of privilege structuring American society. Due to the imaginative scarcity that enforces adherence to this construct of expectation, the future can never be more than an attenuated repetition of the past, and thus the presence of people like "the fat Jewess" at the theater and the "three modish Negroes" in the limousine must be the markers of watered-down taste and pleasure, and of the movement of cash outside of its traditional patterns of circulation.

This goes for cultural forms as well as for individuals: the substitution of the past for the future at work here is exactly what is at work in the misrecognition of "Beale Street Blues" as "hopeless comment." The evacuation from Handy's composition of the positive valence of the future, and its replacement in *The Great Gatsby* by an overweening nostalgia for the past, support Fitzgerald's belief that the only real choice is how to act in a world in which everything lies behind us. The sounds of "Beale Street Blues" and of the jazz produced in its wake are enough in themselves to tell us that this is a choice both impossibly constrained and ultimately false. Fitzgerald's imaginative world is governed by the laws of scarcity and thus invariably presents a series of false choices. In this world one cannot be both Jewish and a connoisseur of the theater, both black and the legitimate cargo of a limousine, both newly wealthy and in possession of "fundamental decencies" (6). Choices must be made between the future and the past, between stasis and decline, and between snobs or criminals.

In sharp contrast to the blues construction of "noncontradictory opposites," the construction of the novel makes all movement dependent on narrow choices between two mutually exclusive opposites that exhaust the entire field of possibility. Among the sharpest of these forced choices is the decision between the future and the past, but this opposition rests on an even more fundamental polarization of the difference between inevitability and decline. In Fitzgerald's world there is sameness and there is a falling off from the level that sameness guarantees. This belief in a sharp and absolute distinction between an inevitable repetition of the same and a dissolute departure from it makes a form of dreary repetition seem like the only movement capable of staving off the constant threat of decline and dissolution. Despite the pronouncements of Fitzgerald and other modernists, this is not the repetition of the "Beale Street Blues" or of the jazz that makes itself heard at Gatsby's parties (even if in a highly attenuated form).[29] It is instead a form of what Nick Carraway might call "snobbish repetition." This form of repetition is given to us as a frame for the entire novel; on the novel's second page, Nick writes, "as my father snobbishly suggested and I snobbishly repeat, a sense of the fundamental decencies is parceled out unequally at birth" (6). Nick makes his father's dictum, and his repetitive adherence to it, the key to his narration of Gatsby's fate. To be snobbish is to have what Gatsby lacks, namely, an acute sense of social form, and of the "right" thing to do at any given time. Snobbish repetition attempts to avoid all awkwardness by unfailingly performing exactly what is expected at each appropriate moment.[30] Unlike the repetition that Snead characterizes as a form of social improvisation, the repetition that Nick inherits from his father inoculates society against change by clinging to an exact repetition of forms inherited from the past.

The entire novel circumscribes an elliptical path around the choice between the reassuring stasis of snobbish repetition and the desultory change linked to other forms of repetition. It does so by blinding itself and those who move to the rhythm of its form to other possibilities. *The Great Gatsby* effaces alternatives that fall between or outside of the narrow choices that it constructs as insuperable and monolithic limits. Between the unconstrained and risible possibility that Nick sees in the back of the limousine and the inevitability that keeps money and power in the proper hands, the main thrust of the novel cannot admit the not unlimited, but still very real, possibilities implicit in new sets of hands having access to money and power. Between the acquisition of wealth through the Buchanans' inheritance (certainly one of the most snobbish forms of repetition) or Nick's selling of bonds, and the sheer criminality of Gatsby's methods (methods racialized by their provenance in the figure of Meyer Wolfsheim), the novel excludes the possibilities for financial gain contained in the new modes of social recreation and the propagation of new types of aesthetic forms. (Here we should remember the association of jazz with criminality in

"The Offshore Pirate.") In a sense, the limousine that makes an all-too-brief appearance moves along a path that cuts right through the middle of *The Great Gatsby*, bearing in it all that must be excluded. For, as I have argued, the most likely occupants of this limousine are the musicians (the W. C. Handys, Eubie Blakes, James P. Johnsons, and so on) who make their living as purveyors and practitioners of a repetition far removed from the snobbish repetition of the Buchanans and Carraways. The sharp opposition between stasis and change behind the novel's substitution of nostalgia for hope must exclude above all the possibility of repetition as a fortuitous force for opening up the future, the imbrication of repetition and change.

The excluded middle between the polarized choices around which the novel shapes itself is the demotic repetition brought to its highest form in jazz. The ability of jazz to use repetition to produce change is a possibility that does not have a place in Fitzgerald's imaginative landscape. The derisive dismissal of the modish Negroes in the back of the limousine is a figural analog for the dismissal of repetitive trajectories that choose both the past and the future, and of the motile sonorities in which these trajectories are encoded.

Despite his commitment to snobbish repetition and his inability to engage the rhythmic and temporal movements of jazz, Fitzgerald still sees himself as someone who has something important to say about "Jazz." His major pronouncement on jazz in "Echoes of the Jazz Age" is that "jazz meant first sex, then dancing, then music" (16). For him, jazz is part of the generalized frivolity threatening the boundaries of taste and judgment in an age living on "borrowed time." The irony of this position is that Fitzgerald's lament over the thinning out of values is something enabled by the very tides of culture that he sees as responsible for this thinning out. Fitzgerald's reputation, the very thing that makes his musings in "Echoes of the Jazz Age" seem worth publishing or reading, was secured by the success of his first novel, *This Side of Paradise*. A much less accomplished work than any of his later novels, the popularity of *This Side of Paradise* was largely due to its being conceived as in tune with the scandalous new attitude of a particularly rebellious generation.[31] This means that the market and its lack of taste deliver Fitzgerald into a position from which he can attack the corrosive effects of the market upon literary quality. His position on the cultural trends of what he calls "The Jazz Age," and on the jazz that he sees as a rather undistinguished component of these trends, is at least partially a disavowal of objects and of trends to which he owes his own position. This is to say that Fitzgerald and his novel need and use the elements that they disavow and dismiss. The movement of *The Great Gatsby* needs modish blackness as a figure for the risible flows of absolute possibility that sweeps James Gatz into the same orbit as Nick and the Buchanans, just as it needs jazz to exemplify the futility of a temporal attitude that ends up serving only as a "shortcut from nothing to nothing" (114). Both are part of the economy of the novel and of Fitzgerald's literary position because they are an unavoidable part of the economy of the cultural situation that gives rise to both. Fitzgerald's exclusions are a decision for one part of a process that is inevitably double. This is the doubleness of exchange societies that Marx first diagnosed, and that Eugene W. Holland sums up as follows: "On the one hand, capitalism devotes itself to production as an end in itself, developing the productivity of socialized labor to the utmost, yet on the other hand, due to the private investment in the means of production, social labor and life are restricted to regimes of production and consumption that valorize only the already existing capital-stock" (536).

In the period in which *The Great Gatsby* is set and produced, American culture finds itself in a situation in which new economic, cultural, and social means of production are taking on a velocity that puts them beyond the purview of traditional means of ensuring society's reproduction (like the limousine speeding past Nick Carraway). The response of *The Great Gatsby* is to figure this velocity as leading nowhere but downward and to promote a kind of stoic clinging to a bare, mechanical repetition of traditional forms of culture as a compensation for loss and a bulwark against decline.

Parties and Repetition

What is interesting about *The Great Gatsby* is its use of a new sense of form to promote very traditional cultural imperatives. Fitzgerald's novel is a compromise formation with new modes of repetition that incorporate these modes into the novel in an attempt to contain them and use them as mere means to its own conventional and conservative (in the full sense of the word) ends.

This strategy is most apparent in the sections of the novel that deal with Gatsby's parties. Nowhere in *The Great Gatsby* is repetition as explicitly confronted as in Nick's description of these parties. To Nick's eyes these parties follow an inevitable pattern that makes them virtually interchangeable. He describes events at these parties as fixed elements capable of serving as time markers: "I lingered in the garden until the inevitable swimming party had run up" (115). Nick's description aims at debunking the supposed spontaneity of events at Gatsby's parties by showing the mechanical regularity with which these enjoyments occur. In Nick's eyes the parties are not Dionysian revels but a concerted effort by a group of rather bored and boring individuals to convince themselves of their own enjoyment, an operation heavily dependent upon the consumption of alcohol.

The conviction that a strict and "inevitable" regularity reigns at Gatsby's parties is evident in the way that these parties first enter the narrative. They enter by way of the iterative, a form that alludes to repetition but avoids actually engaging in it. In *Narrative Discourse*, Gerard Genette defines iterative as "narrating once what happens *n* times" (116). Use of the iterative establishes a pattern by synthesizing multiple occurrences, as in the description of the preparations for Gatsby's parties: "Every Friday five crates of oranges and lemons arrived from a fruiterer in New York—every Monday these same oranges and lemons left his back door in a pyramid of pulpless halves" (43). This pattern continues into the party proper, making Nick's first appearance at one of Gatsby's parties into an event already bearing the mark of uniform repeatability, and revealing the narrative's attempt to function as a synthesizing and somewhat mechanical control of disparate moments. The use of the iterative to describe Gatsby's parties repeats a traditional operation of Enlightenment knowledge production, the dissolution and polemical recombination of events into units of didactic sense that, in Edward Said's words, serve to "illustrate human power . . . to transform nature" (*World* 125). The iterative functions here both to assert definitional control over one of the most unruly situations contained in the novel and to shore up Nick's narrating authority, an authority that, like that of all narrators, depends upon what Genette calls "*the absolute and almost sacred distinction between the narrator and that which s/he narrates*" (236). This distinction is crucial because in order for Nick to show us the dire consequences of Gatsby's temporal delusion and concomitantly unwarranted social and amorous aspirations, he has to demonstrate his ability to separate himself from this delusion. At the parties, Nick is most a participant in the action and most in danger of losing his ability to reliably narrate this action. Hence, the iterative serves as a tool to contain that which most threatens the flow of the narrative to its appointed ending.

In this attempt to stand apart from the activities taking place at the parties, Nick shares something in common with the author of these parties. In his description of the first party he attends, Nick remarks upon Gatsby's isolation at his own party. At the most convivial moment of the party, the conclusion of the "Jazz History of the World," Gatsby stands apart: "no one swooned backward on Gatsby . . . and no singing quartets were formed with Gatsby's head for one link" (55). Gatsby keeps himself detached at his parties because they are for him a mere means to a very specific end. They are not ends in themselves, worthwhile for their ability to entertain or divert Gatsby; they are designed with one very concrete goal in mind: the procurement of Daisy. Jordan Baker indicates to Nick that Gatsby "half expected her to wander into one of his parties," and the parties end as soon as Daisy's dislike of them is made clear (120). For Gatsby, as for the narrating Nick Carraway, the parties are not interesting in themselves but only for the ends they serve. The narration uses them as an illustration of

Gatsby's extravagance and of the unsavory results of the "open door" policy practiced at them. The parties are an affront to Nick's sensibilities and he narrates them in a way that makes this clear: from his fear that he should "begin to address cordial remarks to the passers-by" (46) at the first party to his consistent characterization of the conversation and the conversationalists at these parties as insipid, jejune, and tasteless, the parties are made into a tawdry and tedious menagerie of people one definitely wouldn't want to associate with.[32] Their description is meant to demonstrate the joyless chaos that results from the lack of adherence to social distinctions and the desultory nature of the absolute possibility that Nick laughs at when the limousine passes Gatsby's car.

Gatsby's parties represent a social dynamic unimaginable in the conservative East Egg society, and the kind of social mixing and vulgar behavior most antithetical to the hierarchy of cultural values that motivates the narration of Nick and Fitzgerald. Just as Gatsby has to die for Nick to be able to shape his life into a an allegorical summing up of the American condition, so the chaotic flux of the parties has to be contained, summed up, and dismissed by a narrative treatment that figures them as a repeating pattern of futility with no consequence.

However, the fact of the matter is that Nick's narration does not fully contain the energy of these parties; despite the intention of Gatsby and the narrative to use them as means to further their own ends, it is clear that the parties have a life of their own, a life evident in the passions and activities of the guests present at them. For these guests have aims of their own and the sheer license available at these parties is clearly a source of enjoyment to them. The polemical aims of Fitzgerald and of Nick cannot entirely strip the parties of their allure, a symptom of the ambivalence at the heart of their positions. This ambivalence manifests itself in the narrative, for the iterative pattern with which the description of the first party begins is eventually broken, and broken in a particularly telling way. Witness the following paragraph: "Suddenly, one of these gypsies in trembling opal seizes a cocktail out of the air, dumps it down for courage and moving her hands like Frisco dances out alone on the canvas platform. A momentary hush; the orchestra leader varies his rhythm for her and there is a burst of chatter as the erroneous news goes around that she is Gilda Gray's understudy from the 'Follies.' The party has begun" (45).

The specificity and distinctiveness of what is described here is incompatible with the belief that, like the delivery of oranges and lemons, it occurs regularly at each of the parties Gatsby gives. With the adverb "suddenly" we shift into the realm of the singular and unrepeatable, or in Genette's terms, into the "singulative." What has occurred is an instance of what Genette calls "the pseudo-iterative," a scene or scenes "presented . . . as iterative, whereas their richness and precision of detail ensure that no reader can seriously believe that they occur and reoccur in that manner, several times, without any variation" (121). According to Genette, the pseudo-iterative is a sign that the writer "'lives' such scenes with an intensity that makes him forget the distinction of aspects." In the pseudo-iterative, the writer falls prey to, or engages in, "intoxication with the iterative" (123). This is the intoxication that intrudes on the iterative description of the party, an intoxication in which the sheer delight in the use of what is initially a narrative tool transforms it into something wielded for its own sake. The pleasure immanent in the free play of the pseudo-iterative takes on a momentum of its own and breaks free of subordination to the goal that initially justified its employment.

The initial narrative goal of the iterative was to characterize the events at Gatsby's parties as regular, repetitive, and monotonous, for there is a strong association between the iterative and the habitual or typical (Genette 123, Kinder 5). This goal's forgetting of itself is, as Genette points out, a forgetting of aspects, and in Nick's narration this is a forgetting of social as well as grammatical distinctions. The intoxication with the iterative is aligned with the intoxication that allows Nick to enter into the spirit of the party and to forget, if only temporarily, his judgmental attitude toward the people he finds at it. In these intoxicated moments Nick also finds himself closest to Gatsby, most willing to forgive him his social immaturity, and most willing to forget that Gatsby represents everything for which he feels "an unaffected scorn" (6). These are dangerous moments for Nick's ability to construct himself as a reliable narrator of Gatsby's tale, for in his forgetting of distinctions he risks not only his ability to reliably judge Gatsby but also his ability to stand apart from Gatsby's confusion over time. In Nick's use of the iterative, as well as in his slippage into a present tense incompatible with his narrative detachment from Gatsby, Nick and the narrative for which Fitzgerald makes him responsible participate in Gatsby's confused relationship to time. Gatsby thinks he can repeat the past; the basis of his belief is, as we have seen, a reified vision that sees each moment as exchangeable with any other moment. The iterative is based on a similar vision. According to Genette, use of the iterative to link any two moments leads the iterative narrator "to consider them identical, and to merge them" (143). "This strange equation," in Genette's words, is "the law of the iterative." Implicit in the iterative is not only "a very sharp sense of habit and repetition" but a "feeling of the analogy between moments" (123). In the intoxication with the iterative, this feeling is overwhelming and intense enough to lead to a Gatsby-esque belief in exact repeatability. In making the parties into repeatable patterns, Nick's narration posits the possibility of returning to the past, even if it is only the past staged in Gatsby's desultory parties. The intoxication with the iterative betrays what Edward Said calls "the ironies of repetition," ironies that repetition "can not long escape" (125).

In his desire to sum up the repetitive—and in his mind, therefore epicene—patterns of Gatsby's parties, Nick ends up capturing some of the intensity and individuality that belie his own stance toward these parties. Both Nick's slippage into the pseudo-iterative and the content of this slippage, the drama of the bold dancer, bear traces of the fact that no temporal occurrence is ever just a means. If the past cannot be repeated in the sense that Gatsby intends, or that strict nonintoxicated adherence to the iterative implies, neither can it be consigned to a place without any relevance to, or communication with, the present. In *The Great Gatsby*'s narrative interaction with its readers the force of the unrepeatable intensity of the past events of Gatsby's parties still holds some allure. What is a means for the narrative can still potentially be something else for us. The same is true of Gatsby's parties. Though intended by Gatsby as means for obtaining Daisy, for at least some of the many guests at these parties and some of Fitzgerald's many readers, they undoubtedly live as potent markers of how social interaction might possibly be shaped, or even as living practices of recreation and conviviality attempting to creatively repeat what occurred at Gatsby's Long Island estate.

The use of the pseudo-iterative marks a point at which the text opens itself to two possibilities that threaten the narrative's drive toward self-totalization and toward delivery of its closing homily on Gatsby's failings and ours. The first of these is the possibility that Nick might not be able to separate himself from Gatsby and Gatsby's shortcomings enough to be a convincing deliverer of this homily. The second is that repetition might come to have an attraction that upsets Fitzgerald's valorization of nostalgia and that lets repetition appear as a creative force capable of opening up a fortuitous future. This is a danger because the unmotivated nature of the slippages from past to present tense and from the iterative to the pseudo-iterative speaks of the arbitrariness of judgments concerning repetition. As Genette points out, "repetition is in fact a mental construction," a judgment on an event that "eliminates from each correspondence everything belonging to it that is peculiar to itself" (113). The repetition identified in the "recurrence of identical events" is an abstraction that sees a series of several events "*only in terms of their resemblance.*" It is thus dependent on a single perspective, the kind of perspective valorized in Nick's statement that "life is much more successfully looked at from a single perspective, after all" (9). This perspective is shaken by the diffuse energies active in the relatively uncontrolled space of Gatsby's parties. What the narrative figures as a mechanical and sterile repetition antithetical to the pleasure of the singular looks less univocal from the collective perspective of the guests who come to the parties with aims less concrete than those of Gatsby or Nick. The forgetting of distinctions at work in the pseudo-iterative reveals the dependence of what counts as repetition upon the control of a narrating interest, and blurs the distinct boundary separating repetition from change. The intensity at work in the party and in the intoxication with the iterative that it engenders is the possibility of a repetition inseparable from change, motion, and discontinuity, a repetition that exceeds the secure foundations of primacy and secondariness.

However, neither Nick's intoxication nor that of the narrative lasts. Both are ended by the cold water of Daisy's perspective. Daisy's first time at one of Gatsby's parties is the occasion for the second description of one of these parties, a description that attempts to rectify and contain the excesses evident in the first description. In the second party's description, the awareness of Daisy's disapproval allows Nick to reflect remorsefully on the extent to which he had forgotten himself in succumbing to the charm of Gatsby's parties: "I had merely grown used to it, grown to accept West Egg as a world complete in itself, with its own standards and its own great figures" (110). Nick bemoans the fact that he has let the standards of Gatsby's West Egg parties become his own. The awareness of this lapse and its corrective comes through his ability to look at the world of these parties "again, through Daisy's eyes" (110). Nick adjusts his vision to correspond to the class to which he belongs by birth and upbringing, and the result sobers and saddens him by purging the parties of their vertiginous vitality and making them into tasteless manifestations of a "too obtrusive fate" herding "its inhabitants along a shortcut from nothing to nothing" (114). Characteristically, this adjustment is given a typicality and representative inevitability meant to reinforce the pessimistic devaluation of new perspectives at work in almost all aspects of the novel: "It is invariably saddening to look through new eyes at things upon which you have expended your own powers of adjustment" (111). In adopting Daisy's vision, Nick joins her in her mischaracterization of the complex energies at work in the parties as a "raw vigor" and "simplicity," a mischaracterization following the same pattern as the most prevalent misunderstandings of jazz.

The corrective force of Daisy's judgment ends Nick's intoxication with Gatsby's parties, but it doesn't fully extricate Nick from his ambivalent relationship to Gatsby or from his participation in Gatsby's affairs. For this to occur, another force is necessary, one that also stems from the Buchanans: the bullets that end Gatsby's life, guided to their target by way of Tom Buchanan's aid. Gatsby's death is the precondition for Nick's narration of his tale. The corrosive force of time must be halted, at least temporarily, if the meaningful moralistic kernel of Gatsby's life is to be extracted from it and put into palatable aesthetic form.

In Nick's hands, the knowledge to be gained from the emplotment of Gatsby's life is the truth that everything of value lies behind us. For this to be the main significance of Gatsby's tale, the ending must be fixed; Gatsby cannot be left in motion with the potential of discovering something that doesn't look like the most threadbare repetition of the past. His temporal path must be one that leads to death.

Gatsby's tale is given a sharp and poignant ending, and with this ending he is transformed into one of the discrete commodities in which he always had such faith. Gatsby's death serves as a purging of the improper temporal and social conceptions that threatened to seduce Nick, but it also removes a form of narrative for which Nick has nothing but scorn. Nick may like telling Gatsby's tale, but he has no stomach for the way Gatsby tells it. According to Nick, Gatsby's revelations about himself all come cloaked in an "appalling sentimentality" (118). Named here is the narrative form and mode of ordering affect against which modernists like Fitzgerald defined themselves. Gatsby is deficient in part because he has adopted for himself an outmoded or "old-fashioned" narrative that clings to sentimentality and to the forward and upward motion that Fitzgerald sees as illusory. The reappearance of Gatsby's childhood copy of *Hopalong Cassidy* marks him as the manifestation of an old rather than new logic. This serves to make him easier to dismiss, a dismissal characteristic of *The Great Gatsby*'s construction of time. In the world imaginatively constructed by Fitzgerald, there is the correct, cynical evaluation of time and temporality, and a bevy of other visions of time and repetition that are outmoded because of their deluded investment in a future that offers nothing. The effect is to configure all rival temporalities as already past, already superseded by a temporal conception that is not only the latest thing but is the last latest thing. *The Great Gatsby* thus aligns itself with the snobbish cynicism of the Buchanans, able to say in the same blasé tone: "Ah yes, I have seen that before . . . I have seen it all."[33] The easily discernible elitism implicit in this position, is characteristic of larger trends within modernism itself.

In its insistent desire to "make it new," modernism placed an injunction on the use of well-established techniques and literary formulas. This is the thesis advanced in Jameson's *A Singular Modernity*: Jameson argues that modernism depends more on "an ever-keener distaste for what is conventional and outmoded" than on "an exploratory appetite for the unexplored and undiscovered" (127). The modernism Jameson describes is ascetic rather than expansive, an impulse whose embrace of newness necessitates consignment of most conventions of expression to the scrap heap of obsolescence. What makes this impulse elitist is its assumption of a link between aesthetic necessity and the shape of the social realm that the aesthetic purports to represent. Jameson characterizes this dynamic as follows:

The outmoded and conventionalized literary expression, now identified as sentimentality, can also be seen to designate the obsolescence of a certain emotion in and of itself . . . But most often those outmoded emotions live on in social life itself long after modernism has pronounced its judgment on them; whence the intensifying suspicion of an elitism built into the very framework of this art, and also the sense that, whatever new areas of feeling and expression modernism has opened up, its representational focus spans an ever-dwindling sphere of social and class relationships. (127–28)

Jameson's description of modernism's ascetic and elitist impulses clarifies the positions taken up by *The Great Gatsby* and its first-person narrator. Nick's distaste for Gatsby's "appalling sentimentality" is just such a disqualification of outmoded expression, an elitist attempt to draw an ever-shrinking circle around the realm of the proper.[34] Gatsby, the representative of everything for which Nick feels an "unaffected scorn," is also figured by Fitzgerald as representative of the groups and classes of people whom the accelerating pace of American culture has propelled into social realms for which they are unprepared. Thus, Nick's scorn for the tawdry mawkishness of Gatsby's speech is indicative of the link between narrative desires and social desires. As the narrator, Nick positions himself as a purifier of the language, a filter capable of straining out the distasteful sentimentality that seems to characterize the utterances of all whom he encounters.[35] Nick's disdain for sentimentality is linked to his disdain for the activities and guests at Gatsby's parties; both work to dismiss those social trends whose gambling on "borrowed time" marks them as tasteless and unsustainable. Flowing from a position predicated upon the desire to expunge the "outmoded" linguistic habits of society, the narrative that organizes itself through Nick's perspective is laced with a degree of elitist misanthropy.

The predictable upshot of this misanthropic position is the desire to withdraw, to detach oneself from the vernacular of the multitude. Like the narrator of Johnson's *The Autobiography of an Ex-Colored Man*, Nick sees isolation and aesthetic production as necessarily linked. In *The Great Gatsby*, however, the desire for an isolated space from which to produce is not an explicit consideration of the narrator, as it is in Johnson's text, but the achieved position of the narrator as the novel begins. Nick has already withdrawn himself from the action of which he writes; before he writes anything about Gatsby, he writes about his withdrawal. On the second page of the text we find: "When I came back from the East last autumn I felt that I wanted the world to be in uniform and at a sort of moral attention; I wanted no more riotous excursions with privileged glimpses into the human heart" (6). The combination of removal and the desire for order speaks of the narrative's investment in an order unidirectionally imposed on the outside world, an order like the iterative pattern imposed on the "riotous excursions" of Gatsby's parties. From the very beginning of the text, the desire and necessity for an end to Nick's receptivity are explicitly thematized. Before the narrative can properly begin, Nick's "interest in the abortive sorrows and short-winded elations of men" has to be "closed out," even if only temporarily. When Nick says that he wants "no more riotous excursions with privilege glimpses into the human heart," he is expressing the narrative necessity of time coming to a stop. The "riotous excursions" must end, the listening to which Nick is constitutionally predisposed must end, and the "appalling sentimentality" of Gatsby must end.

Because these preconditions are all met, "Gatsby turned out all right in the end" (6). Gatsby turns out all right because he turns out dead, a suitably stable object for narrative investment. Gatsby's capability for speech ends, and with it any need for Nick to repeat his story, a story he has translated for us by transforming it into an aesthetic object free from plagiaristic and sentimental clichés. The unstable alliance between literary elitism and social elitism at work here is an alliance in which commitment to a modernism based on "tendential elimination of the extrinsic" leads to the elimination of the "extrinsic" social interloper. This alliance is predicated on the investment of both forms of elitism in reifying time and lifting it from its provenance in the play of social interactions. A function of friction, time is generated by the dialogic play between the circle of individual consciousness and anything outside of that narrow circle, whether it be an object or another consciousness.[36] The naturalization of time depends on the suppression of this interplay, a suppression at work in Nick's aestheticizing translation of Gatsby and his speech.

Despite the work the novel does to mute the dissonance of Gatsby's tale and the social vectors resonating within it, the figure of Gatsby takes on a temporal movement irreducible to the main movement of the text that engenders him. This ability of characters and other textual effects to acquire a momentum and life of their own gives novels, even ones whose main thrust is reactionary, a progressive potential. Novels are able to engender characters, actants, patterns, and rhythms that take on a life of their own in a kind of intoxication of the novel with the being-for-self of what are initially created as mere supports for the novel's progress.[37] The result of this is a polyphonic dissonance between the trajectory of the novel and the trajectory of its individual components.[38] It is this dissonance that *The Great Gatsby* works to contain or suppress; part of the way it does so is by ending Gatsby's ability to speak. Removing the impediments to the narrator's ability to speak univocally for all the characters in the novel (and ultimately for all of "us" who read it), the end of Nick's willingness to listen is a closing down of coevalness and dialogue. The time that remains is almost exclusively the self-generated time of the narrative's origin, a time whose subservience to nostalgia strives to make the possibility of a fortuitous future into a childishly deluded wish.

From "I" to "We"

The suppression of Gatsby and of time itself serves to elicit assent to the famous "we" of the novel's conclusion: "So we beat on, boats against the current, borne back ceaselessly into the past" (189). In moving from the narrator's solitary "I" to the aggregating "we," the text performs the traditional maneuver by which a specific configuration of subjectivity is naturalized. According to Étienne Balibar, the possibility "of creating an identity between *I* and *We*" is the fundamental belief licensing political and discursive regimes based on an autonomous subject detached from the natural and social world (9): "The articulation of an identity between an 'I' and a 'We' inscribes the individual in the social structure, and uses the resultant 'We' to install within . . . consciousness a virtual representation of the world of which [the individual] is an 'indivisible part'" (15). Linking the "I" and the "We" together grounds the structure of expectations functioning in any social order, and reinforces the exclusions that this structure creates.

This articulation of "I" and "We" serves the same purpose as the snobbish repetition of traditional social forms, and is the tendential goal of the entire novel. The ending of the novel works to establish a polity based on the verities of which Gatsby was ignorant, but which his death is meant to articulate.

The "We" that manifests itself on the last page of *The Great Gatsby* is a "we" that repeats Gatsby's movements but with the crucial difference that it is conscious of this movement in a way Gatsby never was. This means, among other things, that this "we" and the link between it and the narrating "I" are dependent upon Gatsby.

In order for the narrative to move from Nick's "I" to the concluding "we," Gatsby has to be made into a representative figure. He is representative insofar as the pattern of his life (as given to us in Nick's narrative) is a repeatable template into which all lives that partake of the concluding "we" should fit. At the same time his life is given to us as unique, as an unrepeatable occurrence that can never be surpassed in its ability to express the truth of the American condition. In the figure of Gatsby all the paradoxes of the role of repetition in American culture are played out. Nick's narration repeats Gatsby's story in a synthesizing repetition that stops time and programs the way this story will be repeated in the future. It does so through the establishment of a link between an "I" and a "we," which are, after all, themselves repeatable pronominal shifters. "I" and "we" are pronouns whose content depends on the structure in which they are uttered, shifters whose reference is determined by a relational play and thus subject to a creative repetition bearing the possibility of change, displacement, and subversion as well as of the static confirmation that *The Great Gatsby* wagers on. This instability of "I" and "we," and of the link between the two of them is always present in their use, and the novel attempts to dispel this instability through its treatment of Gatsby. By reducing Gatsby to a lifeless body the novel excludes the possibility of his appropriation of the novel's final collective "we." This "we" depends on the use of Gatsby as a uniquely repeatable example, but it also depends on his exclusion from the community that the "we" establishes. The final "we" both relies on and disavows Gatsby and his confusion about time.

Given stability by the abjection of Gatsby's body, the communal "we" with which the novel concludes derives its constitution from the exclusion of people like Gatsby and his father, the "fat Jewess" at the theater, and the "three modish Negroes" in the back of the limousine. Appearing as an abstract communal enunciation available to all, it has built into it not only the valorization of a particular temporality but the exclusiveness of this temporality as well, an exclusiveness that banishes to the realm of delusion all movements into the future that don't depend on the snobbish repetition of established structures.

"He had come a long way to this blue lawn and his dream must have seemed so close that he could hardly fail to grasp it. He did not know that it was already behind him" (189). This is the truth that the identification of the narrating "I" with the textual and extratextual "we" is intent on communicating. We are meant to realize that the object or situation we seek is behind us, and that our past will always remain unrepeatable and inaccessible. *The Great Gatsby* pushes us to come to terms with our past by weakening its hold on us as much as possible, and to assign both the past and the future to a limited and hermetically sealed place in our psychic life. If we are to learn anything from Gatsby's fate, it is that we should stop our ears to the siren song of the past and to the call of the future "that year by year recedes before us" and that is in actuality only a disguised version of the past.

The past, however, plays an important part in our social life as well as in our psychic life. To acknowledge with Snead that repetition is the means by which cultures maintain themselves is to acknowledge the continuing impact of the past on the way we think and act in the present and the future. That this impact of the past is material as well as ideal is not an occasion for despair, for the continued existence of the past is an opportunity as well as a restriction. As Snead shows us, a direct confrontation with the fact of repetition (and repetition is always the repetition of the past) exposes the truth that the rhythmic starting point of any formation is always "there for you to pick up when you come back to it," always "amenable to restarting, interruption or entry by a second or third player or to response by an additional musician" (67–68). Snead writes of musicians, but his insights apply to all social agents. The past worked upon by repetition is not an inert object but a constantly shifting field reconfigured by the way societies and social subjects perform its movements. The past can be syncopated, can be given a different valence by shifting the accents of its repetition. Gatsby is right to think that the past can be repeated; his mistake is to think that he can repeat it just once, "fixing" it by replacing Tom's exclusive and possessive relationship to Daisy with his own. Gatsby thinks that one can repeat the past, but the truth is that the past constantly and ceaselessly repeats itself, and this repetition is always a function of dynamic relationships between individuals and social formations.

The Great Gatsby tries to teach us how to repeat without changing anything and without listening to the other forms of repetition that coexist with ours and on which ours depend. And yet, despite this, we can hear beating in it other rhythms of repetition. The novel works to give itself a formal autonomy by neutralizing and containing these rhythms, but their repetitive allure continues to whisper to us.

Their voice is full of much more than money, and if we, unlike Nick, do not close out our receptivity to the world, we can hear in them possibilities that exceed the novel's valorization of a unidirectionally nostalgic relationship to the past. Like Gatsby, Fitzgerald does not realize that these possibilities lie behind him, in the past out of which his novel grows and in the jazz that gets figured in the novel as unimaginatively repetitive. In the seams opened up in the text by the representations of Gatsby's parties and the jazz heard at them, and by the intoxication with the iterative mimetically engendered by these representations, a time whose flexibility and capaciousness evades the logic of commodity thinking and abstract temporal sequence makes itself heard, even if only faintly.

Insofar as the Jazz Age was an age in which jazz flourished and not just an age in which jazz could be understood as a puerile obsession with dancing and sex, the future is behind us in a decade that is not just "borrowed time," but is a moment in which American culture opens itself up to a sound that, if properly heard, pushes us to rethink our commitment to a time based upon hierarchy and exclusion. The repetition that jazz endows with such attractive force gives us hope that this is not a moment like Gatsby's encounter with Daisy but one that might fortuitously come around again.

What lies behind us is the initial encounter of American society with the repetitive vibrations of jazz, an encounter that determined much of the consequent reception of the music. The beauty of this missed encounter is that the rhythms that were missed on the first time around are precisely what ensure that they will come around again. Jazz's existence on recordings and its sedimentation in novels like *The Great Gatsby* guarantee that the listenings required to really hear the music are always available. Jazz's performance of a repetition that exceeds exchange guarantees that what is available on these recordings is more than stockpiled use time; it is a time that threatens to intoxicate the listener and draw him or her into the vibratory world of the music. Thus what is "behind" us is also "ahead" of us in a future created by a mode of repetitive performance that creatively repeats the past in order to move past the exclusions of the present.

As a result of its attempt to use jazz for its own purposes, Fitzgerald's structure of nostalgic renunciation contains within it the seeds of a future unimagined by the text and not reducible to the grasping, commodified vision of Gatsby himself.

5
Vibratory Time

Smith and Armstrong's "St. Louis Blues"

But if you look at the phenomenon of rhythm, you find that the beat
consists of sound and not sound, being and not being. The Be & the
At. The pulse of everything. Go. Stop. Yet the Stop is part of the Go.
Dialectical as everything else.

—Amiri Baraka, "Rhythm and Rime"

That-which-is *repels* that-which-is-not and, in doing so, repels its own
real possibilities.

—Herbert Marcuse, "A Note on Dialectic"

W. C. Handy's "Beale Street Blues" is mentioned in Fitzgerald's *The Great Gatsby*,
but it is not allowed to fully sound there. Its resonance is narrowly circumscribed,
incorporated into the text in a way that mutes it and makes of it a force that
moves in only one direction, the direction of the text's final closing off. In his
novelistic meditation on music, barbarity, and Western civilization, Thomas
Mann describes a similar act of resonance constrained: "It was the earliest concern, the first conquest of the musician to rid sound of its raw and primitive
features, to fix to one single note the singing which in primeval times must have
been a howling glissando over several notes, and to win from chaos a musical system" (374). Mann describes the emergence of a rationalized system of
constraint out of the "chaos" of musical liberty. His description resonates with
Fitzgerald's attempt to imagine chaos as the only alternative to existing systems
of social constraint. While Fitzgerald and others would like to see jazz and blues
as primitive precursors to civilized musical and social forms, what the music of
Bessie Smith, Alberta Hunter, and Louis Armstrong actually gives us is a sophisticated critique of the barbarism and irrationality embedded in the forms
of American culture. Their music plays upon the irrationality embedded within
these forms in order to construct a more capacious form of musical and social
performance. A central part of this construction is their sliding and vibratory
manipulation of tone itself.

The codification of a prescribed pattern of tonality that Mann describes is
figured by Western society as a rationalization that facilitates the production of

clear melodic and harmonic forms by purging sound of its "barbaric" propensity to slide across and elude established patterns of musical meaning. Following this institutional prohibition, divergences from established melodic and harmonic patterns are allowed only as ornaments added to notes without altering their solid basis in a rationalized schema of tonality. Chief among these ornaments is vibrato, an etiolated return of the repressed that allows the vibrational nature of musical tones to manifest itself, but only insofar as it is subordinated to the established musical system.[1]

It was Max Weber who first described the dictates and proscriptions of the classical tradition as rationalization. The "first conquest" that Mann describes was seen by Weber as an important early step in this rationalization, a necessary standardization and fixing of notes that moves "beyond a random collection of sounds that someone might make on different occasions" (91). According to Weber, music making is no autonomous region but is subject to the same processes of rationalization that shape the rest of Western civilization. In the service of predictability and calculability, the material of music was as subject to the imperatives of the "Puritan spirit," as were any other aspects of economic or religious life. The tonal system of Western music evolved around the imperatives of securing repeated access to the most consonant of intervals, the octave and the fifth. All other intervals were made to orbit around the inescapable gravitational pull of these valorized consonances. Moreover, only intervals that could be theoretically derived from them were given any place at all within the tonal system. Intervals not reducible to temporary steps away from consonance were banished to the outside of the musical system.

However, according to Weber, despite the provenance of this musical system in a rationalizing impulse, its seventeenth- and eighteenth-century expansion led it into realms in which a narrow reliance on rationality proved insufficient. As the music became more harmonically sophisticated, and as shifts between multiple key centers became more common, the inflexibility of a system that tried to derive pitch values from a single center resulted in problematic harmonic clashes.

A note that functioned as a fifth or sixth tone in one key needed to be bent to serve as a different scale degree (say a second or third) in another key. For example, a b natural in the key of G (where it is the third scale degree) clashes with a b natural in the key of C (where it is the seventh scale degree). These kinds of discrepancies threatened to destabilize the entire harmonic system, and eventually a recodifying adjustment was made in the late eighteenth century. This was the replacement of just intonation with a tuning system known as equal temperament.[2] Equal temperament intonation is a kind of compromise formation that attempts to preserve as much as possible of the consonance of the octave and the fifth while bending intervals to facilitate the smooth transition from one key to another. The result is a harmonic system that retains virtually none of the "purity" of the consonant intervals around which it is organized. As every piano tuner knows, one has to "fudge" the intervals on a piano to ensure the proper functioning of the piano in all twelve key centers.[3] The system of equal temperament, which has reigned in Western music since its institution, is, to paraphrase Weber, a rationalized irrationality.[4] It keeps an orientation toward a few key intervals but does not itself preserve them, sacrificing the beauty of the most resonant of intervals to a system that ensures a frictionless motion between key centers.[5] What is gained in this sacrifice is fungibility, an exchangability of musical elements that mirrors the emphasis on exchange in the society out of which the music emerges.

In *The Rational and Social Foundations of Music* Max Weber describes this pattern of rationalization and the flaws within it. According to him, the Western system of harmony enshrines an amalgam of rationality and irrationality.[6] Certain tones are more irrational than others, primarily the third and the seventh. All careful observations of jazz and blues have noted its tendency to both emphasize these tones and to bend them in ways unknown to the classical tradition.[7] These bent tones are usually called blue notes, which Gunther Schuller defines as "microtonal variant[s] . . . associated almost exclusively with the third, fifth, and seventh degrees of the scale" (374).[8] The jazz imperative to bend these tones to the point of breaking derives from two impulses: from the retentions of African performance traditions and from an African American performance tradition that plays upon the irrationality of the "rationalized" system of Western music making. Jazz performance picks on the soft spots of Western rationality, ironizing a cultural edifice portraying itself as eminently rational but which depends on a subordination of African Americans that is both narrowly rational in its clinging to privilege and power and broadly irrational in its failure to meet the most basic standards of human decency. Like the civilization that produces it, the classical harmonic system is built out of irrationality and cannot legitimately ascribe irrationality or primitiveness to the sounds outside of its prescribed system. Understanding this is key to understanding both jazz and most of its reception. Jazz tugs at the irrational underpinnings of a prescribed form of (ir)rationality. Its performance tropes on these underpinnings as part of an acerbic exposure of the given system's mixture of rationality and irrationality. The primary response of the rational and white American listener is to ascribe to this troping a primitive irrationality having its provenance in a locus absolutely anterior and exterior to a closed Western rationality.

What Thomas Mann describes as "raw and primitive features" outside of and prior to the system of Western music making can be heard in Alberta Hunter's vocal performance of "Beale Street Blues." Accompanied on this 1927 recording by Fats Waller, Hunter engages in a display of the swoops, scoops, trills, and manipulations of vibrato characteristic of the blues tradition. Unlike the vibrato valorized by the classical tradition, Hunter's vocals are not content with the division between the primacy of the rationalized note and the purely ornamental and secondary nature of ornaments. When Hunter trills her voice over the top of Fats Waller's organ (as at 2:23) she is not providing a mere ornament; she is playing upon the very materiality of the note and creating a musical line unfettered by the dictates of a narrowly defined musical rationality. What Hunter and Waller perform is the sound of a tradition suppressed by Fitzgerald's imagining of the music as "hopeless comment" and Mann's imagining of the outside of the classical music system as a "howling" expression of a "raw" and "primitive" "chaos." For what makes itself heard in Hunter and Waller's performance are not primitive survivals or retentions but a countertradition conversant with all the resources of the Western tradition familiar to Mann, as well as with the techniques of a performative tradition that exist outside of the narrowly circumscribed imagination of Fitzgerald and Mann.[9]

To hear the movements suppressed by Fitzgerald's conscription of "Beale Street Blues" into his text, I turn to a recording of another W. C. Handy composition. Recorded and released in 1925, the same year as *The Great Gatsby's* publication, the performance of "St. Louis Blues" by Bessie Smith, Louis Armstrong, and Fred Longshaw engenders a vibrational pattern both inimical to and imbricated with the closed, nostalgic rhythm of Fitzgerald's novel.

One thing, then another. Stop, then start. First there is silence, then there is not. A cornet sounds a solitary but richly expressive note (a richness dependent on vibrato); then it is augmented by a single chord from an organ. This is the way "St. Louis Blues" comes to us, building a structure out of sound, that is, out of the ridiculously tenuous material of vibrating columns of air. Sound is a longitudinal wave, a pattern of stops and starts and thus a pattern of rhythmic vibration. The duration of a sound wave is not simply a matter of maintenance; it takes both pauses and reapplications of force to make a continuous note sound. (*The Science of Sound* on the vibrations that come out of the bell of a brass instrument: "In order to sustain the oscillation, the player must continue to supply puffs of air at appropriate times, not unlike the regular pushes applied to a child in a swing. A steady flow of air into the instrument will not sustain the oscillation any more than a steady force applied to a swing, because energy would be added during half the cycle and removed during the other half. To maintain oscillation, air must be added at the appropriate part of each cycle" [228–29].) The production of the simplest sound plunges one into the complexities of continuity, and the vibratory patterns at work in the performance of "St. Louis Blues" move forward without ever disengaging themselves from these complexities.

First cornet, then organ. First Louis Armstrong, then Fred Longshaw. This is the way that Bessie Smith's 1925 recording of W. C. Handy's "St. Louis Blues" announces itself. Before we hear the "empress of the blues," her arrival has been announced by a cornet fanfare that tails off into a quavering vibrato. This fanfare announces not the arrival of the archon, or of any fixed arche, but the arrival of an unsubordinated vibration. Unlike the vibrato performed in accordance with the demands of the classical tradition, the relationship between note and vibrato announced in Armstrong's an-archic fanfare upsets the priority of discrete notatable tones, spinning the listener into a sound world in which the vibrations constitutive of a note display their affinity with the vibrato ostensibly added to a note as a mere ornament.

The tremulous quality of Armstrong's tone is not an expression of its own wavering; it is the shaking manifestation of a powerful torque quivering with a Faustian need to transmit its energy by putting others in motion. The music aims to make listeners into vibratory responses to a series of forceful questions: How does one hear time? As continuity or discontinuity? Are continuity and vibration compatible? How does the repetition in jazz hold itself apart from the snobbish repetition virtually omnipresent in the world?[10]

To the implacable directness and heedless solidity of the linear, jazz adds the slightest but crucial torsion of an unhoused vibration. Sound is vibration (as is time),[11] and music might best be understood as a system for organizing vibration. Western music is essentially a rationalization of vibration, and jazz puts itself into play on this grid of rationalized vibration. Its ludic manipulations of pitch, timbre, and rhythm are not totally divorced from the system of Western classical music; jazz uses the materials and devices of this music to further its own ends.[12]

Sound and time are the central materials of all music; both are vibrating waves that travel differently in different mediums. Their propagation and their shape are both profoundly impacted by the material, intellectual, and social densities in which they move. According to Hegel, music brings to our attention the normally unnoticed motion of time, and the music that Armstrong's fanfare sets in motion brings to our attention the way that European-derived conceptions of music, time, and subjectivity are distorted when they travel in the medium of African American performance.[13] The vibrational sound world awakened by the cornet and organ fanfare is inhabited by rhythmic and melodic trajectories bearing the weight of the fact that the way we hear time affects its shape. The single note that shakes itself from the end of Armstrong's horn announces the key of the vibrational sound world that his cornet and Bessie Smith's voice will move in for the duration of their performance of "St. Louis Blues."

Armstrong and Smith play creatively upon the dialectic of continuity and discontinuity. They establish a continuity, but it is a syncopated continuity built out of the interweaving of the stops and starts of the three distinct voices and vibratory patterns: cornet, voice, organ. The fabric of their interaction is as tight as the interaction of any three musicians could be, and yet the texture of this fabric is not uniform enough to hide the labor of weaving that produces it: the discontinuity alternates with the continuity rather than being hidden behind it.[14] In "Sound and Sentiment, Sound and Symbol" Nathaniel Mackey describes this form of oscillation between continuity and discontinuity as a form of the mythological Legba's limp. Legba, the lame dancer, is the Fon-Yoruba orisha of the crossroads and "master of polyrhythmicity and heterogeneity" (613). The specific genius of Legba lies in the way that his dance uses his "deformity" (a deformity that Mackey renames as "multiformity") as a springboard to a higher form of virtuosity, a virtuousic movement that evokes a "heterogenous wholeness" through its "rhythmic digestion of dislocation" (Mackey 527). The rhythmic digestion of dislocation thrives on the border between continuity and discontinuity, playing through rather than around the discontinuity that lingers at the edge of every performance, feeding on it to produce a rhythm full of breaks, hesitations, and waverings.[15] In "St. Louis Blues" these negative elements of discontinuity are just as much the raw material for improvisation as are the positive elements of tone, scale, and song structure.

Legba limps because his legs are of different lengths, a discrepancy that makes his motion into a coordination of incommensurate elements. The motion of "St. Louis Blues," of "Beale Street Blues," and indeed of jazz in general is this kind of incommensurate limp, a limp whose power, grace, and lithe dexterity in coordinating incommensurabilities makes the term "limp" seem unsuitably pedestrian.[16] Hearing the loping interplay between Bessie Smith's arching and aching animation of W. C. Handy's lyrics and the pungently elaborative melismas of Louis Armstrong's cornet, one hears a coordination of rhythmic and vibratory patterns as different as one could imagine, and yet the deftness of their interaction and the limpid coarseness of the motion that this interaction generates strikes the listener with at least as much force as any univocal wall of sound.

The principle at work in generating this force is named in the title of an essay by the composer Olly Wilson: "The Heterogeneous Sound Ideal in African American Music." According to Wilson, an essential part of the conceptual framework of African American music making is a preference for the "timbrally heterogeneous," a preference that manifests itself in all aspects of musical organization and that puts melody, harmony, rhythm, and structure in the service of producing "dramatically contrasting qualities of sound" (160). When Bessie Smith's broad, imperious vibrato sounds at the same time as Armstrong's sly, and slightly more rapid, vibrato (as it does at the end of the second chorus, at 2:22), the result is a composite pattern combining the two distinct patterns of oscillation without purging their discrepancies. This is a manifestation of Wilson's "heterogeneous sound ideal," a manifestation that forms what he refers to as a "composite musical texture" and "a mosaic of varying tone colors" (162). The improvised texture that Armstrong, Smith, and Longshaw perform requires no curtailing of individual expression in the service of a greater whole; for despite their attentive attunement to each other, their combination into an ensemble yokes them together with a harness flexible enough to allow an almost infinite play.[17]

Wilson's article makes no direct claims about the extra-musical significance of the heterogeneous sound ideal, but his assertion that the "distinct set of musical qualities" embodied in African American performance "are an expression of the collective cultural values of peoples of African descent" clearly implies that performances like Armstrong and Smith's illuminate aspects of African American modes of sociality (158). In a 1941 interview Duke Ellington makes this link between musical practice and a heterogeneous social ideal explicit. Pointing out a chord in a recording of his, Ellington tells his interviewer: "That's us. Dissonance is our way of life in America. We are something apart, yet an integral part" ("Interview" 150). For Ellington, the clash of different sound patterns embodies the experience of African Americans whose participation in the American polity is essential to it, but whose contributions are always at least partially suppressed. At the same time, the dissonance that Ellington refers to differs in subtle but crucial ways from the dissonance that Max Weber describes at work in classical music. Although both the jazz tradition and the classical tradition conceive of dissonance as discordant vibrations sounding simultaneously, the classical tradition recognizes only dissonances internal to the Western system of rationality and music. In the classical tradition dissonance is something generated entirely by the tonal system itself, a clash of two distinct and codified vibrational patterns or pitches that sounds temporarily before being resolved into a more consonant resolution. Dissonance is seen as subordinate to the harmonic systems' valorization of consonance.[18]

In declaring dissonance a "way of life," Ellington points out that dissonance comes from the outside as well as the inside of the tonal system. The dissonance that he refers to owes its existence to the vibratory patterns and modes of performance evolved by those figured as deficient in rationality and denied access to the most prestigious preserves of Western music making. Ellington points to the existence of an African American dissonance, a blackening of the harmonic

2. Fitzgerald at his writing desk.
Manuscripts Division, Department of
Rare Books and Special Collections,
Princeton University Library.

system that removes the prescriptions for how dissonance can sound and transforms it from a negative principle into a positive principle. In the European
classical tradition dissonance is used as an impetus to forward motion, a thing
to be fled from or passed by on the way to a more stable consonance. This is
the way that Fitzgerald uses the dissonant sight of chauffeured blackness: as a
temporary clash that spurs visions of chaotic dissolution in Nick Carraway but
quickly disappears as the plot speeds on to its appointed end. What Longshaw,
Smith, and Armstrong perform is the full musical resonance of the sound that
Fitzgerald suppresses in his circumscription of conflicting elements. Dissonance
is not Fitzgerald's way of life, and he cannot but mute the polyphonic resonance
of the scene that he introduces. To do otherwise would be to risk derailing the
prescribed forward motion of his plot. In *The Great Gatsby* the curtailment of
listening works in the service of unilinear progress.

The tradition that Ellington, Armstrong, and Smith are a part of has no such
fear of derailment or disarticulation. Like Hurston, they know that "discord is
more natural than accord" ("Characteristics" 305), and their intimate familiarity
with a rhythm identified by Mackey as a "digestion of dislocation" lets them
treat the alleged chaos alluded to in Fitzgerald's non-encounter with blackness
as the site of improvisational opportunity. Their preference for the "timbrally

3. Fitzgerald and Armstrong created competing versions of American temporality. Courtesy of the Louis Armstrong House Museum.

heterogeneous" gives them the clash that Fitzgerald avoids as a positively entropic opening onto a performance that moves in multiple directions at once. Embracing dissonance as "a way of life" means moving past or through a conception that categorizes unresolved clashes as failures and into a realm where no unilinearity can prevail. For implicit in the way that Smith and Hunter's voices and Armstrong's cornet play upon the vibrational constitution of sound is a confrontation of the fact that, despite appearances, no musical performance can move in a line that is straight or uninterrupted.

Given the fact that sound is the indispensable material of music, and that sound is vibration, no performance and no composition can avoid the back and forth oscillation without which they would not exist. Musical time can only pose as unidirectional; it cannot really be unidirectional because sound is not unidirectional. Sound always has an inescapably oblique component, and all music must come to terms with this obliqueness in one way or another. The classical tradition's way of dealing with this is to fit vibration into rigidly prescribed categories of tonality and to enforce these categories so emphatically that they begin to appear as natural or given.[19] Jazz enters into this systematic enforcement of categories as obliquely as the side-to-side oscillation of pitch enters into any music hall; performers like Armstrong and Hunter trope on the Western harmonic system in a manner reflective of the fact that they know it both from the inside and the outside. They know the scales, chords, and valorized harmonic progressions as well as the most well-schooled classical performer, but at the same time they are heirs to a musical tradition that has syncretically bent these formulas to suit the aims of a different conception of sound, of time, and of the coordination of bodies and subjects.

Bending the music to fit their performative needs, Armstrong and Smith inject malleability into the musical system, and part of what their performance communicates is this malleability. What can be heard in their intertwined melodic lines is not only the unique and unrepeatable brilliance of their performance but the planting of a banner for others to rally around. Like the advanced guard of an army that has breached the enemy's walls, the interplay of organ, cornet, and voice is an incitement and a beckoning call. Announcing the permeability of the fortress of rationalized harmony (and of the equally adamantine walls of the music industry), Smith and Armstrong make visible an alternative construction of the aesthetic, a mode of music making and performed sociality that uses a reconceived dissonance to engender a trajectory capable of noncoercive yokings of incommensurate elements and of movements into a future that is neither unbounded chaos nor a snobbish and unbending repetition of the past.

When we hear the ensemble that performs "St. Louis Blues," we hear a forward rhythmic motion created primarily by Longshaw's organ but to which all three performers contribute. At the same time, we hear movements that branch out from and accompany this forward movement. Armstrong's melodic embroidery of Smith's vocal line darts in and out of the rhythmic propulsion signified by the organ, moving in a plane that intersects the plane of Smith's voice and Longshaw's organ but is not reducible to them. His melodies move toward the listener as well as parading themselves in front of the listener, evoking contradictory responses. The heterogeneity performed by the Bessie Smith ensemble creates effects that shock and surprise the listener, pulling them up short, as well as effects that carry the listener along with the ensemble, drawing us into their movement. The effect is a kind of distention that pulls the listener in multiple directions at the same time and invites them to make dissonance their way of life. An embodiment of Wilson Harris's dictum that "wholeness is an insoluble paradox" (viii), this performance of the "St. Louis Blues" makes neither the individual voices (of Armstrong, of Smith, of Longshaw) nor the combined ensemble into points of mimetic identification but throws the listener into a realm in which the most insistently sounded call is an exhortation to mime the difference between the two. Reveling in the clash of discrepant motions, the

Bessie Smith ensemble models a system in which each component part has its own temporal rhythm (Bachelard 75), which urges the listener to hear or identify in themselves a similar system. The coordination and clash of cornet, organ, and voice speak in the imperative voice, and it speaks a message common to much African-derived performance: "Dance all the drums in your body" (R. Thompson 338).

The polyrhythmic nature of "St. Louis Blues" is not aimed at any motionless or placidly self-possessed subjectivity; it is aimed at the polyrhythmic subject that precedes and underlies any such mutely immobile self-possession. The subject that the "St. Louis Blues" aims itself at is an embodied subject, a subject whose bodily surface is a sounding board for vibrations and is thus made up of, in Lefebvre's words, a "packet of rhythms" (75). According to Lefebvre, "the body, or more specifically your body, consists in a packet of rhythms." If one listens sympathetically to "St. Louis Blues," one should hear vibrating within oneself a Bessie Smith component, a Louis Armstrong component, and a Fred Longshaw component, as well as combinations of these that defy identificatory naming. Any vibration that doesn't elicit a sympathetic vibration in the hearing body (a surface much larger than the ears) is simply not heard. A polyrhythmic listening requires that the packet of rhythms constituting the subject be opened and that the different temporalities at work within the self forsake subordination to any univocal temporal line. What is crucial here is that the polyrhythms and vibrational dissonance exemplified in "St. Louis Blues" are not only engendered by the interaction of two discrete patterns or identities but are at work *within* patterns and identities. The resonant sound of Bessie Smith's voice is already a complex interaction of different vibrations before it enters into any interaction with the equally complex interaction that resonates within Armstrong's cornet sound.[20]

The coordination of different rhythms at work in the production of sound or of any utterance has long been clear to those who use, study, or teach the production of vibrato. The renowned vocal coach Richard Miller cites approvingly an article, published in 1958, by the Dutch scientist and researcher Janwillem van den Berg titled "Myoelastic-Aerodynamic Theory of Voice Production." Van den Berg's hypothesis is that "vocal-fold vibration is produced by the coordination of muscle tension and breath pressure" (R. Miller 47). Refuting the belief that vocal-fold vibration stems solely from the excitation of nerve cells (the "neurochronaxic principle"), van den Berg describes voiced phonation in speaking and singing as the result of a communication between the motor of the breath mechanism (that is, the lungs) and the vibratory action of the vocal folds.[21] Vibrato, or any vocal effect—including the production of the "cleanest," most unadorned tone—is produced out of the coordination of at least two distinct physical systems within the body. This means that before there is more than one note, before there are any notes, there is already a coordination of different rhythms, a dynamic interplay of forces that creates the vibration at work in any sound. In the interior of the bodies involved in musical production there is a call and response going on that precedes any exterior call and response. The sounds that emerge from Bessie Smith's throat are a manifestation of what Floyd dubs "Call-Response," a vibrational interplay in which call and response are braided together in a sound and a motion that defies subordination to any unsplit, univocal source.

An acknowledgment of the unavoidably polyrhythmic nature of the processes that occur in the production of sound and music takes away the justification for thinking of any elements of music as solid entities having precedence (in the temporal sense of the term) over vibration. Vibration is never added to a non-vibrational entity; vibration is always woven into the substance of all musical (and cultural) elements. Long before Jacques Derrida, Bessie Smith and Louis Armstrong sound out the implications of the fact that "it is always too late to ask the question of time" (42) and add the corollary that it is also always too late to think of adding vibration or vibrato. This is true not only in the musical world but in the social and physical world as well. Marxists like Marcuse and Baraka describe the vibratory nature of social existence,[22] and modern physics posits a physical world composed entirely of vibrations of transverse and longitudinal waves.[23] According to both Kant and Hegel, matter is an amalgam of attraction and repulsion, and to conceive of this amalgam as stable enough to constitute an object or a thing rather than a motile wave is to suppress the perturbing presence of nothingness within being, the fact that in every moment the energy of an object is exerting itself in order to preserve itself. There is either expansion or contraction but never an absence of vibration or an absolutely regular rhythm.[24]

The movement from stable moment to stable moment without rupture and in a way that maintains the existing forms of society requires a neutralization of the dissonance between subjects and of the dissonant vibrations between subjects and social structures.[25] A linear movement into the future requires the suppression of a nonlocalizable and nonresolvable dissonance and of the side-to-side (and back-and-forth) motion of vibration. Since there is no sound, and indeed no motion, without vibration, this suppression is necessarily a channeling of vibration and dissonance rather than its elimination (which would be impossible). In his critique of Bergson, Gaston Bachelard writes that "the most stable patterns owe their stability to rhythmic discord" (137). Musical, literary, and social structures build themselves out of rhythmic discord and the instability of time; they do so by evading, containing, and/or narrativizing this instability.

The Western harmonic system evades vibrational instability by allowing only a fixed set of pitches (defined in terms of vibrations per second). Expressive possibilities that fall in between the gradations established by this system are disallowed, but as a kind of compensation for what has been lost, vibrato, a vibration added onto a pitch within the system, gives back a modicum of what has been denied. For the system of Western harmony to retain its stability, it is important to keep a rigid distinction between the vibration that constitutes a note and the vibration added to the constituted note as vibrato. Vibrato, then, is a kind of return of the repressed, a vibrational ornament attached to the reified vibration of a systematically defined pitch. What is preserved by maintaining a rigid distinction between stable tone and vibrato added as an ornament is the fixed repeatability of the system and a coverage against rupture and the unplanned. Emerging out of a musical system less invested in stability and less averse to change, the vibrato captured in the recordings of "Beale Street Blues" and "St. Louis Blues" functions quite differently. Bessie Smith's voice oscillates in a way that shakes the distinction between vibrato as ornament and the fixed pitch that it is supposed to ornament. Smith's vocal inflections and Armstrong's high, wordless soarings sing to the fixed notes of the harmonic system the song of their own vibrational constitution and make them dance their own dissolution, unfixing, and extension. Smith and Armstrong's improvisation upon the melodies and harmonies of song structure are intertwined with their improvisation upon the phonic materiality and constitution of notes. Giving a trembling motion to the tools of musical shaping, this strategy of improvising upon the vibrational structure of sound itself necessarily disturbs the predictability of the way that the music unfolds itself. It improvises not only *within* the established harmonic system but *upon* this system, constantly interrogating it and forcing it to justify itself.

Embodied in the sonority of Bessie Smith's voice is an insistently revisionary impulse that shakes the unthinking instrumentality of harmonic and melodic prescriptions and pushes them toward their own self-questioning. Smith's performance folds back upon the music its own questioning nature. According to James Baldwin, jazz is essentially the constant reasking of the questions "Who am I? and why am I here?," and the vibratory power of Smith's voice leaves no musical element immune to these questions ("Of the Sorrow" 89). In her hands the structures of harmony and melody become not only fixed tools for asking these questions but elements that have to justify their own form and existence. When Bessie Smith breaks the line "My man's got a heart like a rock cast in the sea" by pausing unexpectedly after the word "a," she demonstrates the boldness and efficacy of this conception (2:46).[26] Her break allows the questioning power of the music to avoid running strictly in prescriptive and well-worn grooves. Letting the dictates of performance and of her performative tradition clash with the dictates of the composition's melodic and lyrical lines, Smith opens herself and her performance up to the possibilities of rupture and surprise.[27] The shock of surprise delivered by Smith's dramatic phrasing is not part of any conventional system for delivering surprise to the audience, but is part of a performance style predicated on the possibility of an unprepared or unplanned surprise. The surprise lurking as a possibility in Bessie Smith's performance is a surprise not foreseen by either audience or performer, a surprise that interrupts the relentless forward motion of time and rhythm the way cataracts in a river create distortions and explosive interruptions of the water's inexorable downstream flow.[28]

This form of surprise constructs the future out of a recognition that the motion of change vibrates in a way that leaves no element untouched. Against a possessive vision of the future in which an inviolate subject remains unchanged except for its possession of the specific thing that completes it, jazz performs an attunement to the future in which the subject is changed by every encounter with another object or subject.[29] This is a vibration that oscillates across the boundary between subject and object with an unpredictability antithetical to mastery or to self-possessed individualism. The ability to generate dramatically surprising effects and combinations is the sign of jazz and blues' preoccupation with an open form of futurity. The most obvious source of this affinity for surprise and for the open future is improvisation; in jazz, sound is set in motion without foresight concerning the final endpoint of any sound's vibratory motion. This is not to say that Bessie Smith and Louis Armstrong have no control of their sound (and both are absolute masters of sound) or no plan; it is instead to suggest that the improvisational context of their performance precludes a foresight that could be certain of how one's sound will blend or clash with another's. When Bessie Smith sings "St. Louis Blues" or Alberta Hunter sings "Beale Street Blues" their accompanists are improvising at the same time, and no matter how attuned to each other they are or how many times they have performed together the outcome of their performance will not be free of the unexpected.[30] Projecting their sound into a musical landscape susceptible to sudden shifts and unexpected turns, the music makes the unknown and the possibly disastrous into an ever-present component of what is played.[31]

The surprise flowing from the confrontation of two open and partially unprogrammed vibrational patterns also takes some of its impetus from a confrontation between the present and the past. The path carved through the song structure of "St. Louis Blues" by the sound of Bessie Smith and Louis Armstrong is a highly original one, but this is not the originality of fresh tracks on a virgin field of snow. The improvised path of Armstrong and Smith is an exuberant conversation with previous performances of "St. Louis Blues" and of all other blues.[32] Bessie Smith and Louis Armstrong come from different branches of the jazz tradition; Smith from the vaudeville blues tradition of her mentor Mamie Smith, and Armstrong from the brass-oriented New Orleans jazz tradition. This heritage manifests itself in their sound, an example of the vibrations of the past alive in the performance of the present. Part of what one can hear in Bessie Smith's voice is Ma Rainey's voice and Bessie's negotiation between her own voice and the pull of Ma Rainey. Similarly, the notes coming out of the bell of Armstrong's horn resonate with the sound of King Oliver and echo Armstrong's admiration of Oliver and his break with him. The notes and ornaments they play are already choruses built out of the presence of the past within the present. The richness of tone in evidence in "St. Louis Blues"–the complex sound recipe of partials, harmonics, and overtones—is the cohabitation of tone by present performers and past precedents. Cutting across the divide between the past and the present, the performance of sound produced by Armstrong and Smith bears the mark of a pregnant confrontation with the past, a confrontation in which the past does *not* "weigh like a nightmare on the brain of the living" (Marx, "Eighteenth Brumaire" 595). What burdens the performance of Armstrong and Smith is also what gives it its propulsive motion. The past at work in the polyphonic interplay of this particular trio performance of "St. Louis Blues" is a past recognized as vibrational tendency rather than solid entity. This undead past is an unpredictably volatile resource as full of stopping and starting as any actually sounding longitudinal wave. It thus sets up a pattern of interference, an Ellingtonian dissonance that prevents any note from being placidly content with its position in a rhythmic flow. In the sound world in which Bessie Smith and Louis Armstrong maneuver, performance unearths surprising and unheard resources, not just because these performances are improvised but also because the volatility of the encounter between the role of a tone in the past and the vibrational spin that a performer puts on a tone in the present leads to unexpected results. Playing with the forces submerged in the tonal system, Armstrong and Smith stage encounters between past and present vibrations that are incalculable and thus drive the music into futures unseen by the calculations enshrined in the prescriptive rationality of the tonal system. Armstrong and Smith's performance strikes with such force because it is essentially a series of explosive encounters between their productive forces and the productive forces of the past, a series of explosions that rend the veil obscuring the multiplicity of possible and alluring futures. Out of this dissonant consonance with the past flows the yearning timbral momentum of Smith's blues and the inexorable forward momentum of Armstrong's jazz.[33]

What Smith and Armstrong perform is an engagement with the past that opens the present up to an imminent and open future, a future that performance evokes (and provokes) by staging itself as a revisionary qualification of that which has gone before and which needs further revisionary elaboration to realize itself in its movement toward an inherently unrealizable and endlessly deferred goal. Animating the performance in question are confrontations with the past, with other improvisers in the present, and with the not-yet of futurity trembling within the present and the past. In the performance of vibrational masters like Smith and Armstrong, every element of music trembles with an awareness of its own lack of solidity. Harmonic and melodic conventions as well as rhythmic ones vibrate with the not entirely foreclosed possibilities of the past as well as their possible revision in the future. For the established chords and scales out of which W. C. Handy's compositions are formed receive their shape from rhythms invested in maintaining the given order, rhythms that James Snead characterizes as "perpetual repetition[s] of apparent consensus and convention that provide a sense of security" (60). The consistent engagement with the rhythmic and vibrational basis of sound that makes itself heard in Bessie Smith's voice exerts a magnetic influence on these rhythms. Recognizing in Smith's sound their own suppressed rhythmic discord and dependence on repetition, the stable bases of musical performance acquire a new malleability, a loosening of the fetters that subordinate the past to a desire for a stable platform on which to perform in the present and out of which to build a predictable future. The past sounds in the conventions of musical performance (as it does in the conventions of all aesthetic performance). The vibrational virtuosity of Bessie Smith emphasizes this presentness of the past and works its living but suppressed possibilities for innovation and improvisation into a sound cognizant of the fact that the past, as well as the present and the future, has its surprises.

It is the writing of James Baldwin that gives us the most penetrating reading of Smith's music and its focus on the entanglement of different temporal and social registers. In numerous interviews James Baldwin goes out of his way to point out how indispensable to his work the music of Bessie Smith was.[34] Although Baldwin was partial to her recordings with James P. Johnson, his comments on the puissance of Bessie Smith's performance practices are relevant here. For Baldwin, Smith's music is, first and foremost, a performance of imbrication. It was her performance of the imbrication of the present and the past that enabled him to draw upon his own past in creating *Go Tell It on the Mountain* and other works.[35] But Baldwin also points out the way that Smith's music performs the necessity of social imbrication, the imbrication and entanglement of even those elements thought of as antithetical opposites. This imbrication reveals the poverty and impossibility of encountering or understanding "from a safe distance" (Baldwin, "Sorrow" 86). In the music of Bessie Smith we hear sounding the persistent theme of all of Baldwin's work: the radical interdependence of subject and object and of all dichotomies that stem from the separation of subject and object, black and white, straight and gay, exploiter and exploited. Baldwin writes that "each of us, helplessly and forever, contains the other" (Baldwin, "Dragons" 690). The precision of this formulation indicates that what is at stake here is not the interdependence of discrete identities but the ineluctable imbrication of rhythms that move through and across subject positions, tying them together in ways that defy description by any language unaffected by these rhythms. The time that does not hide itself from these rhythms is perhaps best captured in Achille Mbembe's description of what he calls the "time of entanglement." The time of entanglement is, in Mbembe's words, "an *interlocking* of presents, pasts, and futures that retain their depths of other presents, pasts, and futures, each age bearing, altering, and maintaining the previous ones" (16).

"St. Louis Blues" performs an engagement with this kind of time, making music out of the necessity of recognizing both it and the time conception governing American society. Its interlocking rhythms and vibrational patterns both mime a rationalized time and depart from it by miming this time's suppression of, and imbrication with, other forms of time. The result is an improvisation of possible forms of individual and collective articulation, an exploration of the convergences and divergences licensed by the possibilities and impossibilities of social structures of rhythm and sound.

In the third chorus of "St. Louis Blues" (2:26), Armstrong, Smith, and Longshaw bring themselves into a tighter coordination with each other. Like dancers pulling one another closer together, the three play Handy's melody in a puissant but heterogeneous unison. Up to this point in the performance the three voices have pulled against each other by stretching the limits of rhythmic divergence. Here the three come together, and the sharp contrast with what has gone before clarifies the principle of coordination that has motivated their performance all along. They move "in synchrony while out of phase" (Feld 82–83), in a form of coordination owing something to the principles of physical vibration out of which they form their sounds. Individual atoms have what is called a "natural resonance frequency," that is, they vibrate or oscillate with a rhythm that defines them. At the same time, these atoms enter into combinations with one another predicated upon an affinity for one another, an affinity defined as a "force that causes the atoms of certain elements to combine and stay combined" ("Affinity"). The point here is that each atom has its own vibrational rhythm as well as having rhythms that lock it into powerful bonds with other atoms. This is the physical correlate of the social principle that Baldwin names when he writes that "each of us, helplessly and forever, contains the other," and also of the rhythmic principle that allows Smith, Longshaw, and Armstrong to play against each other and still maintain a rough unity. Up to the collective articulation of the melody tied to the line "I've got the St. Louis Blues, just as blue as I can be" (2:26), the three performers have moved in the space opened up by the divergence of their sonic rhythms, but at this point they move into the space of their shared vibrational affinity and they sound the ratio of their divergent but compatible musical trajectories.

Although the three performers come closer together in this chorus of "St. Louis Blues," they do not entirely merge with one another. All three play the melody together, but one can hear the tail end of Armstrong's notes lagging behind the end of Smith's notes and running ahead of Longshaw's chords. The three share the melody without sharing all of the different rhythms that make up their own sonic identities. In doing so they demonstrate what we might call a polyrhythmic intelligence, an intelligence predicated upon the fact that rhythmic coordination does not depend upon identity, that the strangely composite nature of the self—its containment of many drums and many rhythms—allows for a rhythmic coordination not based upon lockstep obedience to a master rhythm that defines all other rhythms.[36] The three musicians use this rhythmic coordination to organize their performance, but the impetus of this music strives to implicate the listener in its vibrational patterns as well. In *Rhythmanalysis* Henri Lefebvre tells us that "to grasp a rhythm it is necessary to have been grasped by it" (83). To relate to another, whether subject or object, is to let a part of yourself vibrate sympathetically with the other, to move part of yourself in the same time and to the same rhythm as the other. Performing together is one such relation, but listening is another. Properly grasped, the rhythmic genius manifest in Bessie Smith's performance resonates within the listener long after the recording stops playing. It lingers more in the body's polyrhythmic procedures than it does in a memory that can be reactivated at will. Once grasped, the rhythmic motions of "St. Louis Blues" enter into the rhythms of the listener's own existence, rearranging and syncopating them in a way that never totally submerges the grasped and grasping rhythm performed by Smith, Armstrong, and Longshaw. To give oneself to the pull of the rhythms performed in pieces like "St. Louis Blues" is to feel the lines of force that come from the past, the present, and the possible. Like the end of Fitzgerald's novel, this particular performance of "St. Louis Blues" ends with a version of "and so we beat on." The final, only partially conclusive, vibrations of voice, cornet, and organ invite us to hear a pattern that continues, but one whose tide carries a polymorphous, nonexclusionary "we" on transverse and longitudinal waves that nibble at the future and the present as well as the past. "So we beat on," the music tells us, pushed ceaselessly by our entanglement in the social webs of time and sound into a repetitive engagement with the vibratory hinge between the past and the future.

6
Rhythmicizing the Novel

Temporal Taxonomies from Larsen to Hemingway, Stein to Hughes

Our very lives are dependent on rhythm, for everything we do is governed by ordered rhythmic sequences.
— Duke Ellington, "The Duke Steps Out"

It's a long way from the underground Harlem club where James Weldon Johnson's narrator encounters ragtime to the Louisville party where Daisy Buchanan dances to "Beale Street Blues." The social and geographical distance between the two scenes speaks of the pervasiveness of jazz in American culture and of the virtual impossibility of entirely avoiding its resonance. In an attempt to capture some of the wide-ranging impact of jazz on the literary field, this chapter looks at works by four different American authors: Ernest Hemingway, Langston Hughes, Gertrude Stein, and Nella Larsen. The impact of jazz registers in the work of all these authors, but it registers in a wide variety of ways. We have seen in the works discussed so far, both musical and literary, an incredible diversity of rhythmic imperatives and a broad range of different relationships to the jazz tradition. This range is even more diverse in the works considered in this chapter.

Although no taxonomy can do justice to the differences and similarities between the works of authors as different as Stein and Hughes, some distinctions between possible ways of treating temporality can serve as an aid to thinking about the impact of these four texts. I am thinking here of the distinction that Henri Lefebvre makes between isorhythmia and eurhythmia. In *Rhythmanalysis* Lefebvre defines "isorhythmia" as "the equality of rhythms," an equality between temporalities that effaces differences by positing an identity based upon equivalence. To this, Levebvre opposes "eurhythmia," a coordination derived from "a living body, normal and *healthy*," a coordination that "presupposes the association of different rhythms" (67).[1] According to Lefebvre, authority often maintains itself by falsely identifying isorhythmia with eurhythmia and by using this collapsed identification in order to suppress the multiplicity of rhythms at work in bodies, social structures, and aesthetic forms. Isorhythmia assumes that outside of absolute equivalence there is only unproductive disorder (which Lefebvre call arrhythmia), while eurhythmia sees all healthily functioning systems—literary, social, or biological—as dependent on the coordination of rhythms not reducible to each other.

While neither novels nor musical performances ever militate unequivocally for any monolithic position, every work does tend toward either a valorization of isorhythmia or a valorization of eurhythmia. The distinction between these two ways of treating rhythmic coordination guide my readings here, but the distinction only serves as scaffolding on which to hang a consideration of the multiple ways each work interacts with social constructions of race and time and of the way each work registers the resonance of jazz.

Hemingway

In *The Sun Also Rises*, Hemingway's novel celebrating traditional bullfighting culture and lamenting its decline, there is a brief but telling encounter with jazz. After dining with Count Mippipopolous, a connoisseur and economic imperialist who shares Jake Barnes's value system, Jake and Lady Brett dance at a club in Montmartre called Zelli's.[2] Only one component of the band that they dance to is found worthy of description by Hemingway: the drummer, a caricatured figure—"all teeth and lips"—who speaks in something approximating dialect and who sings as well as drums (62). Four times the "nigger" drummer sings, and three of these times his lyrical effusions are represented in a very curious way: by ellipsis, the presence of six dots within quotation marks: "' . . . . . . ' the drummer chanted" (64). The barest repetition of all, the repetition of six typographical marks stands in for the drummer's singing, an enigmatic elision that marks both a presence and an absence. For Hemingway's narrative to function properly it both needs the drummer's music and needs to mute its resonance.[3]

This is tantamount to saying that, for Hemingway's novel, the music at Zelli's has a value that is both questionable and unstable but indispensable for the functioning of the text. The value of the music is an important question, for the course of the novel and the conflicts that occur in it both revolve around a well-defined conception of value, a conception that the novel endorses. This is seen most clearly when Jake asserts that "enjoying living was learning to get your money's worth and knowing when you had it" (148). Jake is the central bearer and champion of this position, but its structure is first articulated by Count Mippopopolous: "it is because I have lived very much that now I can enjoy everything so well. . . . That is the secret. You must get to know the values" (60). In this view there are two modes of living, one in the count's past and one in his present. In the first mode one experiences life in order to test it, to find the worthiness or unworthiness of various experiences. This mode is the mode of youth and is a form of apprenticeship in which one "get[s] to know the values." Growth and change have their place in this mode but only as parts of a provisional scaffolding useful for reaching a more permanent and unchanging mode of life. Serving as a prolegomena to a time when the enjoyment value of experience is reliable because predictable, the mode of living as testing ground for experience has value only insofar as it leads to its own end. It is a stage to be passed through. The count has passed through this stage, as has Jake (although Jake is still a bit of an amateur and sometimes wavers in commitment to his "values"). Both have learned "the secret" and have moved into a second stage of living characterized by firmly established systems of value. The count places high value on champagne, cigars that draw well, and food (61); Jake values fishing, writing, and bullfighting. These are valuable because they reliably produce enjoyment and are devoid of the capacity to disappoint so prevalent in the mutable flux surrounding Jake and the count. Their system of values is a bulwark against time and against regression or decay. In this advanced stage the limited role that the movement of time (in the form of growth and change) had played in their earlier mode of learning "the" values has vanished. Jake and the count have both graduated from time and from change and have entered into a world in which values are fixed and from which uncertainty has been purged. The conception of life at work in their reliance on fixed values is one in which the only possible form of growth is the recognition of the unchanging verities of life. One learns to recognize what has value and what does not, and one learns that these values, like the subjects that enjoy them and the world that produces them, are essentially without change or motion. This is the conception that underlies the passage from Ecclesiastes that gives the novel its epigraph: "One generation passeth away, and another generation cometh; *but* the earth abideth forever" (1). For Hemingway and for the characters that ventriloquize his conception of value, the sharp point of this passage is contained in the coordinating conjunction "but"; things may appear to change, but underneath this appearance lies an abiding formal truth. There is a stubborn and immutable pattern of stability that underlies change. Knowledge of this "secret" (in the count's words) is what allows one to "get to know the values" and to disregard whatever keeps one from focusing an undistorted and hardheaded gaze on them.

The Count is upholding the purity and immutability of these values when he prohibits Brett from toasting with the champagne he has had brought up to Jake's room. He tells Brett that "this wine is too good for toast-drinking, my dear. You don't want to mix emotions up with a wine like that" (59). This is not an isolated incident. Throughout the novel Brett stands outside of the masculine system of values espoused by Jake, the count, and Hemingway himself. In her series of affairs with men, she is constantly mixing up emotions with values. She refuses to uphold the prohibition on the affective endorsed by Jake and thus, in the eyes of the novel, has not graduated from time. She has not passed through the apprenticeship to value and thus is an unpredictable and unreliable participant in the patterns of enjoyment engaged in by Jake. Arriving and departing at unexpected times and with unexpected partners, Brett is constantly upsetting Jake's plans. She disturbs his sleep by showing up in the middle of the night, she upsets plans by arriving late in Spain, and, most importantly, her amorous engagements upset the pleasure that Jake derives from the bullfights. Her dalliance with Roy Cohn has created a difficult situation, but her romance with the young bullfighter and her involvement of Jake in this romance make it virtually impossible for Jake to continue making his annual return to Pamplona. His participation in Brett's seduction of Pedro (the young bullfighter) has destroyed Jake's carefully constructed relationship with the local bullfighting aficionado (Montoya).

Throughout the novel, Brett is figured as a recurrent pattern of disturbing repetition. She doesn't fit into the time-construct or value system of Jake and the count. As Kristeva shows in "Women's Time," the maneuver by which Brett is excluded from the values and the temporality of the properly oriented masculine world is a well-rehearsed one. In Kristeva's words, "female subjectivity as it gives itself up to intuition becomes a problem with respect to a certain conception of time: time as project, teleology, linear and prospective unfolding: time as departure, progression and arrival—in other words, the time of history" (192). Kristeva gives a brief sketch of the alignment of women with the repetitive and the eternal and the consequent alignment of masculinity with the linear time of active self and world shaping. These alignments are operative in Hemingway's text, but what gives Brett such an ambivalent charge is Hemingway's attempt in *The Sun Also Rises* to eschew both progress and the threat of a strictly vegetative repetition in which one is a slave to the past. Jake and Hemingway renounce the repetitive temporality that Brett is made to stand for, but they do so in a text that is also a polemic against the Victorian investment in progress.

In "Protestant, Catholic, Jew: The Sun Also Rises" Ron Berman shows how Hemingway employs allusions to religion to argue against what he sees as an idly utopian progressivism identified by him (and others)[4] with Protestantism. Hemingway opposes to this deluded Protestantism an idealized Catholicism seen as a repository of medieval Christendom and fully in tune with the central conceit of *The Sun Also Rises*: character does not change. Taking this into account makes clear the difficulty of Jake's position and the tension-fraught nature of his relationship to Brett. Jake must stake out a middle position between a false belief in progress (embodied in the Jewish Roy Cohn—a man "raised by women" [45]) and an undisciplined repetitiveness that threatens not stasis but regression. Divorcing himself from the consolation provided by belief in progress, Jake struggles to stave off the menace of a meaningless regression threatening to submerge everything in blunt animalistic repetition. He does so through investment in practices that hold out the promise of value without the false illusion of progress. In Jake's quest to forge a reliable pattern of independent writerly manhood, the repetitive shape of Brett's life serves as a background against which this pattern is defined.

As a figure of dislocating repetition, Brett is aligned with the drummer at Zelli's. The exchange of greetings between the two indicates a shared past experience suggestive both of Brett's licentiousness and her confusion of affect and value. In the presence of both of these figures from outside the prescribed temporality of his value system, Jake is confronted with that which most threatens this system. Moving his body in tandem with Brett and the repetitive patterns of the drummer, Jake experiences "déjà vu": "I had that feeling of going through something that has all happened before" (64). Confronted with the fickle inconstancy of Brett (whose mood changes from elation to wretchedness in the space of what seems to Jake to be "a minute") and the insistent repetition of a music that has a visceral impact on its listeners ("the music hit you as you went in" [62]), Jake is struck by a vertiginous feeling of falling into the past, of losing his firm grip on the values that structure his life. In the presence of the drummer's syncopations, value and affect are put together in a way that reopens the past and destabilizes the present.

Announcing itself in the music that gives Zelli's its atmosphere is a form of value oriented around a temporality antithetical to the time of Jake's value system. The tensile ratio of profit and loss in jazz drumming and singing obeys a different imperative than Jake's "getting what one pays for." This is not to say that jazz is without its own system of paying one's dues, but jazz performance knows a form of change distinct from the naïve optimism that Hemingway critiques. This form of change is an approach to the future that works on its technique as diligently as Hemingway worked on his beloved sentences. The difference is that the work of a jazz musician is in the service of preparing one for the magic of an unprepared and unanticipated moment when the deployment of rehearsed patterns results in a genuinely new (and almost necessarily unrepeatable) combination that escapes the gravitational pull of the past and the present. The jazz musician is thus in a permanent apprenticeship to the future. Jake's system of values is predicated upon a temporary apprenticeship that one eventually passes beyond; the drummer at Zelli's is consistently in the mode of "getting to know the values"; his repetitions constantly restage the dialectic of the joy of the new and the joy of the known. Jake's value system prevents him from hearing the drummer, because in this system values are reliably stable and unchanging. In the drummer's jazz resonates Snead's assertion that "beat is an entity of relation" (68); the forms of value and enjoyment set in motion by jazz rhythm are forcefully relational and celebrate the fact that the source of all value and all enjoyment are negotiations between individuals and between individuals and groups. The odd textual representation of the drummer's singing is the mark of Hemingway and Jake's deafness to the relational nature of value; the elliptical blotting out of the drummer's utterance is a protective maneuver intended to inure the text to the rhythm of an African American performative value system. Banishing the past and the affective, Jake deadens himself to the unpredictable life of values that depends on the interaction of individuals.[5]

Despite this deafness to some of the crucial aspects of jazz rhythm's social resonance, there is a real interaction between Hemingway's writing and jazz performance. For Jake, the repetitive drumming and singing are either threatening or inconsequential. But for Hemingway, jazz does have some attraction, and there is an affiliation between the rhythms of Hemingway's sentences and the rhythms of jazz performance. A sign of this affiliation is the way jazz is represented in the text. When the drummer sings ". . . . . .," the quotation marks open up a space in the text through which two things pass: Hemingway's writing and the rhythms of the jazz at Zelli's. At this moment, Hemingway's writing and jazz performance have a dynamic affinity, whether intentional or not; the two rhythms of performance move with each other. This is important because, for Hemingway, writing is the practice most valued for its ability to reliably deliver pleasure free from the illusions of progress and the weight of the past. The true hero of any Hemingway novel is always the solitary individual at his typewriter, and at this moment in the novel, this individual's practice falls into the orbit of jazz. In Hemingway's valorization of the perfectly balanced sentence straining to cut itself free from semantic depth there is an aspiration toward the clean unadorned stroke of the typewriter. Hemingway wants us to be struck by the accents and rhythms of his sentences and undistracted by the semantic richness or affective resonance of the words themselves, as if the bare typographic strokes occurring in his representation of the jazz drummer's singing were the secret (if impossible) goal of his writing.

What this suggests is an attunement of Hemingway's sentences to the formal aspects of jazz rhythm and a similar temporal stance built out of a penchant for displaced accents and unexpected juxtapositions, the result of which is an ability to spin out complex structures without formal processes of subordination. There is thus a formal interaction between Hemingway's prose and the movement of jazz rhythm.⁶ What *The Sun Also Rises* attempts to do is to make sure that this formal interaction is as limited as possible, and that it doesn't lead to an interaction with the social and historical implications of jazz form. We see the attempt to limit these social implications in the novel's treatment of Brett and the black drummer; the novel's narrow engagement with the historical implications of jazz form is suggested by the novel's treatment of its setting.

Besides condensing much of Jake's relationship to Brett and to time, the dancing scene is also a representation of a real set of historical circumstances that are not without their own place in intellectual histories besides those of Hemingway and Anglo-American modernism. Zelli's was a real club; a seedy dance hall operated by Joe Zelli, an Italian American who owned and managed several other Paris night spots. Opened in 1919, Zelli's was one of the first clubs in Paris to employ African American musicians, and although its importance and popularity was soon surpassed by that of Le Grand Duc, several of the major figures of the Montmartre and Paris jazz scene performed there.⁷ Chief among these were the trumpeter Cricket Smith and the drummer Louis Mitchell. After performing at Zelli's in the early and mid-1920s, Mitchell went on to form a number of different bands and to serve as the nucleus of the African American jazz scene in Paris in the 1920s and 1930s. This is important because it speaks of what is suppressed by Hemingway's ellipses and of the way that the singing drummer might resonate in other contexts. Louis Mitchell's role in the Paris jazz scene marks the excised presence of not only an ongoing and vital aesthetic tradition but also a major inspiration and resource of the Négritude movement. Aimé Césaire, Léopold Senghor, and René Ménil were devotees not only of the literary productions of the Harlem Renaissance but also of the music that fueled the exploratory aesthetic and political forms of the New Negro. During their time in Paris, Ménil exposed Césaire and Senghor to jazz, and their enthusiasm for the music influenced much of their aesthetic and theoretical output. Senghor in particular was struck by jazz, and in his employment of terms like "syncopated imagination" and "prospective reflection" the debt to the rhythmic virtuosity of drummers like Louis Mitchell is obvious.⁸

The proximity of the setting of Hemingway's novel and of his site of literary production to the stage on which an alternative model of time, history, and subjectivity worked itself out suggests not only the narrowness of Hemingway's imaginative vision but also the fact that his novel bears within itself the traces of aesthetic and intellectual trajectories that it can neither fully acknowledge nor fully contain.

The rather undistinguished interior of Zelli's also shows up in Langston Hughes's *The Big Sea*. Zelli's employed a group of women whose only duty was to raise the bar tabs of the clientele by inspiring an increased consumption of champagne. Paid to egg customers on with their own drinking, with faked consumption, and with toasting and other types of feigned conviviality, these women lived a precarious economic existence. In 1924 (two years before the publication of *The Sun Also Rises*) Hughes lived briefly with one of these women, Sonya, a Russian dancer. Not knowing a single person in Paris, Hughes seems to have survived only through his partnership with Sonya, who used the last of Hughes's money to secure the two of them a single room and a few frugal meals. This is Hughes's introduction to what he calls "the quick friendship of the dispossessed" (*Big Sea* 150).

In the description of the relationship between himself and the Russian dancer, Hughes sketches an economic relationship that moves to a conception of profit and loss different than that enshrined in Hemingway's novel. Hughes first pays for the place in which they both live; later when she starts to work at Zelli's, she is able to buy food for the both of them. He has wagered on her and the wager pays off; their relationship is a response to the intermittent nature of employment. Their coalition is a contrapuntal working relationship not uncommon among those from outside the realm of respectability and regular employment. It is also not without an affective component; tears mark Sonya's departure from Paris (*Big Sea* 156). This is not highly remarkable except in its contrast to the pathos-laden inability of Jake and Brett to fashion a working relationship in *The Sun Also Rises*. The temporal stance of *The Sun Also Rises* does not countenance the give and take rhythms of Hughes and Sonya; the novel's attempt to secure a temporal space free from both the illusion of progress and the threat of repetition is predicated on a dismissal of the formal possibilities latent in the everyday strategies of those excluded from the realm of titles and exorbitantly expensive champagne and even from the realm of regular employment.

This dismissal includes not only Langston Hughes and the Russian dancer but also the homosexuals in whose company Brett first appears, the prostitute hired by Jake, and ultimately the drummer whose rhythmic utterances are blotted out by the repeated typewriter strokes of Hemingway's conception of writing.[9] For what beats insistently in the rhythm of jazz performance are the psychic and pragmatic maneuvers of black existence in a white America hostile and indifferent to the living vectors of this existence.

The arrangement that Hughes and the Russian dancer make is a way of coping with the irregular employment that quite frequently makes up the life of artists (she is a dancer; he is a writer) before they establish themselves. Rare is the artist in any medium who is steadily employed at the beginning of their career. Thus, what we see in the relationship between Hughes and the Russian dancer is a kind of anacrusis, the preparatory moves prior to the establishment of a regular pattern. The *American Heritage Dictionary* defines anacrusis as "one or more unstressed syllables at the beginning of a line of verse, before the reckoning of the normal meter begins."[10]

The distinction I started this chapter with between novels valorizing eurhythmia and ones incapable of seeing anything outside of isorhythmia besides chaos might well be read as the difference between artists who incorporate this anacrusis into their established artistic career and their conception of form and those who close themselves off from this stage of their life as securely as Jake and the count separate themselves from their time as apprentices to value. This would be the difference between novels (and other forms) that attempt to banish dislocation and rupture and those that attempt to incorporate it into their form. Novels that keep alive the anacrusis out of which they emerge have a sense of their form as provisional, as a syncopated preparation for a future form or rhythm that does not yet exist. This attitude is akin to the form of futurity performed by jazz, and what I am suggesting is an understanding of jazz syncopation as a form of permanent anacrusis. Novels that let jazz temporality exert an influence on them tend to shape themselves as permanent apprentices to the future, adopting something of the rhythm of the relationship between Hughes and Sonya.

Hughes

Hughes is an author intensely devoted to the resources for aesthetic form contained within the maneuvers of demotic life; his works draw much of their power from their ability to translate strategies of everyday African American life into unique and compelling interventions in poetic and novelistic form. His literary production grows out of the space that Hemingway circumscribes within parentheses. In Hughes's novel *Not Without Laughter*, published in 1930, we also encounter an African American drummer. He does not speak or sing, but his drums do, pouring forth a varied stream of comments, exhortations, and commands while almost always keeping up "their hard steady laughter" (100). The difference in treatment of these two drummers is quite telling; the ellipsis of jazz in Hemingway's text speaks of a cloistered temporality intent on securing a present and future free from the erroneous temporal patterns of others, while the extended and extensive treatment of jazz in Hughes's text is the mark of a striving toward an emphatically capacious rhythmic sense, one that builds a temporal movement out of imbrication and interaction.

The chapter in which Hughes's drummer appears ("Dance") is the longest and most important chapter of the novel. Its importance derives both from its role in separating Sandy's aunt Harriet from her attachment to the strict religion of Aunt Hager and, more importantly, from its role as a demonstration of the rhythm of subjectivity that Sandy adopts at the end of the novel. *Not Without Laughter* is essentially a bildungsroman, a tale of the protagonist Sandy coming of age. It tells the tale of the diverse familial influences on Sandy and his eventual synthesis of these influences into a coherent rhythm. With Sandy's father mostly absent and his mother exerting little influence, Sandy's self-definition depends on the strong personalities of his grandmother Hager and his aunt Harriet. Their influence pulls Sandy in different directions; the event that precipitates the break between Harriet and Hager is Harriet's decision to ignore Hager's explicit command and to attend the dance at Chavers Hall.

Aunt Hager's objection to the dance and to Harriet and Sandy's presence at it stems from her association of it with sexual license, "sin," and a class of people who had "ceased to struggle against the boundaries between good and bad" (217). Hager is an upstanding member of a religious community opposed to secular celebrations of the flesh; she embodies a viewpoint that sees this world as preparation for the next. Harriet's worldview is primarily secular. She is intensely attracted to the blues and embodies an orientation toward present-tense pleasure over otherworldly rewards. Sandy's development depends on the possibility of reconciling these two orientations.

Hager sees the dance as an event of questionable morality, but there is another viewpoint in the text that looks with disapproval at both the participants in the dance and at figures like Hager. This is the position of Hager's oldest daughter, Tempy, and her husband, Mr. Siles. Mr. Siles, who Sandy thinks of as "ashamed of colored people," dismisses African Americans in the following terms: "Clowns, jazzers, just a band of dancers—that's why they never have anything. Never be anything but servants to the white people" (289). Tempy and her husband are representatives of a class that looks upon both Harriet's wildness and Hager's antiquated ways as embarrassing reminders of slavery. Siles's dismissal lingers powerfully in Sandy's imagination, and when he recalls it at the end of the novel, it leads first of all to an image of his grandmother "whirling around in front of the altar at revival meetings in the midst of the other sisters, her face shining with light, arms outstretched as though all the cares of the world had been cast away" (289). Sandy then moves from this image to memories of Harriet dancing and his father, Jimboy, singing: the effect is to turn the image of African Americans as essentially dancers into a matrix of cross-generational identification that allows Sandy to synthesize the different legacies of his family members without renouncing any important part of his past. The key to this turn is a positive valorization of Siles's terms of denunciation; in Sandy's imagination, being a "band of dancers" becomes the best possible thing to be in a racially circumscribed world: "A band of dancers. . . . Black dancers-captured in a white world. . . . Dancers of the spirit, too. Each black dreamer a captured dancer of the spirit. . . . Aunt Hager's dreams for Sandy dancing far beyond the limitations of their poverty, of their humble station in life, of their dark skins" (290).

This scene is essentially a fulfillment of the earlier chapter "Dance," putting the resources of the earlier scene at work in coordinating the different aspects of Sandy's existence. In the narrative movement and portraits of social interaction contained in "Dance," there is a sketch of polymetric subjectivity—subjectivity as a center of multiple, constantly shifting affective contacts—that makes possible the latter coordination of dissonant family trajectories.

In the movements on the dance floor, in the musical interactions between the members of Benbow's ensemble, and in the exchanges between the two, Hughes sketches a complex mode of social coordination. His writing strives to catalog the movements of these interactions and to translate them into Sandy's tale of development. The result is a jazz-inflected bildungsroman that militates for an alternative model of subjectivity and social form. Both models depend on three elements that Hughes draws from the movements of Chavers Hall: a heterogeneous social principle capable of coordinating discrepant and divergent movements, a performance practice that tropes on the past as a living vector within the present, and a polyrhythmic self divided between different constitutive rhythms.

At the heart of everything that takes place in "Dance" is the music of "Benbow's Famous Kansas City Band." The interactions of the four musicians in the band form a whole, but it is a curiously polyvalent whole, made up as it is of timbrally and stylistically distinct parts. The band is billed as a "Kansas City" ensemble, yet none of its members are from Kansas City: "Rattle Benbow from Galveston; . . . the drummer, from Houston; his banjoist from Birmingham; his cornetist from Atlanta; and the pianist, . . . from New Orleans" (105). The Kansas City sound that the band generates is a synthesis of regional styles from throughout the South, pointing to the fact that much of the prepossessing force of Benbow's band derives from its ability to create a unified motion out of diverging rhythmic conceptions. Embodying Olly Wilson's "heterogeneous sound principle," Benbow's band performs in a way that provides a musical center for the dance without effacing the forces that go into constituting this center.

This heterogeneity depends on the way the musicians' performative shapings of sound are directed simultaneously at each other and at the dancers. The improvisatory, spontaneous unfolding of the music requires that each musician take his cues from the other members of the ensemble. In the absence of a written score, the musicians follow the dictates of the sounds and sights that strike them. They play for each other in order to play for the dancers. Their responsibility as performers divides them, attuning them to the sound coming from their bandmates and to the motions coming from the dance floor. The form of attention and responsiveness this division necessitates distends and extends the present by making each performer a nexus receiving commanding incitements from sound waves and light waves out of an immediate past.

Out of the past because all waves take time to travel, and by the time these waves strike an individual the individual who produced them has moved on. The power of the rituals taking place at Chavers Hall is that they transform this division of present from past, of individual from individual, and of performer from him- or herself into a resource out of which to build acts of social affiliation. The rhythm of Benbow's band and of the dancers who move to it creates a trajectory whose broadly capacious forward movement draws into itself these divisions, the time lags they create, and the discrepant temporalities that produce them.[11] The condition of possibility of such a trajectory is a specific configuration of the shared past, a configuration engendered by the band's "swing."

In *The Power of Black Music* Samuel A. Floyd Jr. conceives of swing as a troping on past performances as well as on current rhythms and time conceptions. His conception draws attention to the way the past is operative in jazz music and dance and to the fact that the relationship between the present and the past in arenas like the one Hughes describes is always double. The past is present as repetition and as a resource for Signifyin(g). Floyd writes that in events like the one at Chavers Hall, "cultural and 'motor' memories of the mass, circle, and line dances of African societies and of slave culture were operative" (83). In jazz music and dance the past makes itself present in the way that performers will repeat phrases and steps that they have performed before and that they have seen and heard others perform before them. At the same time, they will use these phrases and steps as ways of referring to and signifying on the past, revising, extending, and modifying these tropes in ways that mimic, ironize, and respectfully mock the past.[12] In successful jazz performances repetition and signifying dwell in the same phrases and rhythms. The two are inextricable, joint temporal trajectories yoked together in the polyrhythmic drive of swing. When a drummer or dancer repeats a pattern they have executed in the past, their repetitions do not have to be an unreflective subservience to the past or to a tradition hostile to innovation or change. If a performer swings, their movements are a conjugation of bodily inertia and muscle memory with an alert context-specific kinetic attention to the present.

The point is that in Hughes's "Dance," the past surrounds and enables the present, inhabiting the musicians and dancers as a collective resource productive of a rhythmic coordination tight enough to make the dance an event not to be missed and loose enough to allow each performer as much freedom as they can use. This is a performance, that is, in Floyd's words, "fraught with funded meanings from the Afro-American musical tradition" (409). The music and the dancing perform the presence of the past in a way that makes it available for everyone to pick up on but that doesn't allow the future to be totally circumscribed by the past. It is this performance of the past as a tradition both ritualized and improvisatory that allows Benbow's musicians to respond to the calls of the immediate past flowing from the kinetic troping of other musicians and dancers without breaking off the propulsive rhythmic flow resulting from the inertia of their own performative trajectory. What this means is that the drummer, or any of the other musicians, functions as a multimetric center through which flows several different temporal trajectories. Responding to multiple pasts and multiple calls, Benbow's drummer performs not only a polyrhythmic music but a polyrhythmic self.

Playing responses to a wealth of pasts of varying temporal proximity, the drummer performs (in) a polyrhythmic and anticipatory present. "Bouncing like a rubber ball on his chair," Hughes's drummer is himself a dancer and, like any good dancer, combines attention to his own moves with a sharp anticipatory awareness of what other dancers are doing and are about to do (100). The necessity of finding the proper rhythms to sustain the forward momentum of the band and to match and inspire the movements of the dancers moves the drummer into a space of temporal entanglement, a space in which a deep imbrication of different dimensions of past, present, and future correspond to the entanglement of the drummer's rhythms with those of his bandmates and of the dancers on the floor. The drummer is legion, an embodiment of an attunement that is at least triple. His polyrhythms "articulate a multi-stranded web of social relations" (Walser 210), and these articulations make themselves visible in the movements of his body. One foot on the bass drum, the other on the high hat, an arm working the ride cymbal, and the other managing the snare drum, the drummer is a picture of multidimensional movement.[13] His sharp attunement to the dancers in the hall has made him into a dancer.[14]

Letting the dictates of time, rhythm, and sound work upon the different components of their bodily and subjective integrity, both dancers and drummer disarticulate themselves in order to articulate connections with others. In their danced articulation of the different parts of their body, the dancers give back to the musicians visual responses to what the musicians give them in sound. The musicians and the dancers form a rhythmic social ensemble dependent on a notion of bodily and musical integrity not threatened by the transgression of borders. Everything in Hughes's description suggests that the integrity and cohesiveness of Benbow's band is strengthened rather than weakened by the porosity of the border between it and the dancers. Benbow focuses the energy of the band and of the dancers; he does so by working the proscenium of the bandstand, the articulatory hinge between the two groups. He directs his verbal exhortations both outward, toward the dancers ("Ever'body shake!"), and backward, toward the band ("Benbow turned towards his musicians and cried through his cupped hands: 'Aw, screech it, boys!'" [99]). At a certain point in the proceedings, Benbow leaves the bandstand and crosses over into the physical space of the dancers "to dance slowly and ecstatically" (100). His movement onto the dance floor marks a point at which "the hall itself seemed to tremble," as if the effusions of musicians and dancers threaten to burst its physical constraints. This is also the point at which commands start to flow from the dance floor to the bandstand: "Aw, play it, Mister Benbow!" In the two-way movement from bandstand to dance floor and back, a circularity is established that Jacqui Malone, acknowledging the work of Gerald Davis, characterizes as "a dynamic system of influences and responses whose components include performers, audiences and their tradition" (35). The dancers and musicians organize their intensity into a covalent bond, a lining up of kinetic assonance that lets individuals share rhythms and movements in the way bonded atoms share electrons. The result is a porosity of the individuals in the hall productive of powerful couplings and aggregations that do not impinge upon the space for individual expression.

The porosity of the border between the band and the dancers is predicated upon the porosity of the borders separating any of the individuals in the hall. Giving themselves over to the polyrhythmic imperatives of the music, the dancers explore the many possible kinesthetic ways of moving together. The variety of these maneuvers are given expression in Hughes's catalog of the different kinds of bodily syntax on display at the dance: breasts shake against shirts (96), chins rest on shoulders, arms encircle waists and dangle over haunches (99), and hands hold desperately fast to hips (100). In the circuit of energy flowing through the hall, and "under the dissolute spell of [their own] rhythm" (100), bodies strain against their own self-containment and attempt to merge, meld, and flow into the movements of other bodies. The hall becomes a space of what Jason Stanyek calls "intercorporeality," which George Lewis glosses as "a body-based, face-to-face exchange of ideas and sounds" (13). The rhythms of the hall inspire a heightened bodily dialogue,[15] a series of improvised exchanges in which parts of the self move into the orbit of other selves. After Benbow cries, "Ever'body shake!," bodies "move ever so easily together—ever so easily," "like candy in the sun" (99). This is an image of bodies flowing out of their established patterns of self-consistency.

The first dancer presented in the chapter moves with his "body riding his hips" (96). Describing him in motion requires dissecting him, showing his hips related to his body like a horse under an equestrian or one sexual partner under another. Like the drummer dividing himself between the different components of his drum set, this dancer gets into the rhythm by getting himself out of a stolid unsyncopated coordination of the self. In the bodily dialogue taking place in the hall, the common ground is the felt sense of the self as a sharply articulated unity of distinct parts. Bodies move "easily" with each other and with themselves, because they are, in Lefebvre's words, "a bundle of rhythms." In their response to the heterogeneous rhythms of the music, the dancers embrace the discrepant rhythms within themselves. Benbow's band speaks powerfully to the dancers because it allows them to live the different rhythms that the world outside of the dance hall wants to subordinate to the isorhythmic requirements of labor, of the clock, and of narrow forms of social respectability.

These forms of isorhythmic subordination are forms of objectification; Lefebvre characterizes them as follows: "We *contain* ourselves by concealing the diversity of our rhythms: to ourselves, body and flesh, *we* are almost objects" (10). The treatment of rhythm embodied in Benbow's Kansas City Band breaks this concealment, dispelling any notion that the self is an object and compelling bodies to move in ways that disturb identities predicated on this form of containment. Thus bodies flow out of themselves and into a social space characterized by a dynamic instability that is neither absolute chaos nor strict conformity. Robert Farris Thompson's characterization expresses much of this quite well: "Ideally speaking, multiple meter in the dance is a means of articulating the human body more fully than is possible in ordinary discourse; it makes a person blaze as a living entity at the center of existence" (336).

Thompson's formulation captures the movement of a body that "blazes" without consuming itself, for the merging and melding that takes place at the dance is emphatically not a Nietzschean extinction of the self. In Hughes's description, "the crowd moved like jelly-fish dancing on individual sea-shells" (95). In this description we see articulated a position that Hughes will insistently return to throughout "Dance," the position that despite the intensity of the exhortations to go beyond themselves, each dancer is essentially alone, "on individual sea-shells." The word "loneliness" is repeated four times in three pages, and the music is consistently described in terms of an insuperable and bitterly tinged isolation: a "lonesome sea of harmony," and insistence on "the utter emptiness of soul when all is done"(105, 101). The music insists, as does Hughes, on the sharp individuation of each dancer, musician, and listener in the hall. The mode of sociality performed in the hall is no simple merging that brings people together by extinguishing their differences. This is why the dance chapter is worth dwelling on and why the music in it is such an important resource for Hughes; they figure a complex form of interrelatedness that foregrounds difference rather than attempting to efface it. Each participant floats on a sea of a rhythmicized collective past, yet each registers the pull of this sea's currents in different ways: "It was true that men and women were dancing together, but their feet had gone down through the floor of the earth, each dancer's alone—down into the center of things—and their minds had gone off into the center of loneliness" (104). In "Dance" Hughes conjugates a celebratory pleasure with the "bitter syrup" of loneliness that this pleasure moves with and against. His ability to do this depends on his leavening of novelistic form with imperatives adopted from jazz, particularly jazz's ability to combine seemingly contradictory opposites.

Following the imperatives of the music and the practice of the dancers, Hughes constructs *Not Without Laughter* as a coordination of discrepant trajectories, a packet of rhythms that combines scenes of collective social experience with the coming of age story of Sandy. In addition to "Dance," the tale of Sandy's development is syncopated by narrative lingering in the space of the pool hall, the barber shop, and the forum for tale telling that Aunt Hager's porch provides. In most of these scenes, Sandy barely participates and one almost forgets that he is present. These scenes are clearly important contributors to the shape that Sandy's subjectivity comes to take, but they are not structured around him. The result is that they exist for him not only as representations of the past dwelling within his consciousness but as living practices to be repeated and elaborated by him. Sandy has taken into himself the polyrhythms and collective conversations of life in black Stanton. These contribute to the ensemble of his existence and take their place among the rhythms that constitute his social being, not only as latent possibilities but as cross-rhythms that strengthen and shape the other rhythms of his existence. These scenes exist in a similar relationship to Sandy as the flexible forms of performance and improvisation do to the musicians in Benbow's band. Whether explicitly enunciated or not, they move along as a tacit rhythmic accompaniment to Sandy's movements. Their rhythms shape his and serve as a living resource for his configuration of himself. This is an articulation of the past not as an inert resource but as a packet of living rhythms requiring careful handling. Just like the repertoire of melodic patterns that jazz musicians draw upon, not every past vector will suit each present situation.

Each vector or melody has its own demands and requires a negotiation of the past and the present to effectively (re)enact it. The past is a vast reservoir of syntactic chains as articulate and recalcitrant as the dancing "jelly fish" of Hughes's dance hall.

And that, ultimately, is the point: that the strategies for using the past as a resource in the present is what is being worked out in the movements of the dancers that Hughes describes. The past is available in the present not as an inert and slavishly tractable object, but only as a living pattern requiring a sophisticated temporal askesis.

In the penultimate chapter of the novel, when Sandy comes to articulate his relationship to his social context and his past, he does so in terms of dancing: he sees himself as the embodiment of "Aunt Hager's dreams for Sandy dancing far beyond the limitations of their poverty, of their humble station in life, of their dark skins" (290). Sandy can come to terms with the different legacies handed down to him by the different members of his family (Aunt Hager, Harriet, Jimboy, Tempy, Annjee) only by conceiving of himself as a dancer, by seeing himself as a dancing complex of rhythms and rhythmic exchanges like the ones he witnesses at Chavers Hall.

Dance is the model for the form of subjectivity that Sandy comes to adopt for himself, and it is the model for the relationship between self and social context at work in the form of the novel. The dancers who move to the music of Benbow's Kansas City Band articulate a movement that is at least double in its obedience to the music and to its own prerogatives. The self performed in this movement is polyrhythmic, dancing rhythms that orient it to contexts and movements outside of itself, as well as rhythms that use complicated aliquant ratios to remain in contact with the outside world while creating for the individual a space for rhythmic self-definition.[16] The best dancers combine steps and rhythms acquired from others with revisions and refinements to these steps, a combination highlighting the fact that, in Lefebvre's words, "acquired rhythms are simultaneously internal and social" (75). This ratio of acquisition and refinement gives the formula for the complex performance of sociality and individuality in "Dance."[17]

The most prominent figure for this conjugation is found in Hughes's description of dancers moving apart and then back together: "A long, tall gangling gal stepped back from her partner, adjusted her hips, and did a few, easy, gliding steps all her own before her man grabbed her again" (99). In 2012 this maneuver is rather unremarkable, but in 1915 it is a real break with precedent. Sandy and Harriet attend the dance that Hughes describes in 1915, a time when a dance called the Texas Tommy was spreading across the nation. According to Marshall and Jean Stearns, the Texas Tommy is the earliest example in the vernacular "of a couple-dance incorporating, as did the Lindy fifteen or more years later, the breakaway, or the temporary and energetic separating of partners—a distinctly unwaltzlike and non-European maneuver" (129). The maneuver that Hughes describes is one without precedent in European-derived dancing and without support in the ideologies of civic and social comportment that such dancing upholds. This maneuver, and all the others described in "Dance," moves toward a complex orientation of a composite self to a composite natural and social world.

"Dance" revels in the possibilities of selves that belong simultaneously to the past and the future, to themselves and to others, and to intellectual and corporeal realms.

At the end of the novel, Sandy is rescued from the hopelessness of a life as an elevator attendant by the intervention of his Aunt Harriet. She has become a successful blues singer and is able to finance Sandy's education. Despite her sharp break from Aunt Hager's vision of a life narrowly bound by the dictates of work and religion, it is Harriet who keeps Aunt Hager's hopes for Sandy alive. She counters Annjee's objections to Sandy going back to school by insisting on Hager's ambitions for Sandy: "He's gotta be what his grandma Hager wanted him to be—able to help the black race" (298). Hager's ambition for Sandy takes a dance-step detour through Harriet, whose attachment to dancing and singing gives her the power to finance his education.[18]

Harriet invests in Sandy's future, wagering on a return that is only dimly imaginable and whose profit will accrue to the race rather than to her individually. She passes something of herself on to Sandy, making him into an object of affective and economic cathexis, a bearer of hopes and dreams that he inherits from others. Sandy becomes who he is through a form of psychic and affective ingestion of the familial and social forces pulling at the different components of his being. These forces come to him in ways that exceed the filter of the nuclear family; what he takes in from his mother and father are the least important of the influences upon him. He owes the most to his grandmother and his aunt, and the most important thing he gets from his father he gets indirectly, the wealth of songs and dances that contribute to Harriet's ability to fund his education. Hughes gives us a familial ensemble less like the hierarchical and closed-off structure of a traditional family and more like the expansive organization of Benbow's ensemble. In Benbow's band the different musicians are just as responsive to other musicians and to listeners and dancers outside of the band as they are to their nominal leader. The borders of Benbow's ensemble are porous enough to respond to imperatives from the outside, and this is true of Sandy as well.

The gossip at the barber shop, the movements on the dance floor, and the "lying" of the pool hall all enter into Sandy's makeup. Sandy is legion in the same way Benbow's drummer is; he is not only a member of a social ensemble, he is an ensemble himself. In *In the Break* Fred Moten uses the set of exchanges at work in Duke Ellington's band to elaborate a conception of ensemble resonant with Hughes's construction of Sandy. Moten defines the "ensemble" of jazz performance as "a field of convergence" and as a "lived, sounded philosophical lingering in the cut between the dangers and saving powers of (the refusals of) totality and singularity" (255, 96). According to Moten, the ensemble, an improvised phenomenon encompassing and surpassing the phenomena of "singularity and totality" (98), cuts the social with the musical to arrive at performances of subjectivity in which the rhythm of the individual sounds with and against the rhythm of the social whole. Hager, Tempy, Harriet, Jimboy, and most of the town of Stanton constitute an ensemble that improvises together, and one of their improvisations is the subject bearing the name Sandy.

Hager's dream for Sandy is that he "help [his] race," and despite the apparently limited abilities of a community like black Stanton to enable the education of its members, the role of the community is essential for the productive conjunction achieved at the end of the novel. Sandy imagines a future in which he helps the people of Stanton, but in a reversal typical of the way energy moves at the dance, they also help him. Duke Ellington's description of just such a reversal illuminates the nature of Sandy's relationship to the community. He describes the experience of using an inexperienced drummer in a town known for the quality of its dancers: "On two occasions up there we were using a substitute drummer, but we didn't have to worry about him because the dancers were carrying the band and the drummer. You start playing, the dancers start dancing, and they have such a great beat you just hang on" (qtd. in Malone 287). In Ellington's anecdote, energy and dependence flow against expectations, and the same is true of Sandy's relationship to the black community of Stanton, especially as this relationship is mediated through Harriet. Harriet's role as "Princess of the Blues" allows her to serve as the link between Hager's dreams and Sandy's attempt to realize them, and Harriet's singing and dancing (her last number is a "dance-song") emerge from the ensemble of social relations in which she first learned her steps and vocal stylings. At the dance hall she is carried by the beat of the dancers and musicians, and her later ability to succeed as a performer is a result of the musical and social ensemble's investment in her. As she takes in the musical rhythms and dance steps at Chavers Hall, she is becoming a repository of steps, melodies, and rhythms; her later success depends on this social investment and on her ability to reenact its performative energies on stage. Against expectation, Hager's influence on Sandy is realized by way of a detour through Harriet, the one member of the family most opposed to Hager's emphasis on work, religion, and propriety.[19] Sandy thinks of this detour as a dance step, and so should we. The intricate evasions and elliptical movements performed at the dance are necessary because all of the most simply straightforward paths are determined by the powers of white supremacy and capitalist inhumanity. To avoid what Hughes elsewhere calls "the teeth in the trap of economic circumstance," Sandy must make full use of polyrhythmic performances' power to interrupt expectation without halting forward motion (Hughes, "Cora" 21).

The sharpest illustration of this in the novel is given in the sterility of the path that Sandy finds himself on while living with Tempy. Tempy's enforcement of an arid combination of uplift and Du Boisian exceptionalism initially looks promising, for it keeps Sandy in school and exposes him to canonical works of American literature. On the surface, Tempy looks like the person best suited to enact Hager's ambitions for Sandy, but the novel makes it clear that under her direction Sandy would be a much poorer individual. Tempy's repudiation of vernacular forms of black culture aim at purging what is most Langston Hughes–like from Sandy, and it is telling that an illicit interruption of her influence yields the phrase that gives Hughes's novel its title. Prompted by the taunting of one of his close friends, Sandy puts off finishing *Moby Dick* in favor of a trip to the pool hall, a locale explicitly proscribed by Tempy. At the pool hall the dominant figure is Uncle Dan Givens, by unanimous consent "the world's champion liar" (249). In the world of the pool hall, a form of tale telling far removed from *Moby Dick* reigns, a form belligerent, exuberant, and above all "not without laughter" (249). Sandy removes himself from the cloistered scene of novel-reading solitude in order to find a social and aesthetic form capable of naming the dance-like impulse of Hughes's novel.[20] In the interruption of *Moby Dick* by a trip to the pool hall, Sandy and Hughes have injected laughter into the form of the novel, displacing its accents and making its completion fall on an unexpectedly stressed beat. This is syncopation, an unexpected combination of interruption and continuity that, like the drums in "Dance," constantly "keeps up [a] hard steady laughter" (99).

Everything returns to "Dance," for it provides the matrix of the novel's movement. Dancing is an attempt to fill space, to occupy it, and to repetitively carve out a segment of it that is one's own but that intersects with the space of other dancers. This movement is not limited to situations as obviously suited for dancing as Chavers Hall; in everyday life, one moves through space and attempts to make of this movement a meaningful pattern, a pattern that is enjoyable, productive, and that conforms to certain patterns of social acceptability.[21]

In the movements that Hughes describes and enacts, the goal is to move into a more exact equivalence or counterpoint with the vibrations and sonic patterns of the social space in which one moves. The wealth of movements on display in "Dance" shows that this can and must be a sophisticated adaptation to a social situation, as much a dancing complex of rhythms and rhythmic interchanges as is the self that moves through it. By highlighting this dancing movement of the self and of the rhythms within and without the self, Hughes draws attention not only to the nuances and potential of African American modes of performance but also to the possibilities for coordination, participation, and exchange contained in these rhythmic relations. If a text or an individual can coordinate rhythms as distinct as the religious devotion to work and propriety of

Aunt Hager and the orientation to pleasure and performance of Sandy's blues-singing aunt Harriet, then the possibility of living affinities and bonds outside of narrowly conceived categories of culture, race, or class is immensely expanded. In the figure of the dance, Hughes unites the strict sacrifice of the present to the future at work in Aunt Hager's religion and the immersion in the present at work in Harriet's devotion to the pleasures of singing and dancing. The result is Sandy's ability to see the different temporalities working within him as components of a heterogeneous wholeness rather than as discrete elements at war with each other.

The conception of time governing the larger society in which the black community of Stanton is ensconced is a high abstraction from the movements of capital, labor, and ownership on which the society is founded. This is a time enshrining univocal causal relations and, thus, not a time that can move Sandy out of a racially and economically circumscribed set of possibilities. Hughes opposes to this an experience of time that imagines the imbrication of the past, future, and present as a rhythm to be danced to, a series of demands upon the somatic and intellectual ensemble operative in the dance, with the same cruelness, loneliness, and possibilities as the music that animates "Dance."

Stein

In the *Dialect of Modernism* Michael North calls Gertrude Stein's literary output a "mixture of aesthetic experimentation and racist crudity" (64). The duality that North attributes to Stein is also evident in the criticism of her work, especially in the criticism that deals with *Three Lives* and with "Melanctha," the second of these "lives."[22] Most of the criticism of "Melanctha" (and most of the criticism of *Three Lives* focuses on "Melanctha") is divided between a celebration of Stein's avant-garde prose style, seen as either feminist or more broadly liberatory or both,[23] and a more negative critique of her employment of racial typology.[24] This division is given a final twist by critics like Carla Peterson and M. Lynne Weiss, who link Stein's style to the performance practices of African American music. Peterson writes that "Melanctha" is closely linked to "early folk-blues" (150), and Weiss calls it Stein's "blues lyric" (122). The final voice linking "Melanctha" and jazz is that of Nathaniel Mackey, a poet and essayist who has produced some of the most insightful criticism of jazz. Unlike Peterson and Weiss, Mackey describes the link between the rhythms of Stein's prose and the rhythms of jazz and ragtime in terms of "cover" rather than of influence or inspiration: "Under cover of blackness, Stein mounts an avant-garde assault on conventions of signification." According to Mackey, Stein's rhythms are not ragtime rhythms, they are rhythms licensed by the idea of ragtime and that, like minstrel performers, mask themselves in blackface. Mackey also identifies an early source of the identification of "Melanctha" and jazz: Katherine Mansfield's review of *Three Lives*. Mansfield warns the readers of her review against "Melanctha," writing that "*Melanctha* is negro music with all its maddening monotony done into prose; it is writing in real ragtime" (Mackey, "Other" 527).

Seen negatively, different threats to an existing order often appear as different versions of the same thing. To a conservative vision, feminism, communism, and atheism can appear as necessarily linked, despite the fact that their only real connection lies in the way they embody visions out of step with dominant social values. Mansfield's identification of "Melanctha" and jazz partakes of this logic; they appear the same to her because they have the same opponents. James Baldwin describes jazz as a music that aims "to checkmate the European conception of the world" ("Sorrow" 87), and for Mackey, Stein's prose takes aim at the linguistic conventions that underpin this conception. Despite their targeting of the same enemy, the two aesthetics have quite different positive projects. To ignore this difference and to collapse the two aesthetics (as Peterson and Weiss at times tend to do) is to privilege the vision that looks from the inside of conventions outward.[25] Mackey's reading of Stein's work as a form of minstrelsy highlights the screens of dissembling and power separating Stein's literary representation of fictionalized inhabitants of a fictionalized Baltimore (Bridgepoint) from the blues practices of the African American community of Baltimore.

This is not to say that the two assaults on convention do not share certain strategies, but merely that attention to their differences as well as their similarities puts us more in tune with the configurations of race and time at work in Stein's text. Mackey, Peterson, and Weiss all see Stein's use of repetition as the hinge between jazz and *Three Lives*, and my analysis is no different. What I add to their analyses is an attention to how repetition works on two different levels in *Three Lives*: the sentence level and the larger structural level. Stein's use of repetition within sentences and paragraphs has been well documented; De Koven and Weiss are particularly good at describing this repetition and its effects. What I would like to focus on is the role that repetition on a larger scale plays in structuring *Three Lives*.

All three stories that make up *Three Lives* start *in media res*. "The Good Anna," "Melanctha," and "The Gentle Lena," all introduce their protagonists as ensconced in the middle of an established and fairly stable situation. Anna is already well established with her dear "Miss Mathilda," "Melanctha" is already closely entangled in the lives of Rose and Sam Johnson, and Lena has already been a servant in the same pleasant household for four years. These initial positions are each repeated later in the text, and with the exception of "The Gentle Lena," what occurs between this starting point and its repetition makes up the bulk of the text. In the Penguin edition of *Three Lives*, "Melanctha" takes up 109 pages; 101 of these are devoted to what we might call the text's catching up with itself. When we first meet Melanctha, she has been friends with Rose Johnson for years and is helping Rose with her childbirth. Melanctha's wandering with Jane Harden and her relationship with the doctor Jefferson Campbell, the most significant events in the text, are already in the past. After the text catches up with itself by returning to this initial point, it devotes only eight pages to Melanctha's subsequent life.

"The Good Anna" and "The Gentle Lena" have similar structures. Built into each of the three lives is a structure that returns to the beginning before continuing on to the end. This return is a repetition, but it is a repetition of a different order than that which takes place in Stein's sentences and one having markedly different results. Like virtually everything else in *Three Lives*, this repetitive return to the beginning has at least two different effects. It serves as a marker of Stein's desire to endow the lives of her protagonists with an epic importance, but it also serves to stamp on their lives an inevitability in keeping with Stein's investment in a typological understanding of human character.[26] All of the most venerated epics of the Western literary tradition begin *in media res*, and in her employment of this form of beginning Stein rhymes the comparatively modest lives of her protagonists with the heroes of these epics, giving a weight and importance to them uncommon in the literature of the period. In Stein's attempt to give epic importance to the lives of those at the bottom of economic and racial hierarchies there is an echo of Flaubert's *Tres Contes*, the book that Stein named as the inspiration for her *Three Lives* and that combines a tale of a household servant with tales built on the epic subjects of St. Julian and the biblical Herod.

In the epic, opening *in media res* is linked to a conception of time different from that functioning in the nineteenth-century novelistic tradition out of which *Three Lives* emerges. Lukács describes this epic conception of time when he writes that in epics "the heroes do not experience time within the work itself: time does not affect their inner changes or changelessness; their age is assimilated in their characters, and Nestor is old just as Helen is beautiful or Agamemnon mighty" (*Theory of the Novel* 121–22). In *Three Lives* Stein is not out to recapture the time-conception of past epics, but there is a similarity between the way time functions in her work and what Lukács describes. The characters set in motion by Homer and Virgil are unchanging types rather than individuals, and while Stein's characters are not necessarily types, they are shaped by her investment in typology.

Catharine R. Stimpson calls Stein "an obsessive psychologist, a Euclid of behavior, searching for 'bottom natures,' the substratum of individuality." According to Stimpson, Stein "tries to diagram psychic genotypes, patterns into which all individuals might fit" (498). This diagramming is at work in *Three Lives*: Melanctha, Anna, and Lena don't change; they merely unwind the telos of their typological nature. They are essentially the same in every situation, and they have the Homeric epithets to suit their static nature: Anna is always "good," and Lena is always "gentle."[27] Melanctha has no matching epithet, but she does have adjectives that are consistently and inflexibly attached to her: "blue" and "graceful." The characters in *Three Lives* are unchanging manifestations of their place in Stein's typological system, a fact that goes a long way toward explaining both why Stein feels free to begin in the middle of their lives and why bald employments of racial, national, and class stereotypes play such a prominent part in such a linguistically adventurous text.[28]

Stein feels free to begin *in media res* because her characters are the same at all points of the trajectory plotted for them in the text. One could start anywhere with Lena's life, because at each point of it she exemplifies her sweet, gentle, yielding nature. Consequently, when the tales catches up with themselves, they repeat an unchanged version of their initial beginning. This is most readily apparent in "Melanchtha"; when this life catches up with itself there are repetitions of identical and nearly identical sentences from the opening. The sentence "Rose Johnson was careless and negligent and selfish, and when Melanctha had to leave for a few days, the baby died," appears both on page 59 and on page 159, the only change being the absence of commas in the sentence's second appearance. This kind of exact repetition is quite different from the repetition within sentences that DeKoven and Weiss praise for their destabilizing and liberatory effects.

Not all repetition is created equal. Much Stein criticism loses track of this simple fact and its ramifications. Relevant here is James Snead, whose attention to repetition alerts us not only to the existence of different forms of repetition but to the different cultural and philosophical assumptions that give rise to these different forms. In "Repetition as a Figure of Black Culture," Snead describes a form of exact repetition that dominates the American imagination: "For repetition must be exact in all financial accounting, given that, globally, capital ultimately circulates within closed tautological systems (i.e., decrease in an asset is either an increase in another asset or a decrease in a liability, both within a corporate firm and in relations with other firms)" (66). The repetition that Snead limns here is not limited to the realm of financial accounting; it merely finds its clearest expression there. It is the form of repetition that manifests itself in all fields of an American culture indebted to the ideals of possessive individualism. It repeats in order to confirm and indemnify itself against risk.[29] A type of prophylactic repetition, this mode of repeating subordinates itself to exact returns and attempts to ignore the pleasurable efflorescences of repetition that make themselves their own goal.

When each of Stein's three "lives" catch up to themselves, they repeat with an exactitude that demonstrates their adherence to the ideal of circulation "within closed tautological systems." They repeat in order to demonstrate a fixed truth, the truth of the typology that determines the movements of Lena, Anna, and Melanctha. This typology is not far from Ann Charter's blunt characterization of Stein's "view of human nature as static and unchanging, basically falling into one of two types, either aggressive or passive" (xiv). Anna is aggressively domineering, Lena is tragically passive, and Melanctha has a power capable of dominating Jane Harden and Jefferson Campbell, but that is ultimately no match for the stubborn simplicity of Rose Johnson and Jem Richards. The tale that each of the three lives tells is given its dynamic by an almost clinical devotion to revealing the dynamics of power in relationships. Each protagonist rises or falls to the level that their innate power has marked out for them in advance.

The law of this movement is stated in the first of the three lives: "In friendship, power always has its downward curve. One's strength to manage rises always higher until there comes a time one does not win, and though one may not really lose, still from the time that victory is not sure, one's power slowly ceases to be strong. It is only in a close tie such as marriage, that influence can mount and grow always stronger with the years and never meet with a decline. It can only happen so when there is no way to escape" (35). "Power always has its downward curve": this is the law that circumscribes the ambit of Stein's "niggers and servant girls and the foreign population,"[30] a law whose "always" announces the horizon of necessity against which the divagations of the three character's lives unfold. The "downward curve" of power establishes a finite limit to relationships by figuring them as zero-sum exchanges within which one is either increasing one's power over one's partner or losing it. "Only in a close tie such as marriage" can the inevitable decline of power be avoided. This corollary to Stein's law of power seems to hint at the possibility of a relationship not doomed to end up in an inevitable split, but the marriages portrayed in *Three Lives* look less promising than even abject loneliness. The marriage of Rose and Sam Johnson functions through the total acquiescence of the passive Sam to all of Rose's wishes, a pattern that is more brutally reenacted in the short unhappy marriage of the gentle Lena to Herman Kreder. Marriage appears in *Three Lives* as a trap in which the weaker partner is increasingly subordinated to the stronger. As a critique of marriage and its crippling heteronormative and patriarchal teeth, this depiction of marriage does serious liberatory work.

What is less productive in Stein's critique of marriage is her assumption that the domination working in marriage is part of the same power dynamic that shapes all relationships, whether heterosexual or homosexual, erotic or platonic. The power struggle that makes Lena's married life far from gentle is the same struggle that forces Melanctha's breaks with Jane Harden, Jeff Campbell, Rose Johnson, and Jem Richards. The "downward curve" of power ensures that Melanctha outgrows the mentorship of Jane Harden and that her domination of Jeff Campbell will eventually expire. Power shapes all the relationships in *Three Lives*; in each one it is always clear who has the most power. When this relationship changes, when one partner's power waxes or wanes to the point at which the original equation between quantities of power no longer applies, the relationship ends.

The "power" of Jane Harden is one of the chief things that draws Melanctha to her and secures the bond between the two of them ("she had power and she liked to use it" [73]). When they break, it is because Melanctha's power has superseded Jane's: "Slowly now between them, it was Melanctha Herbert, who was stronger. Slowly now they began to drift apart from one another" (74). The same is true of the break with Jefferson Campbell, although this break is much more complicated and more troubled by uncertainty (123, 130).

The last two relationships of Melanchtha's life are even more clearly dominated by this law of power. With both Rose Johnson and Jem Richards, "Melanctha never had any way that she could ever get real power" (149). Rose and Jem both have much greater power than Melanctha, a fact that makes it easy for both figures to abandon her. Power differentials govern all of these relationships; what this shows is that while Melanctha and Stein's prose may wander in ways that make Stein's text a seductive and productive incitement, the endpoint of each of the three lives and of each of their protagonists is marked out in advance by a law that channels this wandering and ensures that it functions only as a temporary detour away from a path that leads to an inevitable end.

The power that assigns each of Stein's characters their proper end is a sharp and one-sided force whose impetus is to separate subjects. In the terms utilized in political theory, it is a distributive rather than collective power. Giovanni Arrighi characterizes this distinction as follows: "Distributive aspects of power refer to a zero-sum game relationship, whereby an agency can gain power only if others lose some. Collective aspects of power, in contrast, refer to a positive-sum game relationship, whereby cooperation among distinct agencies increases their power over third parties, or over nature" (6–7).[31] The power that drives the movement of *Three Lives* is one-sided because it has no collective aspect. It is purely distributive, a configuration perfectly suited to Stein's desire to separate herself from the United States and to her conception of herself as a genius exempt from assumptions about the putative intellectual weaknesses of women.[32]

By excising the collective aspect from power, Stein makes isolation into a telos and allows power to function as a unidirectional force moving all in its path toward this telos. Melanctha's isolation at the end of her tale is given in advance; she cannot remain in any relationship to Jane Harden, Rose Johnson, or Jefferson Campbell because the discursive world of *Three Lives* admits no exceptions to the "downward curve of power." The result is a relentless pressure on the protagonists of *Three Lives*, driving them, in Catharine R. Stimpson's words, from "a moment of happiness to death" (500). The flat uninflected time that speaks itself in the text licenses no creative departures from its movement; it sounds an austere form of necessity in keeping with exact repetition and the impossibility of sustainable collective structures. Unlike the breaks that James Snead describes in jazz, each break is final. They are not temporary separations that can lead the two figures involved in them back to each other.

In "The Remaking of Americans: Gertrude Stein's 'Melanctha' and African-American Musical Traditions" Carla L. Peterson asserts that "a blues sensibility permeates 'Melanctha,' determining the story's geographic setting and shaping the destinies of both Melanctha and Jane Harden" (151). For her, the bleak ending of Melanctha identifies it with a blues tradition that persistently concerns itself with themes of hardship and suffering. The problem with this identification is that it places undue weight on the "what" (content) of literary and musical performance and disregards the essential realm of "how" (style).[33] The protagonist of a blues performance never ends up dead because blues narration occurs in the first person. Bessie Smith never sings of trouble that belongs to someone else; she always articulates these troubles as if they were her own.[34] The consistent use of the first person in blues performance is a marker of the blues aesthetic's commitment to the participatory values of imbrication and entanglement. The detachment that characterizes the relationship between Melanctha and the narrator of her tale is totally foreign to the blues aesthetic. When Stein's narrator looks down on Melanctha with detached pity, the effect is to create a safe point of view for the reader far removed from the vertiginously affective response the blues pulls from its listeners: "Poor Melanctha, surely her love had made her mad and foolish" (159).[35] What is marked in the detached un-blues-like position of the narrator and Stein's use of a truncated conception of power to shape *Three Lives* is the element that most separates Stein's text from the African American musical tradition: the horizon of isolation and singularity grounding Stein's text. *Three Lives* gives each character a distinct and compelling rhythm of their own, but it does so by assuming a social ontology in which these rhythms cannot be shared for long and in which each rhythm is ultimately incompatible with other rhythms. In her commitment to the downward curve of power, Stein betrays her investment in a time whose telos suits her typological impulse. Each character and each race has its own rhythm, and the passage of time makes each rhythm amenable to analysis by isolating it from its surroundings. Melanctha can wander with Jane Harden and Jefferson Campbell, but the temporal movement of the text insures that their time together will not lead to a new cooperatively formed rhythm. In *Three Lives* time isolates and in doing so takes each character to an end that most reveals their "true" nature. This is a conception of time hostile to imbrication and merging, a conception that gives us a text constructed as a triptych of discretely framed lives. Melanctha, Lena, and Anna share the same narrow temporal and geographical arena, but there is no hint that their movements might overlap. Here aesthetics and racial separatism come together in a way that is both superficial (that is, textual segregation is not absolutely comparable with physical segregation) and telling.[36] Stein's conceptions of character and rhythm are best displayed in a simple textual context, that is, one in which each character moves against a background of characters from their own race.[37]

Exposed here are the predictable limits of functioning, in Mackey's words, "under cover of blackness" ("Other" 527). Stein's simultaneous use of blackness and utilization of a conception of time and of distinct unmixed entities antithetical to the practices of African American music is of interest because it suggests that, while race is central to modernist literary production, there are sharp conceptual limits to the way African American voice has entered into high modernist texts. Despite its idiosyncrasies and wandering prose, Stein's text is symptomatic of the way that, as Lawrence W. Levine puts it, "American society has done far more than merely neglect jazz; it has pigeonholed it, stereotyped it, denigrated, distorted its meaning and its character" (432). *Three Lives* has both an announced and unannounced traffic with aspects of black performance, and yet it ultimately fails to meaningfully register the sharply interactive and cooperative nature of jazz rhythm. This failure can be located in Stein's one-sided conception of power and the isolating time that it motivates; her suppression of the collective aspect of power is of a piece with modernism's suppression of the uniquely collective aspect of jazz performance.

Amiri Baraka refers to the cultural rhythm of jazz and jazz-inspired performance as "a multi rhythmic thrust . . . with many individual rhythms, harmonically joined in that collective forwarding" ("Rhythm" 30). What is salient here is the coordination of individual rhythms with a movement beyond the individual. Stein handles "individual rhythms" brilliantly, but she banishes the "collective" aspect of their multi-rhythmic thrust from the realm of possibility. *Three Lives* shapes itself "under cover of blackness" but in accordance with temporal assumptions that enforce a deafness to the most powerful possibilities of black musical performance. These possibilities have less to do with the surface features of blues lyrics, which Peterson stresses, than they do with the social and temporal shaping that blues performance enacts. Unlike Stein's text, the blues shape time as a movement that aggregates as well as separates. In *Three Lives* the law of power ensures that characters move past each other in a series of irrevocable breaks necessitated by the antagonistic nature of relationships conceived of as power struggles.

The relationships engendered by jazz temporality, on the other hand, are described by Albert Murray as obedient to the principle of "antagonistic cooperation" ("Function" 574). Antagonistic cooperation allows for forms of coordination not dependent upon subordination. This kind of coordination or cooperation is hinted at in "Melanctha" when wandering figures as an activity engaged in by more than one person. Both Jane and Melanctha and Jeff and Melanctha wander together, thematic suggestions that power might have a collective aspect. However, these forms of wandering do not last and ultimately fall prey to the downward curve of power that makes them unsustainable. The abortive nature of these wanderings à deux is a sign of the missed opportunities in Stein's text and the unheard rhythm of blues performance. For what condemns these nonindividualistic forms of wandering is lack of a structure capable of sustaining them, that is, a blues structure. Angela Davis characterizes the power of blues structure as follows: "What gives the blues such fascinating possibilities of sustaining emergent feminist consciousness is the way they often construct seemingly antagonistic relationships as noncontradictory opposites" (xv). The power to let wandering lead somewhere besides death and isolation lies in the aesthetic that Stein uses as a cover or mask for her linguistic innovations. This is to say that *Three Lives* is not a genuine encounter between Anglo-American modernism and African American culture, but that it comes tantalizingly close to being one. This, I think, explains the enthusiasm of figures like Richard Wright and Nella Larsen for "Melanctha," and why I think John Rowe is correct when he writes that "Melanctha Herbert represents, along with Anna Federner and Lena Mainz, missed opportunities for a modern, hybrid American subjectivity" (10).

These opportunities are "missed," not only because Stein's text has not gotten the right kind of attention, as Rowe implies, but, more importantly, because the dominant time of *Three Lives* is a static, tautological time productive of isolation and yoked to typological characterization. To push these characters into full-blown realizations of the pluralistic possibilities that Rowe sees in them, what is needed is the dynamic flow of a time that precipitates antagonistic cooperation and the coordination of noncontradictory opposites. The most compelling and relevant performance of such a time lies in the jazz, blues, and ragtime that critics like Carla Peterson are eager to hear in Stein's text but that don't fully sound there. To say this is to point to the fact that the source of *Three Lives'* potential opportunities is also the source of what blunts these opportunities: Stein's narrow conception of blackness as a mask rather than as a source of novel temporal and aesthetic models.

This narrow conception and the crabbed, one-sided form of temporality it produces structure *Three Lives*, but they are present throughout her entire oeuvre. A particularly telling example is the essay from *Lectures in America* titled "Plays." An essay devoted to solving the "problem" of "syncopated time" in the theater, "Plays" uses jazz as an exemplification of the form of temporality that has to be banished if "Art" is to fulfill its proper function: "to live in the actual present, that is the complete actual present" (251). The problem with the traditional theater is that in its "syncopated time," there is a lack of coordination between the action on stage and the audience's emotion. The emotion of the audience members is "always behind or ahead of the play," a lack of coordination that prevents the play from achieving the culminating completion Stein sees as necessary to a successful work of art. According to these criteria, jazz is even more deficient than the theater: "The jazz bands made of this thing, the thing that makes you nervous at the theatre, they made of this thing an end in itself. They made of this different tempo a something that was nothing but a difference in tempo between anybody and everybody including all those doing it and all those seeing and hearing it" (245). Underlying Stein's dismissal of jazz is the assumption that syncopated time is incapable of coordinating emotion and action or any other set of disparate elements.

What is disregarded here is the type of coordination of disparate temporalities performed by jazz, a moving-with that neither yokes different elements rigidly together or leaves them floating in asynchronous chaos. The exclusion of jazz temporality is a constant in Stein's work. It is as present in *Three Lives'* one-sided conception of power and downward telos of isolation, as it is in the more explicit exclusion of "Plays." What has changed between the two is the downward telos at work in *Three Lives*, an element replaced by Stein's "actual present" without future or past. This constancy is significant because it means that Stein's placement of race at the center of *Three Lives* is not a vanishing mediator but a move constitutive of the way time will function in the rest of Stein's work. As a result, questions of race are constantly at play in Stein's works and not just in those works that have overtly racialized subjects.[38] The beat of the continuous present in Stein's work bears the trace, therefore, of its provenance in Stein's donning of the mask of blackness. This enabling condition is at the same time a limit to the potential of Stein's wandering prose. In its employment of a downwardly teleological and decidedly unsyncopated time, *Three Lives* suffers from Stein's eagerness to affiliate herself with the painterly tradition of Cezanne and Picasso. The result is a triptych in which the three lives exist in well-framed spaces that parallel each other but do not participate with each other.

The desire to hear ragtime or the blues in Stein's text is the desire to let these three lives sound at the same time and to exist in the same polyphonic performative space. Stein's text is a missed opportunity, but it is a tantalizing and productive one. What Mansfield describes as "writing in real ragtime" still awaits its proper antiphonal response (qtd. in Mackey, "Other" 527).

Larsen

Like "Melanctha," Nella Larsen's *Quicksand* is ostensibly the tale of a protagonist who cannot "make her wants and what she had, agree" (Stein, *Three Lives* 62). The epigraph to Stein's *Three Lives* suggests that neither Melanctha nor the society in which she lives is to blame for her fate; *Quicksand*, on the other hand, seems to suggest that both Helga Crane and society are at fault for the novel's unhappy end.[39] In its movement of Helga through a wide range of settings, Larsen's novel critiques both the social impediments that inhibit Helga's development and the strategies that Helga uses to move past these impediments. The product of an interracial marriage, Helga Crane is a sharp critic of hypocrisy and an ardent partisan of her own pleasure; the restlessness that this combination engenders displays the slim possibilities for an independent, educated, black woman in the cultural landscape through which the novel charts her movement.

Helga Crane's life is beset by the powerful pull of the future and the terrible power of the past. The future exerts its influence on her in the form of the "sweet silent music of change" that Helga finds so compelling (57). Real music she has a much more ambivalent relationship to. The "jungle music" of the cabaret and the ragtime songs she hears in Copenhagen elicit a powerfully mixed response from her. In the cabaret Helga feels an intense and visceral reaction to the music she dances to; she enjoys being "drugged, lifted, sustained, by the extraordinary music, blown out, ripped out, beaten out, by the joyous, wild, murky orchestra" (59). Moments later, after the music temporarily pauses, Helga struggles to distance herself from this enjoyment, "cloak[ing] herself in a faint disgust" and chastising herself for having behaved as if she were "a jungle creature."

In Copenhagen, when she hears a couple of "American Negroes" perform "Everybody Gives Me Good Advice" and other familiar and well-worn songs from Helga's past, her distaste is even more pronounced: "Helga Crane was not amused. Instead she was filled with an intense hatred for the cavorting Negroes on the stage. She felt shamed, betrayed, as if these pale pink and white people among whom she lived had suddenly been invited to look upon something which she had hidden away and wanted to forget" (83). Despite this sharp revulsion, Helga is compelled to return "again and again" to the Circus to see these two American Negroes perform.

These two scenes—spectatorship at the Copenhagen Circus and dancing in the Harlem cabaret—are points at which Helga Crane's struggle with herself and with the constraints of racial and gendered expectation are sharply condensed. Helga Crane's struggle takes many forms, but two of its most insistent and antagonistic coordinates are the pull of pleasure and the weight of the past. Helga is a bit of a sybarite; her relentless desire for pleasurable things and pleasurable experiences makes her one of the most compelling characters in American literature. However, her pursuit of pleasure is never untroubled by the disturbing weight of the past. Her "inconvenient" family history and "the skeletons that stalk lively and in full health through the consciousness of every person of Negro ancestry in America" (96) are elements that Helga constantly and unsuccessfully struggles to suppress. This past haunts Helga and prevents the "sweet silent music of change" from ever making itself audible in a form adequate to her desire (57).

Helga Crane is pulled by these two forces, torn between the future that her desire pushes her toward and the past she struggles to repress. Hers is a particularly acute case of the need to balance the weight of different temporal orientations.

Helga Crane's attempt to productively balance the pull of the past and the future can be understood as a search for what Reinhart Koselleck calls the "elusive present." Koselleck characterizes the importance of the "elusive present" as follows: "The compulsion to coordinate past and future so as to be able to live at all is inherent in any human being. Put more concretely, every human being and every human community has a space of experience out of which one acts, in which past things are present or can be remembered and, on the other, one always acts with reference to specific horizons of expectation" (111). Koselleck's formulation hints at the difficulty of coordinating past and future, and this difficulty is multiplied considerably when, as in Helga Crane's case, subjects have to constantly confront discourses that write their past and future for them. In *Quicksand* Helga Crane finds no free space in which to articulate her own temporal orientation. Expectations of race and gender have already mapped her trajectory in advance, figuring her as an abject outsider with a narrative rhythm already known and dismissed. Her self-articulation is blocked by a set of powerful discursive expectations: those of "primitivism," "uplift," and "exoticism."

What these discourses stand in the way of is, as Saidiya Hartman puts it, a "(counter) investment in the body as a site of need, desire, and pleasure" (75).

4. Duke Ellington at the piano. Duke Ellington Collection, Archives Center, National Museum of American History, Smithsonian Institution.

For Hartman, this (counter) investment is not just a therapeutic strategy centered on the individual but is also an essential component in articulating a community of needs and of building affiliations necessary for communal redress.

This communal aspect is important because it circumvents readings of *Quicksand* that focus on the shortcomings of Helga Crane, readings that pathologize her "dissatisfactions" or "self-delusions" without situating them in the context of the strivings for self- and political articulation characteristic of the period.[40]

Nella Larsen's presentation of Helga Crane needs to be read as a sophisticated critique of social forms. Helga Crane's restless desire and "ironical" detachment point toward a rhythmic attunement to a society with a more capacious sense of time and of social organization than the one she finds herself in.

The most compelling model for this rhythmic attunement is the music of Duke Ellington. Ellington was the most important purveyor of "jungle music" in the 1920s, and his compositions were sophisticated responses to the same primitivist assumptions that stand in the way of Helga Crane. Larsen's allusion to "jungle music" highlights the extent to which Larsen and Ellington were engaged with the same social and aesthetic problems. Both Larsen's novel and El-

5. Nella Larsen. Yale Collection of American Literature, Beinecke Rare Book and Manuscript Library.

lington's music challenge the primitivist assumptions built into the adjective "jungle," and both reflect on the ways that the right forms of temporality and irony can create a space for alternative constructions of African American (and American) selfhood.

Jungle Music

Although Helga Crane often appears to be in pursuit of concrete "things" or specific people, what she is ultimately after is a temporal orientation capable of articulating her desires as a sustainable project and herself as a member of a sustaining but noncoercive collective. The allure of this goal and the power of the elements blocking its achievement are both present in the cabaret scene that immediately precedes Helga Crane's relocation to Denmark. This scene occurs when Helga has been in Harlem for over a year and her roommate Anne Grey's hypocritical approach to "the race problem" (48) is wearing on her nerves. Helga accompanies Anne Grey and other friends to a cabaret. As soon as they enter the cabaret, Helga is immediately unsettled by its vertiginous motion, which confounds her habitual detachment. As she dances, she moves farther and farther away from her normal self: "Helga was oblivious of the reek of flesh, smoke, and alcohol, oblivious of the oblivion of other gyrating pairs" (59). Helga Crane is powerfully moved by the jazz music in the cabaret; at no other point in the novel does Helga enjoy such intense pleasure. As the band plays, Helga Crane puts herself into her body in a way that had not previously been possible. Rather than relying on the elaborate framing of her body that her prowess at shopping and dressing allows, here Helga articulates herself through the motions of her body itself.[41]

The pleasure made accessible to Helga in the cabaret serves as more than a temporary diversion; it suspends the racial antipathy that Helga had been struggling with in the previous weeks and months. As her irritation with Anne's obsession with race increases and her discontent with Harlem grows, Helga experiences sharp flashes of revulsion for those she feels she should regard as her "own people" (55): "It was as if she were shut up, boxed up, with hundreds of her race. . . . Why, she demanded in fierce rebellion, should she be yoked to these despised black folk?" (55).

Helga's distaste is directed both at those who share "her racial markings" and at the claims that race makes on her most intimate interiority. The result of this distaste is an intensification of Helga's insularity, a sharp emphasis on her difference from others, both black and white.

This willed apartness is in evidence as Helga approaches the cabaret, moving through a sea of heterogeneous sounds: "cackling phonographs, raucous laughter, complaining motor-horns, low singing, mingled in the familiar medley that is Harlem" (58).[42] These are the sounds of a fecund and heterogeneous social milieu, but from their reverberations "Helga Crane felt singularly apart" (58). Only as she dances to the "extraordinary music" in the cabaret is Helga able to abandon her aloofness and enter into the unsettling motion of things outside of her own control.[43]

Carried by the rhythms of "the joyous, wild, murky orchestra," Helga moves past her racial antipathy and antagonistic self-division as she improvises a version of herself that begins with "bodily motion." In this expansive and elusive present, the forces that had previously troubled Helga are not so much banished as they are woven into a syncopated counterpoint with other elements of her subjective and racial existence. Everything takes on a new weight in the presence of the cabaret orchestra's sonic topographies. At the cabaret, the existential tessitura of Helga's existence is opened to a host of higher and lower frequencies, a veritable Pandora's box of previously suppressed overtones and undertones. The duration of this alternative present, however, is brief. When the music halts, Helga's will to make its trajectories her own has disappeared.

She reasserts her detached subject position, and when she reflects on her experience with the orchestra's music, her former revulsion returns: "a shameful certainty that not only had she been in the jungle, but that she had enjoyed it, began to taunt her" (59). Larsen's description of the mental operations Helga uses to remove herself from the music reveals much: "She wasn't, she told herself, a jungle creature. She cloaked herself in a faint disgust as she watched the entertainers throw themselves about to the bursts of the syncopated jangle, and when the time came again for the patrons to dance, she declined" (59). The language employed here makes it clear that what is occurring is an active reconstruction of her experience rather than a passive realization of what actually occurred. Helga "cloaks herself" and "tells herself," constructions revealing that she is talking herself into a convenient interpretation of what has just happened. Helga talks herself into a disavowal of jazz and its effect on her by saddling the music with the derisive adjective "jungle." Helga is most assuredly not a "jungle creature," and by figuring jazz as "jungle music," she denies any claim that the music might make on her.

It is important to note two things about Helga's strategy: it is neither unique nor is it simply an irrational manifestation of her innate contumacy. In referring to jazz as "jungle music," Helga is participating in one of the most prevalent discourses concerning the music.

While Nella Larsen was writing *Quicksand*, Duke Ellington was rising to national prominence as the leader of Duke Ellington's Jungle Orchestra, writing and performing music for jungle-themed floor shows at the Cotton Club. As Mark Tucker and Grahm Lock have pointed out, application of the appellation "jungle" to jazz was ubiquitous in the 1920s (and into the 1930s). Tucker notes that "'jungle' songs were a standard part of black musical revues in the 1920s" ("Ellington's 'Jungle Music'" 13), and Lock adds that the jungle theme was equally prevalent in the movies (80). In the September following the release of *Quicksand*, Ellington provided the music for a production at the Cotton Club titled "Congo Jamboree" and billed as "an exhibition of unrestrained Nubian abandon" (G. Lock 246n30). Nella Larsen's employment of the term "jungle" places her novel in the midst of an ongoing attempt to contain the implications of jazz by caricaturing it, making it seem as if it was the production of a time and place far removed from the Harlem of Duke Ellington, Nella Larsen, and Helga Crane. Larsen's novel comments on the forces conspiring to figure the modern hyper-sophistication of Ellington's music as a product of the jungle, placing Helga Crane and *Quicksand* in the midst of the same social possibilities and limitations facing Ellington and letting his composed and improvised responses to them sound within the text.

The association of jazz with the jungle is part of the discourse about African

Americans and their music that makes any assertion of female desire so problematic. In the sphere created by the music at the cabaret, Helga seems to find a place in which to articulate a self capable of negotiating the contradictions that plague her, but the fact that jazz is figured as "jungle music" by dominant discourses means that by participating in it, Helga makes herself susceptible to being constructed as a "jungle creature." Instead of finding a space in which to work out a (counter) investment of her body and herself, Helga encounters an abject music, and her participation in it works to mark her as a lascivious and innately sexualized being whose availability and willingness can be safely assumed. In dismissing this music, Helga is attempting to inoculate herself against being consigned to the role of savage and oversexed "negress."[44]

Although Helga's willed detachment of herself from participation in the music at the cabaret seems disingenuous, it is a perfectly rational reaction to the dilemmas confronting Helga's attempt to forge an independent construction of herself.

Uplift

Helga reacts against the dominant representations of African American women as sexualized beings divorced from rationality. In recoiling from the possibility of being written in this way, Helga is attempting to surmount what Kevin Gaines calls "a major obstacle to the assertion of bourgeois black selfhood" (68). In *Uplifting the Race* Gaines describes the dilemmas of black self-assertion in a way that makes it clear that Helga's situation is not unique. Helga's desire to free herself from racist and sexist expectations is isomorphic with the desire of an African American elite to rid the race of a "narrowly racialized identity" constructed through demeaning stereotypes. Despite Helga's antipathy to "uplift," she shares its desire to abolish "demeaning white images of blackness" (67).[45]

Moreover, at times she also evinces attitudes similar to the less appealing aspects of uplift ideology, namely its tendency to "assent to the racist formulations of 'the Negro problem' by projecting onto other blacks dominant images of racialized pathology" (Gaines 75). This is the strategy she uses to detach herself from the music in the cabaret and from the cabaret's kaleidoscopic parade of color and sound. What makes Helga's application of a primitivising stereotype to jazz so surprising is that her earlier comments on Anne Grey's hypocrisy demonstrate a keen understanding of the shortcomings of uplift ideology. Helga Crane is aware of, and irked by, the discrepancy between Anne Grey's loud proclamation of "the undiluted good of all things Negro" and her "disdainful contempt" for "the songs, the dances and the softly blurred speech of the race" (48). Despite her reactions to this hypocrisy, Helga still shares Anne's unwillingness to embrace cultural forms associated with the "unrefined" black masses.

The reason that Helga wants to separate herself from jazz is because it doesn't conform to her sharply developed "aesthetic sense."[46] This aesthetic sense is the main thing that attracts Helga to Anne Grey; both Helga and Anne are drawn to the purchase of commodities as a proving ground for their highly cultivated sense of taste. The two share a taste for carefully selected objects and for the tasteful construction of protective environments built out of these objects. They use their aesthetic sense to distinguish and separate themselves from their surroundings.[47] This necessarily entails a negative relationship both to those without their kind of aesthetic sense and to the past. The objects that they tastefully select are those detached from their history by the movements of the market. In the selection, purchase, and display of these objects, Helga and Anne participate in the fantasy of a consuming subject unfettered by the past.[48]

The aesthetic stance evidenced here also shapes Anne Grey's taste in music, dance, and drama. She wants the same thing from her aesthetic experiences as she does from the objects in her home: a reflection of her class status and the excision of anything suggesting her imbrication in the tortured racial history of the United States. She wants a sharp detachment between herself and the things she witnesses on stage. Performances that suggest a similarity or kinship between her safe position in the audience and the movements of the things presented on stage as objects of aesthetic approval do not conform to the aesthetic sense of Anne Grey or of Helga Crane.

Practices like jazz call for some participation from their audience and in this way are unlike the objects that Helga prefers. Helga's rejection of jazz also stems from her rejection of the past, a rejection determined by her and Anne's approach to the world as if were an array of discrete objects from which they can freely choose.[49] For them, the past is one more of these objects, and one whose rejection is crucial to their life in Harlem: "But when mental doors were deliberately shut on those skeletons that stalked lively and in full health through the consciousness of every person of Negro ancestry in America . . . life was intensely amusing, interesting, absorbing and enjoyable" (96). The painful unpleasantries of Anne and Helga's racial and familial histories make the past an object unsuited to the tasteful arrangement of their lives. The two of them have fixed their conceptions of themselves to an aesthetic detachment from the world and from the past.[50] In doing so they mark their participation in the ideology of uplift, for uplift maps a path toward a fortuitous future accessible only through repudiation of the past.

The ideology of uplift uses that most American of mythemes, "the evolutionary idea of progress" (74), to attempt to secure for African Americans participation in a common humanity. Insofar as Helga participates in this attempt, she attempts to forge for herself a secure present built over a past rendered inert rather than an elusive present built out of the inevitable contamination of the present by the past and the future. Once she has decided in favor of progress and its secure present, her unwillingness to countenance jazz is already determined. The vertiginous pleasure that Helga finds in jazz is a mark of the music's ironic mocking of progress and its mobilization of the heterogeneous present. Jazz does not ignore the stalking "skeletons" of the past but puts them into motion, staging a confrontation with the past that Helga wants to avoid at all costs.[51] The rhythm that Helga finds herself moving to in the cabaret threatens to unsettle both her temporal appeasement of the demands of the past and the passivity of her aesthetic sense. The music holds out the possibility of an alternative configuration of time and of the present; Helga, unwilling to give up the protective sense of herself as a discerning and detached consumer, removes this alternative from the realm of possibility by throwing the cloak of primitivism over it. By making it into "jungle music," Helga mentally transforms the music from an alternative performance of the present to the survival of a primitive and uncivilized past.

This kind of conceptual operation is a constant and pernicious companion of evolutionary ideas of progress. Progress figures the motion of time as a movement forward through space, a tenuous metaphorization in need of tangible support.[52] Progress almost always shores itself up by figuring some present element as a past against which to define itself. It makes for itself a tangible past against which to mark its movement into the future by designating something other than itself as a present past.[53] The exclusionary nature of this conceptual operation is readily apparent. It is a form of temporal othering that discourages full participation or understanding by presupposing the limited relevance of an already surpassed practice or people to the needs of those on the royal road of progress. Primitivism and progress embrace each other in confirming American society's image of itself and in excluding elements that might force a revision of this image. In Helga's expedient labeling of jazz as "jungle music," she partakes of the primary strategy by which American society has attempted to preclude the possibility of shaping itself according to the temporality sounding in jazz.

Although Helga seems reassured by her consignment of jazz to a jungle past, there is a cruel irony in Helga's position. She embraces an exclusionary movement that excludes her and her past. (The fact that Helga has to hide her past from Anne Grey is a symptom of this.) When Helga directs the terms of primitivist discourse at jazz, she strengthens the force of this discourse, which is, ultimately, a discourse aimed at establishing invidious distinctions between white people and people who share her phenotypical markings.

In her haste to reestablish the security and balance disturbed by the music, Helga seizes the most readily available distancing mechanism, which turns out to be the progressive and exclusionary discourse aimed at disqualifying blackness from participation in civilized society.

Moreover, in addition to setting herself apart from demeaning stereotypes, Helga Crane sets herself apart from the large mass of black individuals whose actions and entertainments don't conform to her aesthetic taste. Throughout the text, Helga Crane is constantly oppressed by "the feeling of smallness which hedge[s] her in" (46). A major contributor to this sense of constricted possibilities is the way in which she walls herself off from the lower classes and from the past.[54] Facing the dense thicket of prescriptions and expectations that the white world imposes on the black world, Helga Crane responds through a defense mechanism that further increases the smallness of her field of action.

In Helga Crane's response to jazz, Nella Larsen gives us a condensation of the agon that is constantly restaged throughout *Quicksand*. Helga Crane only encounters jazz music once, but in this encounter she comes into the most intense proximity to a possibility present throughout the text. The jazz at the cabaret affects Helga so powerfully because in its presence she is face to face with both the past she denies and the class she distances herself from. In addition, the space created by the music's rhythmic shaping of sound presents Helga with the most promising scene for staging a performance of herself as a complexly desiring and powerfully embodied subject.

The text moves Helga through and around a consistently forestalled encounter with those elements of herself that she attempts to evade in her aversion to the past and to the black working class. This movement is a repetitive dance, the gravitational center of which is an African American performance tradition that restages the presence of the past in order to enable a revalorization of the (black) body and an elusive but puissant rhythmic coordination of the past and the future.

This is the possibility occluded by Helga's class bias and the denigration of the past that it enforces. In a passage early in the novel, Helga expresses her awareness of this possibility and its suppression by the forces of uplift. In her reflection on those "manifestations of race" excised by the ruthless machinery of Naxos, she gives primacy to "joy of rhythmic motion" along with "love of color" and "naive, spontaneous laughter" (18). This lament over the suppression of rhythm anticipates Helga's later experience in the cabaret and suggests the extent to which her disavowal of jazz puts her at odds with her own deeply held beliefs.

Additionally, after having fled jazz and left its Harlem environs for distant Copenhagen, Helga Crane experiences her first twinge of regret at having left

America when she realizes that she misses dancing: "At first, she had missed, a little, dancing" (77). Before learning of Anne Grey's engagement to Robert Anderson and before her response to the fragments of spirituals in Dvořák's New World Symphony, Helga feels the pull of the past and of racial identification in her longing for the movements that she had labeled as the acts of a "jungle creature."[55]

This longing for dancing is of a piece with Helga's comments on a racial "joy of rhythmic motion" and with the yearning for "sophisticated, tuneless music" expressed on the novel's final page. From the beginning to the end of *Quicksand*, the possibilities most powerfully experienced in the cabaret shadow Helga, sounding a faint background rhythm to her struggle for self-definition.

Watching the Minstrels

Helga's nostalgia for dancing is eventually buried in the flood of jewelry, clothes, and adulation that characterizes her life in Copenhagen, but another manifestation of the "Negro's joy of rhythmic motion" soon presents itself. This manifestation takes the form of the "two American Negroes" who appear on the stage of the Circus, Copenhagen's vaudeville house. Helga has gone to the vaudeville house with a number of white Danes; at the end of the evening's performance, she and her companions witness the two performers singing and dancing.

The performers are remnants of the minstrel tradition; they perform old ragtime songs and throw their bodies around with an exuberant abandon that thrills the Danes but leaves Helga nonplussed.[56] Her response to the minstrels is deeply ambivalent. On the one hand, when the Danes eagerly drink this performance up, she comes to the awareness that she too is performing a version of blackness on the Danish stage. As she watches the minstrels perform, Helga is ashamed that she shares their status: entertaining and exotic versions of uncivilized abandon for a group of people who feel themselves to be overcivilized. On the other hand, Helga knows these songs from her past, and on some level she knows that no matter how much the two performers pander to racist expectations, there is still a part of their performance with a real link to important African American practices of singing and dancing. It may be hackneyed and may give too much of itself to racial expectations, but the minstrels' performance still has a kinship with the more sophisticated jazz of Harlem.

The recognition and admiration that the Danes bestow on the two performers at the Circus are heavily attenuated and of questionable worth—based as they are on primitivist assumptions and racialized projections—but they inspire in Helga a sharp reevaluation of herself.

In a critical appraisal of herself and her aesthetic sense, Helga returns to her

critique of the hypocritical values implicit in Anne Grey's version of racial uplift. Helga contrasts the Danes' admiration with the disdain that Anne Grey
and her entire class have for African American cultural expression. She suspects
that the Dane's recognize something, in no matter how distorted a form, that
she and other middle-class African Americans ("the enlightened, the intelligent
ones" [83]) had missed.

Helga is deeply affected by what the two black performers at the Circus have
set in motion inside her. She returns "again and again" to the Circus, each time
alone and each time silently and ironically dwelling on the performance's significance.[57] Part of what draws Helga back is the familiarity of the songs the two
black men sing. Helga knows these songs from her childhood, and in her reflection on her disdain for African American expression she comes to see that she
has cut herself off from her past as well as from the vibrant present fashioned
by jazz and other contemporary forms. She is both drawn to and repulsed by
these performances; her deep ambivalence is the result of her struggle with the
contradictory claims of the past. Helga rebukes herself for her repudiation of
the past, but both her aesthetic sense and the primitivising mindset that determines the reception (and production) of the ragtime songs she listens to make
her recognition of any part of herself in these songs deeply problematic to say
the least. Helga does not embrace the minstrel's performance, but it has (re)
awakened in her an awareness of the value of the past and sharpened her discontent with the middle-class aesthetics she shares with Anne Grey.

The importance of this scene and the way that it persistently haunts Helga
Crane is reinforced by the fact that her solitary return to the Circus is one of
the few scenes in *Quicksand* that makes use of the iterative. Helga Crane's silent spectatorship is given to the reader as a repeated event that continues ("it
was at this time" [84]) throughout the rest of her time in Copenhagen. During
the same period in which Helga learns of Anne Grey's engagement to Robert
Anderson and goes to a performance of Dvořák's New World Symphony, she is
constantly returning to hear the ragtime songs performed, dwelling on her relationship to her past and the ideological barriers blocking productive access to it.

It is in this meditative mindset that Helga finally decides to return to America.
After hearing the "wailing undertones of 'Swing Low, Sweet Chariot,'" in a
performance of Dvořák's New World Symphony, Helga tells herself that she is
"homesick, not for America, but for Negroes" (92). Larsen's description makes
it clear that this realization is an acknowledgment of what she has already been
feeling: the music "cut[s] away her weakening defenses" and allows her to see
"what it was that had lurked formless and undesignated these many weeks in
the back of her troubled mind" (92). What is described here is the way in which
Dvořák's symphony provides Helga with a suitable object onto which she can

cathect her earlier reflections. The respectability of the symphony and its treatment of African American musical material allows Helga to arrive at a concrete formulation of the feelings and attitudes aroused in her by her repeated exposure to the ragtime songs at the Circus.[58] Between the admired but disreputable ragtime songs and the more dignified form of the symphony, Helga makes a circuit that allows her to articulate, for the first time in the novel, an unreservedly positive identification with her father and with her father's race.

She forgives her father for his flight and comes to understand and even adopt "his yearning, his intolerable need for the inexhaustible humor and incessant hope of his own kind, his need for those things, not material, indigenous to all Negro environments" (92). In Helga's declaration of identification with her father and of desire for the company of "Negroes," there is a doubleness that indicates the entanglement of the Dvořák performance with that of the ragtime songs. What Helga misses are "the incessant hope" and "inexhaustible humor" of "Negro environments"; if the first of these sounds in Dvořák's utilization of an African American spiritual, the second of these most definitely does not and can only have been heard in the ragtime songs to which Helga repeatedly returns.

There is a strangely asymmetrical and subterranean communication between the performance of the minstrels and the performance of Dvořák.[59] The minstrels sing a song composed by a white Canadian in a manner that utilizes the resources of an African American performance tradition; in the New World Symphony, Helga hears a truncated version of an African American spiritual, transposed into the form of the symphony by a Czech composer and played by a symphony trained in a performance style having little in common with that of the spirituals.

Irony and Performance

All the music presented in *Quicksand* sounds itself under the cover of masks. Jazz music appears under the sign of the jungle, Dvořák's symphony appears as the performance of the "irresistible claims of race," and the performance of the only two African American musicians visible in the text appears wearing the mask of minstrelsy. To negotiate such a complex play of appearance and performance, a sharp sense of irony is necessary. Irony is Helga Crane's most consistent attribute; her consistently ironic stance is what makes her so sharply attuned to the presence of hypocrisy and serves to keep her detached from too close of an identification with any position. This irony fails only when Helga talks herself into belief in God and marriage to the Reverend Pleasant Green. The brutal consequences of this failure—Helga's transformation into an incarcerated womb—make clear how valuable Helga's irony is to her. Without it she is vulnerable to conscription into the various unsavory roles available to African American women in the cultural landscape that Larsen diagnoses. At the same time, the detachment resulting from her irony, and its complicity with her aesthetic sense, keeps her from participating in performances like those enacted in the cabaret.

A strategy keeping her from being submerged by unpalatable identifications, Helga's irony enforces a detachment so severe that it threatens to entomb her in absolute insularity. It is this form of irony that enforces her detachment at the cabaret and that fuels the racial antipathy that drives her from Harlem. Standing on the deck of the liner bound for Denmark, Helga savors the freedom that her ironic detachment has won for her, reveling in "that blessed sense of belonging to herself alone and not to a race" (64).

The two poles between which Helga must chart her course are either submersion in a collective identity deaf to her desires or a painfully desolate and asocial isolation. The irony that Helga depends on protects her from the dangers of the former, but it allows her no mode of engagement that would stave off the latter. Helga's ironic mode is one that mocks, but one that doesn't allow her to mock and participate in what is mocked at the same time. What Helga is lacking is a participatory mode of irony, a mode of irony enabling participation without the kind of unreserved commitment that characterizes her disastrous marriage to Pleasant Green. Helga comes closest to voicing her desire for this form of engagement with the world in her musings on the possibility of dividing her life between Copenhagen and New York. As she prepares to leave Copenhagen, she asks: "Why couldn't she have two lives . . . ?" (93). And back in New York, Helga comes to feel fully aware of "the division of her life into two parts in two lands, into physical freedom in Europe and spiritual freedom in America" (96). She mocks an image of herself "moving shuttle-like from continent to continent," but her desire to claim as her proper home not one but two places expresses a very real need. In laying claim to two homes, Helga gives herself the ability to feel both at home in and apart from the social milieus of Harlem and Copenhagen. Her expression of self-division is an ironic doubling of the self aimed at achieving a sense of being both in any given situation and apart from it at the same time.[60] In her musings on the possibility of living two lives, Helga gives voice to what Duke Ellington considers to be the musical core of African American existence. Pointing an interviewer's ears to a chord in one of his compositions, Ellington characterized its significance as follows: "That's us. Dissonance is our way of life in America. We are something apart, yet an integral part" ("Interview" 150). In his music Ellington presents the sonic equivalent of what Helga can only think of as spatial division, an ironic and dissonant play with possibilities productive of a space that is not external to society's oppressive categories but within which one can improvise a self and a rhythm not subsumed by these categories.[61] Ellington is important here, not only because he is a figure for the possibilities of rhythmic and ironic self-shaping present throughout *Quicksand* but because his music is part of the historical field of possibilities that make up the warp and woof of the text. Ellington was the foremost practitioner of "jungle music," as well as the performer most actively engaged in circumventing the limitations that the label "jungle" and other primitivist characterizations placed on cultural expression. In contrast to other performers of the 1920s such as Louis Armstrong or Bessie Smith, Ellington consistently presented himself and his music as primarily "sophisticated," partially in order to short-circuit the primitivising assumptions governing the reception of African American art.[62]

Like Helga Crane and Nella Larsen, Ellington was intensely aware of the trap that primitivism and stereotypes derived from minstrelsy constituted. In his sartorial elegance, love of sophistication, and well-developed sense of irony Ellington shares some of Helga Crane's strategies for avoiding this trap, but in his performance practice he employs irony in a much different and ultimately much more successful manner.[63] Ellington's aesthetic sense is much more like Nella Larsen's than it is like Helga Crane's. Unlike Helga Crane, Ellington does not flee the label "jungle" by retreating into an ultimately self-defeating middle-class taste. Instead, he works the label for all its worth, ultimately transforming it into a marker of sophistication rather than of the crudely primitive.[64] In his utilization of "jungle music" to achieve an unrivaled musical excellence, Ellington took a real risk, a risk parallel to the one Nella Larsen undertakes in investing her protagonist with an intense relationship to her own desire.[65]

Both Larsen and Ellington take the risk that Helga avoids, entering into the ring with primitivising stereotypes in an attempt to undercut or attenuate their power. While Helga practices an isolating irony that strives to obtain security through detachment, Ellington and Larsen militate for a participatory irony, a dissonant participation that avoids the sterile self-possession to which Helga feels drawn. Helga is never able to fully embrace this kind of participatory irony, but it is a possibility that constantly haunts her. Her reflection on geographical self-division is one marker of this, but its most powerful presentation is in the cabaret scene. As we have seen, Helga's immersion in the music in the club sets aside her isolation and racial antipathy, but the unsettling power of the music is ultimately too much for her. She feels almost possessed by it rather than empowered. With no guide to follow, Helga is lost in its rhythmic power, but after she removes herself from the music, she witnesses another way of participating in it. After an argument with Anne Grey over the propriety of interracial dancing (and interracial relationships), Helga shifts her attention to the movements of Audrey Denney. Audrey Denney serves as a kind of alter ego for Helga Crane, as a bête noir for Anne Grey and her narrow conception of racial propriety, and is the source of Anne and Helga's argument. Audrey Denny rises to dance as if on cue, as if her dance gives a rhythmic shape to the refutation of Anne Grey that Helga would like to give.

In its nonchalance and assurance, Audrey Denney's dancing is distinct from the frenzy that seems to have seized Helga: "Her long, slender body swayed with an eager pulsing motion. She danced with grace and abandon, gravely, yet with obvious pleasure, her legs, her hips, her back, all swaying gently, swung by that wild music from the heart of the jungle" (62). In her movements Audrey Denney enacts a stance that Helga finds intensely appealing. Audrey responds to the music but does not let it dominate her. Helga's response to the music had been almost entirely passive; she had been "lifted, drugged, sustained . . . beaten out, ripped out, blown out." In contrast, Larsen's careful description of Audrey Denney's dancing gives us a mixture of activity and passivity, detachment, and engagement: her body sways to the music, but she is in control of the dance, a division evident in the description's grammatical construction. "She" is the active subject of the dancing, while the different parts of her body are passively "swung" by the music. She is both in the music and floating on top of it, simultaneously giving herself to the music and "gravely" holding part of herself back.[66] Audrey Denney is a terpsichorean version of the double-voiced imperative sounding in Ellington's music.

The significance of the difference between Helga Crane's and Audrey Denney's reactions to the music are illuminated by a comment that Albert Murray makes on the conduct of "blues-idiom merriment." He writes: "As downright aphrodisiac as blues music so often becomes, however, and as notorious for violence as the reputation of blues-oriented dance hall records has been over the years, blues-idiom merriment is not marked either by the sensual abandon of the voodoo orgy or by the ecstatic trance of religious possession. One of its most distinctive features, conversely, is its unique combination of spontaneity, improvisation, and control" (*Stomping the Blues* 50).[67]

Murray's comment shows us that Helga's experience of the music as "sensual abandon" is nonidiomatic and doesn't allow her access to the "unique combination of spontaneity, improvisation and control" at the heart of the music. It is Audrey Denney whose moves are most in tune with the music, and it is she who exhibits the "nonchalance" that Murray sees as the characteristic stance of both jazz drummers and the dancers most responsive to them.[68] When Helga sees Audrey Denney dancing, she sees a participation in the music both like and unlike her own. Audrey Denney indulges her "joy in rhythmic motion" without appearing as "a jungle creature." The significance of this is more than terpsichorean; both Murray and Ellington read kinetic alignment with the music as participation in its modes of organizing experience and staging identity. The extramusical significance of Audrey Denney's relationship to the music is also attested to by Larsen. Her description of Audrey Denney's movements is coupled with Helga Crane's amazement at Denney's "assurance [and] . . . courage . . . to so placidly ignore racial barriers" (62). Helga's gaze at Audrey Denney combines admiration for her physical movements with an envy of her ability to negotiate boundaries and expectations with the same grace and gravity with which she negotiates the dance floor.

Part of Audrey Denney's dance-like social "grace" is suggested by the fact that she dances with white men and with Robert Anderson, a figure whose troubling appeal haunts Helga throughout the novel. Audrey Denny is able to handle both cross-racial relationships and figures like Robert Anderson because she engages them without surrendering herself to them. Following the ironic imperatives of "jungle music," Audrey Denney participates in the world while managing to evade its attempts to fix her in reifying definitions. She does not end up married to Robert Anderson, but the possibility of her having some form of relationship with him is strongly suggested by the text.

The significance of this lies in the way it demonstrates the temporal stance exemplified in Audrey Denney. Partaking of what James de Jongh calls the "flexible sexual morality of the cabarets," (24) Denney exhibits an ability to interact with Anderson without totally giving herself to him. This is a temporal stance because it evinces an ability to give oneself to the moment without sacrificing the future. Unlike Helga, Audrey eschews the claims of absolute stability and adamantine permanence as well as the "consolation of possession" (Monda 31). Translating the combination of "spontaneity, improvisation, and control" evident in her dancing into the social realm, Audrey Denney gives herself the power to try things out, to engage in activities without letting them define her. It is for want of precisely this power that Helga consigns herself to her worst fate. Unwilling to imagine her fling with Pleasant Green as part of an ongoing but dissonant rhythm, Helga decides in favor of permanence and transforms herself into a subservient member of the Reverend Green's flock, defined entirely by her role as preacher's wife.

When Helga chooses marriage and permanence (and God), her irony vanishes (122). Throughout the text, Helga has constantly wavered between the poles of ironic detachment and committed participation, and this choice is a slightly more severe swing of the same pendulum. Helga is never able to combine irony and participation in a rhythm other than a ragged flight from one to the other. The closest she comes to achieving such a combination is in the cabaret. In her reaction to the jazz performed there and in her fascination with Audrey Denney, Helga is in tantalizing proximity to a temporal arrangement that gives the best chance for transforming the powerful contradictions of her social existence into productive tensions. A dynamic alternative to her static and isolating form of irony, this is the participatory irony characterizing the musical operations Ellington conducted under cover of the term "jungle" and reflective of the most advanced conception of social interaction to be found on the American scene.

In the jazz at the cabaret and in the way that Audrey Denney dances to it, Helga is confronted with both a powerful alternative to her detached and skeptical irony and a mode of acknowledging the past without proclaiming fealty to it. Audrey Denney's ability to blithely ignore racial boundaries admits the possibility of the past that Helga has to deny in order to retain her skeptical detachment and to remain a part of proper Harlem society. Helga's access to the past is blocked by the impossibility of imagining her mixed parentage as anything more than a source of shame, but in Audrey Denney's movement across the racial boundaries that mark the borders of Helga's social world the past is opened up in ways that Helga finds both appealing and troubling.

Ellington's Jungle

The link between the performance of participatory irony and the possibility of a productive traffic with the past are even more pronounced in the music. Ellington's employment of participatory irony is what allows him to work under the rubric of "the jungle" without allowing it to circumscribe the music or its development, but even more remarkable is the way he uses the label and its primitivist overtones as an excuse to work out his music's relationship to the past and to revise the significance of tradition. Here is how Ellington characterizes his music's relationship to the jungle label: "During one period at the Cotton Club, much attention was paid to acts with an African setting, and to accompany these we developed what was termed 'jungle style' jazz. (As a student of Negro history, I had, in any case, a natural inclination in this direction.)" (*Music* 419–20). Ellington makes a passing reference to the specious nature of the term "jungle," but his interest lies more in how he was able to use the label to pursue his "inclination" to make "Negro history" the very substance of his music. In his music Ellington cunningly maps what he knows he can make signify as "jungle" onto a key element of the African American musical tradition, namely, its tendency toward timbral heterogeneity.[69] Ellington again: jungle music's "most striking characteristic was the use of mutes—often the plumber's everyday rubber plunger—by Bubber Miley on trumpet and Joe 'Tricky Sam'

Nanton on trombone. They founded a tradition we have maintained ever since. This kind of theatrical experience, and the demands it made upon us, was both educative and enriching, and it brought about a further broadening of the music's scope" (*Music* 320–22). The element that the Ellington band used to form their jungle style was the tradition of "growling" or "gutbucket" brass playing most prevalent among New Orleans musicians and most forcefully articulated in the playing of Louis Armstrong's mentor, Joe "King" Oliver. In this tradition the trumpet or trombone is played in a style that bends the instrument's timbral possibilities far away from the clear bell-like tones characteristic of their playing by non-jazz performers. Using mutes and other techniques that increase resistance to the flow of air through their horns, performers like Joe Oliver and Tricky Sam Nanton strove to make their sound display its affinity with the stylings of the African American vocal tradition. Part cry of disarticulated pain[70], part mockery of social impediment, the extravagant timbral concatenation of the brass in Ellington's band hollers, whinnies, and shouts in ways that evade any stable boundary between the past and the present.[71]

Bubber Miley and Tricky Sam Nanton bend and disfigure tones and melodies in a way that ironizes the rational structure and assumed mind-body distinctions congealed in the Western harmonic system.[72] Ellington's compositional genius lies in the way that he created a musical space that allows for these timbral possibilities and incorporates them into his "jungle sound." Here, Ellington's career and the sonic structures of his music mirror each other: Ellington's growling jungle brass play upon musical expectations in the same way that Ellington bends the primitivist denigrations of the "jungle" label into a license for a stylistic exploration and reshaping of traditional African American musical practices. Both strategies diverge from the imperatives of outward adversity by productively ironizing them rather than overtly rejecting them.[73]

In Ellington's words this music reaches back into the past and "founds" a tradition by repeating and revising an existing tradition. The growling brass of Ellington's "jungle style" displays the complex valence of the past in the temporal strategies of the music. Like Audrey Denney's dancing body, the sound of Nanton's and Miley's horns are swung by the tradition out of which they emerge, but they swing in a style that is all their own. Gathering the past into its own sonic identity, their sound works over and plays upon the persistence of the past in its insistence on the richness of the present and in its insuperable sliding away from itself. This is a performance practice that exemplifies a notion of tradition as a spur to elaboration, a repetition of the past in all its contradictory incompleteness that calls for improvisation and innovation rather than obedience.

Ellington's description of Tricky Sam Nanton's style attests to the complexity of this form of tradition: "What [Tricky] was actually doing was playing a very highly personalized form of his West Indian heritage. When a guy comes here from the West Indies and is asked to play some jazz, he plays what he thinks it is, or what comes from his applying himself to the idiom" (*Music* 108–9). The subtlety of the interplay Ellington establishes in this passage between the terms "heritage" and "idiom" is highly suggestive. According to Ellington, Nanton plays a form of his heritage more by the oblique manner of his approach to the jazz idiom than by any recourse to concrete practices from his own past. It is, thus, an ironic, rather than a reverential, approach to the music and to the past that marks one as a proper part of it. What Nanton brings to the music is a mode of divergence, a mode of ironic play, rather than any quantifiable collection of melodic or rhythmic phrases.[74]

The interplay between inside and outside characteristic of participatory irony and Ellingtonian dissonance is on display here. Nanton plays himself into the jazz tradition by playing productively upon different trajectories from the past. Yoking his ethnic "heritage" to his musical "idiom," he forges a style crucial to Ellington's performative irony and to the critical musical reflection upon African American history sounded in Ellington's music. He does so by bending what he receives from the past into a highly personal and unprecedented sound signature. The jungle sound emerges out of his ironizing of the past, his situating himself within the contradictory musical and social expectations that attempt to define him.

Nanton's and Ellington's performance of tradition depends upon the way in which jazz's repetitive temporality fosters a relationship of the individual to the collective and to the past that has to bend dominant constructions of time to make any sense. Ellington's "jungle music" performs a repetitive restaging of the past that disorients the present as a stable entity detachable from the past and the future, reorienting it toward its own repetition as an elusive mixture of past, present, and future. Rendered dissonant in this way, the present becomes a platform for an ironizing of the self that lives dissonance as a way of life. This is the goal of Ellington's ironic play with the term "jungle" and with the tradition of African American sound production. Ellington uses the label "jungle" to license a plunge into the past of black performance that founds a new tradition by repeating an old one, in the process expanding the tonal palette of his orchestra and the range of possible African American subject positions.

Ellington's description of the genesis and vicissitudes of the jungle style, both in the signifying effects of his recordings and in his autobiography, alerts us to the significance and complexity of what Helga reacts to when she reacts to the music in the cabaret. Nanton's and Ellington's aesthetic strategies speak powerfully to Helga because their creation of a rhythmic space out of received expectations is their way of circumventing the kind of racist impediments that confront Helga. Like Helga, Nanton and Ellington know how easy it is to be labeled as jungle creatures. They are sharply aware of the dissonance between the sounds of the African American musical tradition and the dominant (mis) hearing of these sounds. They know what counts as "jungle music," but, more importantly, they know the slim boundary between the facile misunderstanding implicit in the "jungle" label and an important element of the African American musical tradition. Their response is the one that any recognition of "dissonance [as a] way of life" is bound to engender: irony. Not an irony that holds itself apart from actual conditions, but an irony that plunges into the dissonant contradictions of these conditions in order to realize the real, but far from unlimited, possibilities within them.

The possibility of adopting such a mode of irony is what makes the cabaret scene such a crucial one. In her construction of this scene, Larsen places Helga Crane in intimate proximity to a mode of irony adequate to the debilitating impediments she faces. Helga chooses to reject this mode of irony, and her flight from the cabaret is narratively figured as a decision in favor of self-possession over participatory irony, of Denmark over Harlem. For Helga, Denmark is a land characterized by "formal calm" and an unironic preference for "security and stability" (92). Helga's geographical removal is an attempt to maintain her mode of ironic detachment from the world, but she quickly finds that the Danes are just as determined to see her as a jungle creature as are the Americans. She soon realizes that the only place for her in Danish society is as an exotic figure on display, a rare item that her aunt and uncle can use to increase their prestige. A prefiguration of her unsatisfactory existence in Alabama, Helga's time in Denmark marks the impossibility of her finding a place for herself unscored by primitivising racial assumptions. Larsen suggests that there is no pure place from which Helga can stage herself. She is always preceded by limiting discourses of race and gender, and in the absence of any untroubled platform for self-fashioning, the paramount importance of Ellingtonian irony is made emphatically clear. Since there is no unracialized space from which Helga can dismiss the expectations that limit her, her only choice is to engage these racialized expectations and make a dissonant music out of them. This is the possibility she sees in Audrey Denney, that she hears in jazz, and without which she is rendered virtually powerless.

Inexhaustible Humor and Incessant Hope

In Denmark, Naxos, and Alabama, Helga is confronted by discourses that radically circumscribe her possibilities, but in each location she hears traces of the cabaret music's ironic restructuring of these discourses. In Copenhagen her contentment with Danish "stability and security" is troubled by her memory of dancing, her experience with the American minstrels, and the fragments of "Swing Low, Sweet Chariot" she hears in Dvořák. The last of these leads her to reflect on her father.

In "The Aesthetics of Race and Gender in Nella Larsen's *Quicksand*" Ann Hostetler asserts that Helga's father is a "black jazz musician" (35). Although there is no textual evidence for this claim, I believe that Hostetler is essentially, if not literally, correct.[75] In *Quicksand* Helga's father serves primarily as a figure of a past that Helga cannot bring herself to contemplate and secondarily as the focus of her racial identification. Helga's relationship to her father marks one of the most troubling aspects of Helga's past: her father's abandonment of Helga and her mother marks the problematic nature of any simple embrace of the past or of racial identity. Larsen uses Helga's relationship to her father to suggest the painfully contradictory nature of the racial past available to African Americans and the sophisticated social rituals worked out by people like her father to make this past both bearable and productive.

There is thus a homology between Helga's troubled relationship to Ellingtonian irony and her troubled relationship to her father. When Helga decides to return to Harlem, Larsen makes this homology apparent: Helga tells herself that she is "homesick, not for America, but for Negroes," and at this moment she feels "sympathy rather than contempt and hatred for her father" for the first time in her life. The culmination of Helga's revelation is her ability to understand "his yearning, his intolerable need for the inexhaustible humor and the incessant hope of his own kind, his need for those things, not material, indigenous to all Negro environments" (92). At this moment, Helga feels the way in which Ellington's dissonant irony functions as a bulwark against isolation and as a guide through the minefield of American racial dynamics.

Thinking of her father as a jazz musician (and Nella Larsen's father shares Tricky Sam Nanton's West Indian background) allows us to see that Helga's strongly felt aversion to jazz is also her intense aversion to a past that is always described as deeply unsatisfactory, full of "torturing stabs" and "tragic cruelties" (49). It also highlights the fact that when Helga articulates her own racial identification, she articulates it in terms of repetitive social rituals. The permanence of the racialized "hope" and "laughter" is of a qualitatively different kind than the "security and stability" of Danish society. The hope and laughter that Helga sees as having an almost "sacred" nature derive their permanence from repetition; they are incessant and inexhaustible because they entail a recognition that nothing is ever permanently achieved and that a space for one's self and one's desire must be constantly re-created. Incessant hope and inexhaustible laughter have built into them a bias toward repetition that allows one to face a recurrence of the same obstacles and foes day after day.[76]

When Helga voices her identification with her father, she admits to herself the possibilities inhering in jazz performance as a performance of the self. Larsen gives us Helga's decision to return to Harlem as a decision in favor of Ellingtonian irony. Present in Helga's meditation upon her "homesick[ness] for Negroes" are all the elements of this form of irony: laughter, hope, rhythm, and repetition. In Helga's identification with her father, Larsen gives us the most explicit formulation of a positive path for Helga, a rhythmic shaping of the self that abandons commitment to security and stability in favor of a rhythm that both laughs at the absurd vectors determining present existence and actively hopes for a recombination of these dissonant vectors into a new and more productive combination. Larsen's formulation prefigures the definition of rhythm given by another devotee of Ellingtonian possibilities, Leopold Senghor. Helga identifies with her father's "need for those things, not material, indigenous to all Negro environments" (92), and Senghor tells us that the foremost of these things is rhythm: "It is the most perceptible and least material thing" (qtd. in Chernoff 23).

Senghor and Larsen redact the unique puissance of rhythm: it is forcefully present, but it is not a material thing. It is both an immanent component of musical and social forms, and something apart from these forms. It is not transcendent, but neither is it coterminous with those stable entities to which Helga is most often drawn. It moves through and around melodies, discourses, and all the determinants of musical and social existence in a way that is both inside and outside of these determinants. It cannot dismiss the power of these determinants in the way Helga often dreams of, but it can, like Helga's father, laugh mockingly at the presumed power of these determinants. The hope of such an ironic rhythm is not an unfounded yearning for a place beyond contradictions but an awareness of the "ceaseless" nature of these contradictions and of the way they can lead to unexpected places. Ellington's use of the "jungle" label is a case in point. His ironizing embrace of this label is informed by a knowledge of the primacy of rhythm and the tendency of rhythm to move beyond the given. Ellington writes: "Our very lives are dependent on rhythm, for everything we do is governed by ordered rhythmic sequences" ("Duke Steps Out" 46). In Ellington's world everything articulates itself rhythmically, and Larsen's novel is no exception. As Claudia Tate points out, there is an isomorphic relationship between the "repetitive pattern" engendered by Helga's desire and the "pattern of repetition, inherent in the novel's development" (250). Larsen makes repetition the structuring principle of her novel, embracing the kind of temporality that Helga can only temporarily countenance. Helga Crane might not partake of the ironizing repetition that restages the past's insuperable entanglement with the present, but the form of the novel that tells her tale does. *Quicksand* is a picaresque, structured according to Helga's movement from place to place rather than according to the progressive development of character associated with nineteenth-century novels.[77] In every place Larsen restages the central agon of the novel, the struggle with an ironic configuration of the self that is so powerfully present at the cabaret. The text moves Helga through and around a consistently forestalled encounter with those elements of herself that she attempts to evade in her aversion to the past. The repetitive nature of this movement is quickly apparent to the reader, even if Helga only realizes it in her final location. Helga comes to reflect on the repetitive pattern of her experience only in the final chapter of the novel ("it wasn't new" [134]), and her delinquency in coming to a realization that Larsen has already made clear to the reader implies a critique of Helga's position. This is a form of dramatic irony, a discrepancy between what the author allows the reader to know and what she allows the character to know. Larsen uses dramatic irony to put the reader face to face with the fact of repetition long before Helga Crane faces such an encounter. In doing so she illuminates the gap between Helga's restless dissatisfaction and the restless forward motion of the repetitive irony that she can't quite embrace.

One of the most salient features of this kind of irony is its resistance to locatability, and Larsen stays true to this unlocatibility by keeping it just out of Helga's grasp. Helga is drawn to it in the cabaret, in her decision to return to Harlem, and on the last pages of the novel, but she never fully adopts its rhythms as her own. Instead Larsen presents it to us as elliptically as Tricky Sam Nanton plays his way into the jazz tradition. That is, she works the conventions of dramatic irony in a way that plays upon the hinge between a hopeless acknowledgment of Helga's situation and a hopeful embrace of an escape from these situations.

Larsen's ironization of Helga's dismissal of jazz translates the performative resources of the music into literature. The importance of this move lies in the way that jazz condenses the maneuvers of a vast and multifarious social realm, including the entire range of intellectual and pragmatic practices implicit in forms of ironic participation and detachment. This is why the intersection of jazz and the novel that Larsen stages is worth the most careful of considerations. When jazz sounds in *Quicksand*, or any other novel, even in the most attenuated and fleeting form, what is entering into the novel are traces of a rival aesthetic and a rival form of cultural practice, in the broadest sense of these terms. Larsen's articulation of the novel with the aesthetic imperatives of jazz is a part of an intensified attempt by African Americans to found new aesthetic traditions capable of redefining their cultural identity and reforming the culture responsible for defining them as without real worth or significance.

This is how jazz sounds in *Quicksand*, as a productive mode of ironic accommodation to the past and as a form of temporal being cognizant of the constant making and remaking that shapes culture and identity. The coupling of Helga's proximity to this mode of existence with her repeated rejection of it gives a sense of both the possibilities encapsulated within Ellington's music and the dense array of barriers standing in the way of any realization of these possibilities.[78] Helga's middle-class and ultimately passive aesthetic sense leads her to repeatedly choose a form of rebarbative stability antithetical to the syncopated irony of jazz; the final result is Helga's virtual incarceration in marriage and her separation from death by only the slimmest of threads. In choosing the stability that has put her in this miserable situation, Helga has divorced herself from jazz's performance of a rival form of stability and from the allegiance to repetitive African American practices she adopts in her identification with her father.

And yet, even in her most abject conditions, this divorce is never total. Like the incessantly restaged combination of hope and laughter making up the rhythm of jazz, Helga's restless dissatisfaction is never permanently extinguished.[79] Although she initially submerges herself in the religion of rural Alabama, Helga's irony and dissatisfaction eventually reemerge. After the childbirth that almost kills her, Helga has nothing but disdain and revulsion for her husband and for his religion's belief in a recompense available only in another world. She mocks him and his small town, and she begins to dream of the future again. What reemerges is the combination of "inexhaustible humor and incessant hope" suppressed by Helga's choice of permanence and marriage. Helga dreams the "sweet silent music of change" again, but this time it takes a takes a slightly different form (57).

This time her construction of the future is no longer conditioned by a desire to totally discard the past and transcend the present. Realizing her complicity with the kind of "pie in the sky" mentality that she mocks in the residents of rural Alabama, Helga transforms the valence of the future in her imagination in accordance with the rhythmic truths of "jungle music" and her father's "incessant hope." Tempered by their proximity to Helga's denunciation of the futile belief in "pie in the sky . . . by and by" that characterizes the religion of Pleasant Green's small town, her dreams of the future are no longer the dreams of a stable, noncontradictory future that share so much with the religious attitude that she critiques. There is a slight shift in her ironic stance, an admission that the contradictions of this world have their charm and that they make legitimate, but not peremptory, claims on the self.

Her love of the sweet silent music of change is now linked to a tangible desire for "sophisticated, tuneless music" and for "the sweet mingled smell of Houbigant and cigarettes" (135). Helga's desire is not directed at a world beyond time, but neither is it directed at discrete commodities in the same way it previously had been. The objects she desires are not cigarettes and perfume but the most evanescent of their qualities, their scent. Throughout the novel things have served Helga as barriers against the motion of time and against the fleeting nature of pleasure, but here the juxtaposition of the most transitory of arts with the ephemeral shadow of objects shows that Helga's recognition of repetition and her reconfigured irony have at least partly altered her attachment to permanence.[80] This is not to say that Helga's dreams are entirely separable from the religious attitude of rural Alabama but only that the slimmest of differences is evident here. The extremely slender nature of this difference is matched by the perhaps even slimmer hope to which Helga clings. In a situation that offers no material basis for hope at all, Helga clings to her dream of "sophisticated, tuneless music" as a barrier against absolute despair.[81] While this music may or may not be jazz, Helga's use of it to keep alive the possibility of a better future without any justification from her surroundings and without the support of belief in a world beyond this one gives it some of the valence of the music she heard in the cabaret.

Helga's hope is clearly overblown, but as Fred Moten points out in *In the Break*, overblowing is part of the ensemble of techniques that jazz uses to produce its unique treatment of sound: "Maybe hope is always overblown, but the overblown produces an unprecedented sound, overtones of the heretofore unheard (of)" (83). In his production of a music and a form of irony neither naively hopeful nor cynically resigned, Ellington used the cover of the "jungle" to create a new musical vocabulary out of just such overblown effects. The sophisticated brilliance of what Ellington was able to create out of the quicksand of racial primitivism and the tonal manipulations of musicians like Tricky Sam Nanton suggests that hope cannot only be overblown but it can be other-blown, sounded in such a way that the impediments to its existence and realization become integral to its form. This kind of incorporation of impediments is the timbral equivalent to jazz's ironic embrace of contradictions, and it is the very method that Nanton and Williams used to create their contributions to Ellington's jungle style. They used mutes, tongues, and ridiculously pedestrian items like toilet plungers to block the free flow of air that produces a "proper" brass sound, and in doing so they created gripping and unprecedented tonal impurities.[82] Ellington's genius lies in his ability to make music out of impediments, and the achievement of Larsen's novel does something similar. *Quicksand* forges a repetitive novelistic form out of the barriers that stand in the way of Helga Crane's and Nella Larsen's self-articulation. Repeatedly restaging Helga's problematic relationship to the past and the future, it sounds the overwhelming impossibilities of Helga's situation and intimates the impossibly elusive path that leads through them.

Ralph Ellison once described America as a country "locked in a deadly struggle with time" (243). The period in which Stein, Larsen, Fitzgerald, and Johnson wrote was a period in which this struggle became most overt. In attempting to come to terms with both a newly urban and industrially employed populace and a newly mobile and self-assured African American population, American culture found that the traditional modes of waging this struggle no longer sufficed. Forced to accommodate new rhythms of work and play, America set about shaping for itself a new consciousness of time. These attempts ranged from narrow constructions of hopelessness and exclusion to rich attempts to conjugate egalitarian rhythms out of the imbrication of the past, the present, and the future. Every text considered in this study, musical or literary, is an attempt to work out some mode of waging the struggle with time and of negotiating the changing temporal landscape of American culture. While every novel and musical performance that I have read offers some hints at how to best wage this struggle, in their time and ours, it is those texts that most shape themselves according to jazz temporality that have contributed the most to a productive construction of time.

I chose to end with Larsen's *Quicksand* because the bleakness of her protagonist's end evokes the persistence and power of the barriers that stand in the way of letting the social and subjective structures implicit in jazz become real political and pragmatic possibilities. Helga Crane herself blocks this kind of realization through her aesthetic orientation toward commodities and consistent recourse to "the fantasy of self-containment" (Cornell 221); the fact that these two attitudes are pervasive in contemporary culture betrays the extent to which the encounter between jazz and mainstream American culture has yet to fully take place. The encounter with jazz in the 1910s and 1920s is not so much failed as it is incomplete. Incompleteness is, of course, the thing that Helga Crane admits to herself when she comes closest to consciously identifying herself with jazz temporality. It is an acknowledgment of incompleteness that gives jazz its distinct rhythmic impetus, and part of what my study argues is that not only does attention to the imbrication of this impetus with the shape of the American novel do much to restore the full resonance of the novels in question but that jazz's rhythmic treatment of incompleteness offers a compelling model for our study of the past and of the past's impact on the present.

The impossible return to an incomplete past is what should inform our understanding of the present, the past, and the movements that link the two. Every novel and every musical performance examined in this study suggest that without this kind of apprenticeship to the past, we are left without the resources necessary to coordinate the disparate rhythms of American existence. Repetitively working over the traces of the past within the present dispels any notion that the present can ever be anything but a loosely heterogeneous whole. In the absence of such a heterogeneous present, a deluded belief in the possibility of a secure, unmixed present inevitably finds support in the kinds of social hierarchies and modes of exclusion encountered by Helga Crane and still working to constrict the possibilities of her current day equivalents. The jazz impulse gives us a model for how discrepant rhythms can lead to compelling and capacious aesthetic and social formations; it makes music of the "deadly struggle with time" and attempts to forestall the impulse that would translate this struggle into an even deadlier struggle with difference.

Discography

Ten Recordings that Every Scholar of the Harlem Renaissance and of Modernism Should Know:

Louis Armstrong	"Hotter Than That"	(1927)	"Weather Bird"	(1928)
Bessie Smith	"Yellow Dog Blues"	(1925)	"Backwater Blues"	(1927)
Jelly Roll Morton	"Black Bottom Stomp"	(1926)		
Duke Ellington	"East St. Louis Toodle-oo"	(1928)	"Black and Tan Fantasy"	(1927)
James P. Johnson	"Keep Off the Grass"	(1921)	"Charleston"	(1925)
King Oliver	"Dippermouth Blues"	(1923)		

The following albums give a more complete picture of jazz in the 1920s and early 1930s:

Armstrong, Louis. *Portrait of the Artist as a Young Man, 1923–1934*. Sony, 1994 (4 Discs).
Bechet, Sidney. *Young Sidney Bechet: 1923–1925*. Timeless NL, 2005.
Dodds, Johnny. *Definitive Dodds, 1926–1927*. Retrieval Records, 2009.
Ellington, Duke. *The Okeh Ellington*. Sony, 1991 (2 Discs).
———. *The Original Decca Recordings*. Decca/GRP, 1994 (3 Discs).
Europe, James Reese. *James Reese Europe featuring Noble Sissle*. IAJRC, 1999.
Handy, W. C. *W. C. Handy's Memphis Blues Band*. Memphis Archives, 1994.
Hunter, Alberta. *Beale Street Blues (1921–1940)*. Magnum Music, 1996.
Johnson, James P. *Running Wild (1921–1926)*. Tradition, 1997.
Morton, Jelly Roll. *Birth of the Hot: Red Hot Peppers Session*. RCA, 1995.
———. *Jelly Roll Morton 1923/24*. Milestone, 1991.

Oliver, King. *Off the Record: The Complete 1923 Jazz Band Recordings*. Off the Record, 2007 (2 Discs).

Rainey, Ma. *The Best of Gertrude "Ma" Rainey*. Blues Forever, 2004.

Smith, Bessie. *The Essential Bessie Smith*. Sony, 1997 (2 Discs).

Whiteman, Paul. *Greatest Hits*. Collector's Choice, 1999.

Notes

Chapter 1

1. There are excellent works of literary criticism on the novels of the period in question, and there are excellent works on the jazz of the period. However, there really is no work devoted to discussing the formal workings of these novels in relationship to the formal workings of jazz performance. Articles treating the relationship between jazz and the novel, or containing insightful asides about this relationship, include Raussert, Mackey, "Sound and Sentiment" and "Other," and Gysin. There have been several works about jazz *in* the novel (the best is Cataliotti), but my argument is that the relationship *between* jazz and the novel is much broader than the presence of jazz *in* the novel.

Also, most critical and theoretical work on jazz, and on the relationship between jazz and the novel, focuses on the postwar period. Works that have insightful sections on the 1910s and 1920s include Gebhardt, Werner, and Grandt.

2. For descriptions of the social and historical context of jazz's emergence see Shipton, Jones, Floyd, *Power of Black Music*, and Perreti.

3. See Watt, McKeon.

4. The question of the degree of similarity between the extremely sophisticated, harmonically complex, and listener-oriented music of Miles Davis and the harmonically simpler, dance-oriented jazz of the 1920s and 1930s is not a simple one. Although both are clearly jazz, the cultural valence of the term "jazz" is quite different in the two different time periods.

5. One of the implications of my argument about the impact of jazz on American culture is that the 1910s and the 1930s are as much a part of a Jazz Age as are the 1920s. The restrictive reading of the Jazz Age is based mostly on Fitzgerald's character-

ization of the 1920s, a characterization that I critique in chapter 4. To the point here is Alain Locke's assertion that "the Negro, strictly speaking, never had a jazz age . . . he was born that way, as far as the general response went" (Locke, *Negro and his Music* 87).

6. Here I am working with Snead's assertion that "the terms 'European' and 'black' effectively exhaust the major manifestations of culture in contemporary America" (78n8). I adopt Snead's position as part of the methodological structure of my study, but clearly this position does a disservice to the cultural production of Asian Americans, Latinos, and others. The terms "European" and "black" do not "exhaust" the field of early twentieth-century American culture, but they do go far in delineating the dynamics I am interested in.

7. There are a couple of key moments in chapters 1, 2, and 4 where I turn to the work of Theodor Adorno. When I do so, it is *not* in order to find any theoretical tools capable of elucidating the form and function of jazz. Instead, I use Adorno as a resource for critiquing the society into which jazz emerges. Adorno is a relentless and insightful critic of the ways in which commodity thinking and narrowly circumscribed versions of rationality dominate Western culture. As such, his writings are a useful guide to some of the intellectual maneuvers that license and subtend racial subordination in the United States. Adorno's writings on jazz, however, fail to engage the music's real significance.

8. Here I rely on the analysis and terms of E. P. Thompson.

9. See Early, "Pulp and Circumstance."

10. "Jazz, to them, had simplistic melodies and syncopated rhythms characteristic of popular, and therefore inferior music. They did not conceive of it as an alternative aesthetic" (Ogren 155).

11. The best referent for what Johnson calls ragtime in his novel is the improvisatory stride style of James P. Johnson rather than the more formal notated music of Scott Joplin. See Brown and Fell and Vinding. Note that the word "jazz" did not come into widespread use until 1913, a year after *The Autobiography of an Ex-Colored Man* was first published. Before 1913 the term "ragtime" was used to refer to almost all improvised African American music. Many musicians (particularly Sidney Bechet) never adopted the term "jazz" and referred to everything we now think of as jazz as "ragtime." While we tend to think of the two terms as designating distinctly different forms of music, this was not the case in the period in which Johnson and Fitzgerald wrote.

12. No greater crime exists in jazz performance than dropping the beat; Miles Davis kicked his own nephew out of his band for violating this rhythmic law (Davis and Troupe 377–84).

13. See Stuckey, for an account of these forms of sociality. Particularly relevant to my study is his account of the ring-shout, a precursor to jazz.

14. According to Raussert, jazz rhythm "embodies an accommodation to Western time in its progressive element, while it also counteracts it through rhythmic flexibility and its aesthetic emphasis on movement" (533).

15. This rather broad generalization of an incredibly diverse genre aims at laying out, in broad strokes, the difference in temporal emphasis between the novel and jazz. The novel does many things, but it is still important to outline the major temporal im-

petus of the novel's form. This impetus is something that many, if not all, of the most interesting novels struggle against, especially in the twentieth century. Uncovering the way they do this is one of the main goals of this work.

16. Compare this to Bechet's characterization of jazz: "But that's what the music is . . . a lost thing finding itself." (48).

17. Odysseus is a Gatsby who believes in "the green light, the orgastic future that year by year recedes before us" (Fitzgerald, *Gatsby* 89). See chapter 4.

18. "Repetition is a characteristic of what has been reduced to the animal plane" (Adorno, *Quasi una Fantasia 175)*.

19. These reflections on the form of the novel are more fully worked out in chapter 2, where I link Adorno and Horkheimer's propositions to the work of Georg Lukács and Paul de Man.

20. Snead points out the dependence of this (mis)representation on the suppression of repetition, for the conclusion of his essay posits that the emergence of repetition leads to a realization that "the separation between the cultures was perhaps all along not one of nature, but one of force" (75).

21. In 1912 H. E. Krehbiel, the music editor of the *New York Tribune*, criticized Europe's performance at Carnegie Hall for being "inauthentic." See Badger 73–74.

22. Hammond insisted that Ellington and his music had lost touch with "the troubles of his people" and that his orchestra suffered from the presence in it of "slick, un-negroid musicians" (120).

23. Arthur A. Schomburg states that "the American Negro must remake his past in order to remake his future" (qtd. in Early 413).

24. For more on James P. Johnson and "ragged time," see chapter 3.

25. Schoenberg's rigid and complex twelve-tone method led to a situation in which injunctions against repetition (no note in the twelve-tone row or scale could be repeated before all had been sounded) required that all aspects of a composition be derived from the same conceptual schema. In creating a system that allowed him to break away from the hackneyed conventions of the classical tradition, Schoenberg excised all possibilities of free expression from music. See Adorno, *Philosophy of Modern Music*. In this work, Adorno sees jazz and Schoenberg as responding to the same twentieth-century temporal predicament: "Late Schoenberg shares with jazz—and moreover with Stravinsky—the dissociation of time" (60). The complexity of jazz's treatment of repetition and form outdo Schoenberg in their ability to productively couple innovation, repetition, and expression.

26. See Anne Shaw Faulkner (August 1921) in Walser, *Keeping Time* 32–36.

27. This is not to say that Koussevitsky's (or Roger's) praise for jazz, despite its form, is not without its specific merit or courage. As a rare valorization of jazz by a distinguished member of the established cultural elite, it is of course quite valuable. My aim is not to reproach individuals (who are dead anyway) but to critique the discursive conventions that licensed their comments on jazz.

28. Ernest Newman states that "jazz is not a 'form' like let us say the waltz or the fugue, that leaves the composer's imagination free within the form; it is a bundle of

tricks—of syncopation and so on" ("Summing Up Music's Case Against Jazz," *New York Times*, March 6, 1927, Section IV, pp. 3, 22).

29. For an extended consideration of ideas concerning sublimation and their links to music, race, and the novel, see chapter 2.

30. Early repeats the commonplace of almost all jazz history that the Original Dixieland Jazz Band's recordings represent the first instance of recorded jazz. I see no reason why this priority should not go to James Reese Europe's 1913 recordings. James Reese Europe's music is usually figured as a form of proto-jazz, but in *Along the Way*, James Weldon Johnson, who attended Europe's 1912 Carnegie Hall concert, clearly refers to his music as "jazz." James Weldon Johnson was involved enough in the New York music scene to know jazz when he heard it.

31. Whiteman saw his entire concert as "a stepping stone which will be helpful in giving the coming generations a much deeper appreciation of better music" (117).

32. I take up the imbrication of consumerism and racial primitivism more explicitly in my reading of Nella Larsen's *Quicksand*. See chapter 6.

33. According to Cross, "consumer expenditures for the same amount of disposable income were generally about $5 billion higher in the years after 1920 then before" (117).

34. Unstructured leisure was seen as having "a corrosive cultural effect" by many critics of the period, and this threat was often linked with the threat of jazz ("Think of the old folk dances, and folk music, compared with the modern dances and jazz!" [Cutten 75]) and described in the rhetoric of race ("It is certainly true that leisure has not yet become an art with us. . . . We are similar to some negroes after emancipation, who tried to exhibit their new possession of freedom by elbowing the white people off of the sidewalk" [Cutten 66]). It is clear that the desire to restrain leisure is closely tied to the desire to maintain existing hierarchies, racial and otherwise.

35. In *History of Bourgeois Perception*, Donald M. Lowe characterizes a belief in developmental time as embodying a vision in which "one could calculate progress with the intellect and verify its accomplishment with the eye" (46). In this conception, a version of what I am calling Puritan ideology, progress is always tangible and measurable. Also relevant here are the connections E. P. Thompson makes between Puritanism and capitalism: "Puritanism, in its marriage of convenience with industrial capitalism, was the agent which converted men to new valuations of time; which taught children even in their infancy to improve each shining hour; and which saturated men's minds with the equation, time is money" (E. P. Thompson 95; for Thompson on Benjamin Franklin, see 85).

36. On the number of lynchings during this period, see Redding. Given the role that the dynamics of the early twentieth century have played in shaping the outlines of our own period, the argument that I make here will not be without its relevance to the current status of jazz and other forms of African American music, and of racial and cultural politics today. The extent to which Eminem can be considered a contemporary analog of Paul Whiteman I leave to my readers, but the correspondence of widespread lynching with the popular acceptance of jazz cannot be without some resonance for a

contemporary situation in which the pervasiveness of African American music coexists with a paucity of African American economic and political power.

Chapter 2

1. Although the narrator never explicitly names his planned work a "symphony," both the epic scope he envisions for this work and his self-aggrandizing tendencies make it clear that it can be nothing less. His aim is to "voice all the dreams, all the joys and sorrows, the hopes and ambitions, of the American Negro, in classic musical form" (147–48); nothing less than the broad structural and instrumental resources of the symphony will suffice. The symphony is the most prestigious form of the classical tradition with which the narrator becomes enamored, and, as Salim Washington notes, "Johnson's protagonist was not interested in recording an expert musician's neo-spiritual . . . but was reaching for the top of the musical hierarchy as both Locke and Johnson understood it" (253).

2. Locke's language shows that the sublimation under consideration is more Paterian than it is Freudian. In *Deep River* Paul Allen Anderson gives a thorough description of the presence of the rhetoric of sublimation in the writings of Harlem Renaissance intellectuals and of the debt this rhetoric owes to the writings of Walter Pater (47–54, 147–50).

3. For Du Bois's relationship to the German philosophical tradition, see Anderson's *Deep River* and Zamir. See also Du Bois's description of Wagner's music in *The Souls of Black Folk*: "A deep longing swelled in all his heart to rise with that clear music out of the dirt and dust of that low life that held him prisoned and befouled" (252).

4. What Johnson calls ragtime is much more improvisational than what is usually referred to as ragtime today. In 1912 when Johnson published his novel, the term "jazz" was not in wide use, and the term "ragtime" was used to refer to a broad array of rhythmically complex, improvised musics. See note 11 to chapter 1.

5. This aversion to the new is supported by the pronounced tendency of Western philosophy to focus on time's corrosive force: Locke calls time "a perpetual perishing," Schopenhauer defines it as "that by the power of which everything at every instant turns to nothing in our hands," and Aristotle states that it "is in itself above all cause of corruption." (Zuckerkandl 223; Negri 164).

6. The link between the narrator's passing and the generic passing of Johnson's novel is made in Kawash.

7. In "Autobiography as De-Facement," de Man draws on Philippe Lejeune's assertion that "What defines the autobiography . . . is above all a contract of identity that is sealed by the proper name" (Lejeune 19).

8. The importance of the picaresque is bound up with the special value that travel and motion have for African Americans in the 1910s and 1920s. As a transplanted Southerner, Johnson would have been especially attuned to this value, a value perhaps best expressed by Cornel West: "In the space-time of New World African modernity, to

hope is to conceive of possible movement, to despair is to feel ossified, petrified, closed in" (xiv). Also, see Snead, who in "Repetition as a Figure of Black Culture," sees the picaresque as a form that highlights repetition in a manner not dissimilar to the methods of jazz and ragtime (72).

9. My reading of the encounter between the narrator and the patron's German guest is in chapter 1.

10. This is a position put forth by Adorno in *The Philosophy of Modern Music*, "Late Beethoven," and elsewhere, but which is perhaps most succinctly stated in Said, *Musical Elaborations* 64–70.

11. The patron's appreciation of the music as something novel and exotic shows his participation in the primitivism that characterizes much of the response to jazz and ragtime. For accounts of this primitivism and its distorted vision of the music, see Anderson, *Deep River* (esp. ch. 2), Ogren, and Anderson "White Reception."

12. The patron's refusal to dance is, of course, only a figure for his nonparticipation in the time of the narrator's music. There are ways of dancing that uphold this nonparticipation and sublimated mastery as much as the patron's blunt immobility does. Amiri Baraka suggests as much in the distinction he makes between dance as performed in the "black aesthetic" and "Arthur Murray footsteps" ("'Blues Aesthetic'" 107). Langston Hughes makes a similar distinction between hearing and listening at the end of "The Negro Artist and the Racial Mountain." What is at stake in both cases is not any specific physical action but whether or not the listener or dancer opens himself or herself to the time and rhythm performed in jazz or ragtime.

13. In *The Power of Black Music* Floyd contrasts this emphasis on surprise with a "European musical orientation," pointing out that in improvised African American musical forms like ragtime, "the *how* of a performance is more important than the *what*." Eschewing "nostalgia" and a "preference" for the familiar, the "musical experience of ragtime orients itself around the expectation that an unprecedented "something will *happen* in the playing of the music" (96–97).

14. This pessimism is shared by many of the major Anglo-American modernists. Eliot refers to "the immense panorama of futility and anarchy which is contemporary history," while Pound writes that "a tawdry cheapness shall outlast our days." T. S. Eliot "Ulysses, Order and Myth"; Ezra Pound "Hugh Selwyn Mauberly."

15. This recalls Koussevitsky's comments on jazz. See chapter 1.

16. Although in its canonical form the symphony militates for a progressive and unidirectional time, it is not without its own polyvalence. For a treatment of some of the other ways in which the symphony works on listeners, see Said, *Musical Elaborations*, esp. chapter 2, "On the Transgressive Elements in Music."

17. For theorizations of time as a function of social friction, see Durkheim 20, Fabian, *Time and the Other* 162–65, and Lukács, *Theory of the Novel* 122.

18. The emphasis on separating the listener from the vicissitudes of everyday life was reinforced by trends in the acoustical design of concert halls concurrent with the writing and dissemination of Johnson's novel. These trends are described in Thompson, *Soundscape of Modernity*, a work documenting the use of acoustical science to create concert

halls that deadened space in order to match the new habits in listening and music making. Thompson describes the premium placed on silent and respectful decorum, and on concentrated attention to music alone. According to Thompson, concert hall design between 1900 and 1933 was the culmination of a fifty-year trend away from treating concert halls as spaces for a variety of forms of socialization and toward an attempt to make halls into what Leon Botstein describes as "windowless social morgues" ("The Fine Art of Listening," *LA Times Book Review*, October 19, 2003).

19. One merely has to think of the work of William Grant Still, James P. Johnson, Nathaniel Dett, Scott Joplin, and others to see that an entirely other relationship between classical form and African American music is possible. What stops the narrator from practicing what Houston Baker calls "the deformation of mastery" is his assumption that classical form is neutral (15). Without his susceptibility to the ideological force of his patron's ideals, the narrator could have approached classical form in the same way that Johnson approached novelistic form, with a wariness in service of deforming and reforming it so as to make it do an entirely different type of cultural work than it has traditionally done. (The similarity between Johnson's use of the novel and his narrator's use of the symphony is pointed out in Gates, introduction x–xi.)

20. As Hortense Spillers asserts in "'All the Things You Could Be by Now,'" "symbolic economies . . . are directly tied to the sociopolitical sphere" (113).

21. In Nathaniel Mackey's words, "every concept, no matter how figural or sublime, had its literal, dead letter aspect" (*Bedouin Hornbook* 231).

22. For a description of the New York stride and ragtime scene in the 1910s and 1920s, see Brown, Fell and Vinding. See also the next section of this study on James P. Johnson and "Carolina Shout."

23. This present-tense literary consciousness shares much with the observing position responsible for generating racial taxonomies. Hortense Spillers description of this position highlights these commonalities: "there is in this grammar of description the perspective of 'declension,' not of simultaneity, and its point of initiation is solipsistic—it begins with a narrative self, in an apparent unity of feeling" ("Mama's Baby" 7).

24. The irreverence toward boundaries exhibited by sound is attested to by Hegel's definition of music as "the obliteration of spatial objectivity" (*Aesthetics* 889), as well as by the unfixed ambiguity of the lexicographical definition of sound. The *OED* gives three different definitions of sound, each locating it at a different point on the trajectory from creation to reception: "The sensation produced in the organs of hearing when the surrounding air is set in vibration in such a way as to affect these; also, that which is or may be heard; the external object of audition, or the property of bodies by which this is produced." This definition locates the vibrations of sound in the listener, in the producer, and in the air separating the two, an indication of sound's ultimately unfixable location and of the fact that sound is not an object but a motion.

Also, see Shepherd's *Music as Social Text*: "Sound (and therefore music as text) is the only major channel of communication that actively vibrates inside the body . . . the human experience of sound involves in addition to the sympathetic vibrations of the eardrums, the sympathetic vibrations of the body. Sound is thus felt in addition to being 'heard.' As a consequence it transcends actual tactile awareness and the particular form of erotic awareness at the surface of the body which then finds internal resonance. Sound, however, is in the body and enters the body" (179).

25. Bataille: "A fundamental principle is expressed as follows: 'communication' cannot take place from one full and intact being to another: it requires beings who have put the being within themselves at stake, having placed it at the limit of depth, of nothingness" (qtd. in Derrida, *Writing and Difference* 263).

26. See Ogren, esp. the introduction and chapter five.

Chapter 3

1. See Vincent (esp. the introduction and chapter one) for a critique of the Jazz Age as a "broad identifying term for . . . a period symbolized by 'flappers', fedora hats, [and] the Thompson sub-machine gun" (2).

2. Many jazz critics see this emphasis of rhythm at the expense of melody as a kind of shortcoming in Johnson's playing (even Schuller, who writes about this emphasis favorably considers it to be a kind of "vanishing mediator," a necessary clearing of the ground if jazz is to go forward), but if we take Nietzsche's evaluation of melody seriously, this judgment strikes one as rather unfounded. Nietzsche writes: "For melody delights so openly in lawfulness and has such an antipathy for everything that is still becoming, still unformed and arbitrary, that it sounds like an echo of the *old* order in Europe and like a seduction to go back to that" (160).

3. Johnson consistently characterized the patterns played by his left hand as metronomic: "a solid bass like a metronome" (Brown 87).

4. Johnson was fond of boasting about the bag of virtuoso techniques he was able to employ in coming up with fresh and unexpected ways of repeating sections: "I could think of a trick a minute; double glissandos, straight and backhand; glissandos in sixths, and double tremolos" (qtd. in Southern 389).

5. The Jungles Casino was also known as Drake's Dancing Class, a pseudonym that attempted to circumvent some of New York City's rather irregular liquor laws. See Brown 54.

6. This notion of causality is inadequate because, as Gaston Bachelard notes, "the principle of causality is always seen as playing between two distinct and very clear-cut figures, eliminating both accidents and details" (74). Johnson's performance embraces details and improvises past any distinction between "clear-cut figures."

7. For an extended discussion of this rhythm that precedes origin, see Fred Moten's brilliant book *In the Break*. Moten's work is an extended improvisation on Nate Mackey's description of "an insistent previousness, evading each and every natal occasion" at work in jazz (Moten, 6, 1–24). "Carolina Shout" is also a perfect example of an originality conceived of as "treatment of . . . borrowed material" (Hurston, 304) ("What we really mean by originality is the modification of ideas" [Hurston 304]).

8. LeRoi Jones describes a version of the same thing in *Black Music*: "If you play James Brown (say, 'Money Won't Change You . . . but time will take you out') in a bank,

the total environment is changed. . . . An energy is released in the bank, a summoning of images that take the bank, and everybody in it, on a trip" (186).

9. The phrase "demands response" is James Weldon Johnson's; it appears in his characterization of "Carolina Shout"–like music in *The Autobiography of an Ex-Colored Man* (98). Also, in his introduction to *The Book of American Negro Poetry*, James Weldon Johnson refers to the "response-compelling charm" of improvised ragtime as one of the music's most characteristic features (16).

10. The connection between Hegel's conception of time and jazz performance is made in Amiri Baraka's essay "The 'Blues Aesthetic' and the 'Black Aesthetic': Aesthetics as the Continuing Political History of a Culture." Although Hegel is not mentioned in this essay, Baraka follows the logic of the Hegelian time of negation when he writes that "what is not drives what is, and transforms itself. What is becomes what is not and what is not becomes what is and what is not" (255). (This time of negation most likely reaches Baraka through Marx, or Lenin [who is mentioned in Baraka's essay]).

11. See Marcuse, *Reason and Revolution*.

12. See Adorno, *Negative Dialectics* 331–38.

13. Jacques Derrida: "according to . . . Hegel's fundamental assertion . . . , time is the existence (Dasein) of the concept, absolute spirit in its automanifestation, in its absolute disquietude as the negation of negation" (*Margins* 36).

14. The most intense example of "dynamic suggestion" in literature is probably the ending of Toni Morrison's *Jazz*. The novel ends with a direct first-person address of the reader, an address that comes directly from the novel itself rather than from any of its characters and which attempts to both seduce the reader ("I have been waiting for this all my life") and to draw attention to the physical connection between the reader and the novel ("Look where your hands are. Now" [229]).

15. Morrison: "There is something underneath time that is incomplete. There is always something else that you want from the music" (McKay 429).

16. A National Urban League study of rents in New York in 1924 "found that Negroes paid from forty to sixty percent higher rents than white people did for the same class of apartments." See Byrd.

17. Adorno's propositions on the link between classical musical form and modes of social organization are articulated most succinctly and directly in Said, *Musical Elaborations*. In the recording of the lectures that make up this work (available in the Critical Theory Archive housed at the University of California, Irvine, library) there is a particularly dramatic moment in which Said (a very accomplished amateur pianist) hammers out the beginning to Beethoven's Fifth Symphony on the piano and insists that "there is primitive hoarding here." For the link between form and social organization, see chapter 2, "On the Transgressive Elements in Music," 66.

18. That the music under discussion was recorded in a studio rather than at a rent party does little to vitiate its commitment to effervescent sociality. Johnson strove to transform even the studio recording into a social event, as is evidenced in Pops Foster's description: "Jimmy always wanted someone to come to the studio with him when he cut the piano rolls or made records just to have some company. He'd want you to go out

and get his booze and you'd sit and drink and joke" (151). A more extravagant version of this practice later characterized the recording sessions of Sly and the Family Stone. See Davis and Troupe 321.

Chapter 4

1. Three of the most important treatments of time in *Gatsby* are Stallman, Holquist, and Berman. None of these critics link their discussions of time to either jazz or race (although Holquist comes close).

2. "Things were getting thinner and thinner as the eternal necessary human values tried to spread over all that expansion" (Fitzgerald, "Echoes of the Jazz Age" 22).

3. Suggestive of the way that Gatsby's hyperbolic extension of the traditional American futural orientation borders on an entirely new temporal orientation is Amiri Baraka's poem "Gatsby's Theory of Aesthetics" (*Transbluency* 132–33), which was published in 1964. The aesthetics expressed in this poem are essentially Baraka's.

4. See Franklin 86–87.

5. See Marx, *Capital* 329–36.

6. As Lukács writes in *Theory of the Novel*, "every form is the resolution of a fundamental dissonance of existence" (62). There is an interesting resonance between Lukács's assertion that the novel is the one (literary) form that attempts to incorporate dissonance into its form rather than banishing it and Snead's treatment of the way that African American forms like jazz make the disjunctions of repetition and "the cut" a part of their treatment of temporality. My assertion in this chapter is that Fitzgerald's novel strives to banish both dissonance and repetition and, in doing so, ends up militating against the possibilities inherent in the dissonant clash of traditional and emergent forms of American culture.

7. This echoes Hegel's assertion that America "is a land of desire for all those who are weary of the historical lumber-room of old Europe" (*Philosophy and History* 86).

8. "Gatsby who represented everything for which I have an unaffected scorn" (6).

9. It is probably not necessary to remind anyone that the North American continent was far from uninhabited, or that the explorers' vision that Fitzgerald lyricizes produced unspeakable violence.

10. The cynicism of those accustomed to possession shares much with what Deleuze and Guattari describe as "the basic 'cynicism' of capitalist axiomatization": a cynicism that makes all "beliefs and meanings strictly subsidiary to the conjunction of quantified flows and continually subject to decoding as capital transforms itself in the process of self-expansion" (Holland 528–29).

11. See Morris Cohen: "the major effect of property in land, in the machinery of production, in capital goods, etc. is to enable the owner to exclude others" (159).

12. When Gatsby wants Daisy to renounce her past with Tom, she responds by saying, "You want too much of me" (139).

13. Albert Einstein seems to be describing a similar phenomenon in his book on relativity published in 1916: "Every reference-body (co-ordinate system) has its own time;

unless we are told the reference-body to which the statement of time refers, there is no meaning in a statement of the time of an event" (26).

14. Like the conservatism of the novel, whose very form is, as Said writes, "on the side of institution's preserving, transmitting, confirming not only the process of filiative repetition by which human presence is repeatedly perpetuated" but also the "joining of people in a nongenealogical, nonprocreative but social unity" (*World* 118).

15. These ideas are, of course, not Tom's alone. Two markers of their wider currency are the allusion to Lothrop Stoddard's *The Rising Tide of Color* and the chronological coincidence of *The Great Gatsby* and the 1924 Johnson-Reed Immigration Act. For a description of the nativism enshrined in Johnson-Reed, see Ngai.

16. Anthony Braxton refers to jazz improvisers as "re-structuralists." See Lock, *Forces In Motion* 162.

17. Here I am trying to extend Houston Baker's suggestive comments on *Gatsby* in *Modernism and the Harlem Renaissance*: "Alas, Fitzgerald's priggishly astute Nick has only a limited vocabulary when it comes to a domain of experience that I, as an Afro-American, know well. . . . If only Fitzgerald had placed his 'pale well-dressed negro' in the limousine" (6).

18. In the use of jazz at his parties, Gatsby is not unlike the elite society he aspires to join. In the years before and after World War I, James Reese Europe's band was the preferred music for New York high society's social functions. See Badger 83–85.

19. See Ogren 91.

20. Racial exclusiveness is bound up with other forms of exclusiveness. What the figure of Jay Gatz shows us is that the boundaries of propriety and privilege, although absolutely dependent upon race, foster exclusions that go beyond race. Race supports a hierarchy that does not privilege all who fall on the proper side of the racial divide.

21. The novel also references Paul Whiteman's "Three O'Clock in the Morning" and "The Sheik of Araby," a 1921 Ted Snyder composition originally recorded by the Club Royal Orchestra. The Club Royal Orchestra was, like Whiteman's band, an all white ensemble that played fairly saccharine dance music. In the 1930s "The Sheik of Araby" became something of a jazz standard and was recorded by Fats Waller, Jack Teagarden, Lionel Hampton, and others.

22. For a treatment of the way the blues offer possibilities for "sustaining emergent feminist consciousness," see Angela Davis, *Blues Legacies* xv.

23. Even the young Amory Blaine's future lies behind him at the end of *This Side of Paradise*.

24. An individual's attempt to control her own identity may be foredoomed, but so is any novel's attempt. This is the point of Said's essay "On Repetition": attempts to repeat the identical always engender deviations, and the novel's form of repetition is no exception.

25. "Like a children's party taken over by the elders" (Fitzgerald, "Echoes of the Jazz Age" 15).

26. See, for example, Fitzgerald's "My Lost City": "all these benefits did not really minister to much delight" (30).

27. Youth is a category here, not a biological age, despite Fitzgerald's attempt to conflate the two.

28. This is the claim of modernism and modernity in general, as well as the specific claim of Orlando Patterson's phillipic against the claims of a racialized past.

29. Waldo Frank: "Jazz is the moment's gaiety, after which the spirit droops, cheated and unnurtured. This song is not an escape from the Machine to the limpid depths of the soul. It is the Machine itself!" (119).

30. Gatsby's lack of this sense is demonstrated most clearly when he is unable to read through the stated desire of the wife in a visiting couple to have Gatsby over for dinner (109).

31. In a certain sense it was the *Bright Lights, Big City* of its time.

32. "They conducted themselves according to the rules of behavior associated with amusement parks" (45).

33. This is the condescending tone of the conductor of the orchestra at Gatsby's parties, capable of both announcing the "sensation" caused by the performance of "Tostoff's Jazz History of the World" and of deflating his announcement with the remark "Some sensation!" (54).

34. This same elitist impulse is also at work in the denigration of Gatsby's parties and the behavior of his guests that I describe above.

35. In this, Fitzgerald shows himself to be a modernist in the Pound-Eliot mode, concerned with restoring the value and efficacy of a language debased by misuse. See Jaffe.

36. For theorizations of time as a function of social friction, see Durkheim 20, Fabian, *Time and the Other* 162–65, and Lukács, *Theory of the Novel* 122.

37. Again, Baraka's poem, "Gatsby's Theory of Aesthetics," is a prime example.

38. This is related, but not identical, to the dissonance that Lukács identifies in the novel: "The composition of the novel is a paradoxical fusion of heterogenous and discrete components into an organic whole which is then abolished over and over again" (*Theory of the Novel* 84). A more apt theory of dissonance and form is put forth by Ellington. See the following chapter.

Chapter 5

1. In *Solutions for Singers*, Richard Miller, a renowned tutor of classical voice, assumes the rigidity of the distinction between the vibrations that produce a tone and any vibrato added to a tone (143–45). Despite the lack of justification for such a claim, this assumption is shared by an overwhelming majority of those who write on music, particularly those who write on classical music. Miller's insistence is representative of received ideas of vibrato and pitch production. For a more recent approach to these issues, see Titze.

2. Weber describes this as a shift to "mean intonation," a system used widely in the eighteenth century but eventually replaced by the equal temperament system "now

widely regarded as the normal tuning of the Western, 12-note scale" (Oxford Music Online).

3. The piano is the key instrument in the system of rationalization that Weber describes. It is Bach's "Well-Tempered Clavier" that most forcefully argues for mean intonation; the piece is literally unplayable in just intonation. The piano militates for mean intonation because, unlike the wind and string instruments that make up the bulk of the symphony, it cannot adjust (or bend) notes. The trombone, the cornet, and the voice can all shift the pitch of notes upward or downward as the harmonic or resonant demands of a performance require. Notes on the piano, however, are fixed, and the central role of the piano in the classical tradition is quite telling, particularly when we take into account Weber's assertion that the piano and the tuning associated with it are both closely linked to northern European ideals of domesticity (Weber 23–24). The fixing of tones prescribed by the harmonic system of classical music is also the fixing of certain social ideals and the proscription of others.

This is one of the reasons why, despite the key role of virtuoso pianists like Ellington, Bud Powell, James P. Johnson, and a host of others, the jazz tradition is so heavily dominated by vocalists and horn players. Jazz improvises on a social ideal radically different from that enshrined in the tuning associated with the piano; it celebrates what Paul Allen Anderson calls an "aesthetic of tonal impurity" (55). This aesthetic demands the kinds of glissandos, growls, and other timbral manipulations that are difficult to achieve on the piano. In the most radical period of jazz performance (the late 1960s and early 1970s—although Ornette Coleman started recording without a piano in 1959) the piano is less and less an integral part of the jazz ensemble. Throughout the history of jazz, pianists have developed a whole series of techniques that make the piano sound in unexpected and non-domesticated ways; to my ear the most successful bending of the piano to the jazz aesthetic are the remarkable manipulations of the pedals heard in Thelonius Monk's playing. In listening to some of his recordings, one would be justified in believing that Monk is playing a piano that has been mechanically altered.

Another way that jazz pianists have gotten away from the cultural baggage built into the piano is by performing on the organ, an instrument taken up at various times by Fats Waller, Count Basie, Jimmy Smith, Larry Young, and others. The quavering tonal center of the organ sound introduces an at least minimal amount of vibrational play into the otherwise fixed note.

4. It is quite remarkable how even the most iconoclastic of classical composers have been reluctant to question the dominance of mean intonation: figures like Schoenberg, Stravinsky, Boulez, Ligeti, and others have all left the core of this harmonic system untouched—only figures like Cage and Stockhausen have seen it as anything but a fundamental limit to music making.

5. Weber: "practically, [mean intonation] for purely melodic music is essentially a device to accomplish the transposition of melodies into any pitch without retuning the instruments" (98).

6. Martindale and Riedel: "Basic to the system is a residual irrational division the

consequences of which form a primary object of theoretical reflection for Occidental musical theorists" (xxvii).

7. These are the notes referred to as "blue notes." An excellent example of a blue note can be heard by listening to the way Bessie Smith sings the word "sun" at the very beginning of "St. Louis Blues" (nine seconds into the recording). She is bending the flatted third degree of the key, moving both above and below the prescribed pitch.

8. The flatted fifth is characteristic of later periods of jazz and blues and is relatively rare in the 1920s.

9. Albert Murray: "the great body of European Art Music was already in existence and already a part of the heritage of blues musicians. It was already there to be played with, and blues musicians did just that" (*Stomping the Blues* 188–89).

10. Baldwin: "*Who am I? and what am I doing here?* This question is the very heart, and root, of the music we are discussing" ("Of the Sorrow Songs" 89).

11. The National Institute of Standards and Technology uses an atomic clock that defines a second as 9,192,631,770 vibrations of the cesium atom. Even this clock is not strictly regular but loses a second every 20 million years. See Callendar and Edney 17.

12. Exemplary here is the way that the great stride pianist James P. Johnson plundered the European classical tradition for techniques that he used to heighten his pianistic animations of Renaissance-era Harlem rent parties; according to Eileen Southern, "Johnson spent many hours listening to recordings of European piano compositions, so that he could use 'concert effects' in his playing of jazz piano" (390).

13. For Hegel's views on the relationship between time and music, see *Hegel's Aesthetics* 904–9.

14. This performance plays upon the heterogeneities that make up any continuity or any duration. As Bachelard writes, "duration is a complex of multiple ordering actions which support each other. If we say we are living in a single, homogenous domain we shall see that time can no longer move on. At the very most, it just hops about. In fact, duration always needs alterity for it to appear continuous. Thus, it appears to be continuous through its heterogeneity, and in a domain which is always other than that in which we think we are observing it" (65).

15. W. C. Handy also wrote a "Hesitating Blues."

16. The term "limp" is important because it draws attention to the violent past out of which these rhythms emerged. See Mackey, "Sound and Sentiment" 613–14.

17. An excellent example of the flexible coordination I am discussing occurs in the second chorus, 2:08 into the recording, when Longshaw and Armstrong improvise an interlocking contrapuntal response to Smith.

18. This attitude toward dissonance was undergoing a serious challenge from Arnold Schoenberg and his followers at the beginning of the twentieth century. The composers associated with Schoenberg radically reconceived the role of dissonance in the classical tradition, but they still saw it as something internal to the Western harmonic system. See Ringer.

19. Opera would be a possible exception.

20. Rossing, Moore, and Wheeler 35.

21. Van den Berg's account of vocal production is far from the latest word in the field. For an account of the way in which van den Berg's theory has been revised and reworked, see Titze.

22. See Baraka, "Rhythm and Rime," and Marcuse, "A Note on Dialectic."

23. Bachelard: "It is now one of the most important principles of modern physics that matter is transformed into wave motion and that conversely, wave radiation is transformed into matter" (136).

24. Bachelard: "If a particle ceased to vibrate it would cease to be. . . . substance . . . is *regular* rhythm which appears in the form of a *specific* material attribute" (138).

25. This is isomorphic with Attali's description of music as a force that "creates political order because it is a minor form of sacrifice." Attali stresses the way music has been used to "symbolically signif[y] the channeling of violence and the imaginary, the ritualization of a murder substituted for the general violence, the affirmation that a society is possible if the imaginary of individuals is sublimated" (25–26). Jazz, of course, does something else.

26. Breaking phrases in unexpected places was an important part of Smith's style. See Gunther Schuller for her "unique ability to break phrases into unexpected segments and to breathe at such phrase interruptions without in the slightest impairing over-all continuity, textual or melodic" (232). Smith's phrase breaks, are a form of what James Snead calls "the cut": "The ensuing rupture does not cause dissolution of the rhythm; quite to the contrary, it strengthens it, given that it is already incorporated into the format of the rhythm" (71).

27. Recall that both James Weldon Johnson and his narrator describe surprise as one of the key elements of improvised ragtime.

28. These cataracts are often quite beautiful.

29. The comparison implied here is with Gatsby's relationship to Daisy, in which Daisy serves as the final piece completing Gatsby's "platonic vision of himself."

30. Examples are the nearly fumbled rhythm as Armstrong rushes to finish his improvisations at 2:42 and 2:57.

31. For a dense and rich theorization of the relationship between foresight and improvisation, see chapter 2 of Moten's *In the Break*.

32. In other performances, Armstrong marked the conversational quality of his improvisations by quoting snatches of melody from other tunes (opera, jazz, popular music, show tunes, and so forth).

33. In "Ring Shout, Signifyin(g), and Jazz Analysis," Samuel A. Floyd Jr. describes the jazz soloist as always signifying on past performances and past performance traditions. My thinking of the presence of the past in jazz performance owes much to this article and to his book *The Power of Black Music*.

34. See "An Interview with James Baldwin," "James Baldwin Comes Home," and "*The Black Scholar* Interviews James Baldwin" (all in *Conversations*).

35. Baldwin: "It was Bessie Smith, through her tone and her cadence, who helped me to dig back to the way I myself must have spoken when I was a pickaninny, and to remember the things I had heard and seen and felt" (*Conversations* 4).

36. Here I utilize Gramsci's formation "the person is strangely composite" (Gramsci 324). For the relevance of Gramsci's notion of the self to jazz performance, see Mackey, *Bedouin Hornbook* 178.

Chapter 6

1. This bears a close resemblance to the distinction between African-derived and European-derived senses of rhythm: African rhythms are additive; they exceed the regular metric divisions of any performance; European rhythms are divisive; they conform to these metric divisions. See Nketia 128–29.

2. The count shows Jake the arrow scars he received while undertaking a business venture in Abyssinia, suggesting his involvement with European colonizing forces in Africa. For Hemingway's views on the Italian invasion of Ethiopia, see Cooper 54–55. According to Cooper, Hemingway's main criticism of the war in Ethiopia was that "poor, ordinary Italians would have to face these horrors in order to fulfill Mussolini's absurd ambitions" (55).

3. The truncated lyrics in the chapter suggest that the drummer is singing "Aggravatin Papa," a song composed by J. Russell Robinson, Roy Turk, and Addy Britt. In 1923 the song was recorded by Alberta Hunter, Bessie Smith, and Sophie Tucker. See Hays 139.

4. Berman aligns Hemingway's critique of a progressive Protestantism with the writings of Reinhold Niebuhr and Hillaire Belloc.

5. Hemingway's willed deafness to the syncopated presence of the past within the present is a major impetus behind his valorization of the discrete form of the well-formed and balanced declarative sentence. On Hemingway's valorization of the sentence see Jameson, *Marxism and Form* 408–12.

6. It is worth noting that three of the most important critics of jazz (Ralph Ellison, Albert Murray, and Kamau Brathwaite) all take the link between Hemingway's prose and jazz rhythm quite seriously. See Ellison *Collected Essays*, Brathwaite, and Murray (*Stomping*).

7. For a description of Montmartre's clubs and its jazz scene, see Shack.

8. For the influence of jazz on Cesaire and Senghor, see Baraka's "Cesaire" (*Daggers and Javelins* 195), Irele, and *Aime Cesaire: A Voice For History*. For Senghor's aesthetics, see "African-Negro Aesthetics."

9. For a reading of the group of homosexual men who show up with Brett, see Moddelmog 92–100. According to Moddelmog, "Jake relies upon the homosexuality of the young men to define his manhood" (93).

10. In music, anacrusis is "the note or notes preceding a downbeat."

11. Hughes's description of the Benbow band's performance is in accord with Gaston Bachelard's assertion that "all true duration is essentially polymorphous, the real action of time requires the richness of coincidence and the syntony of rhythmic effects" (55).

12. "Indeed, much goes to show that what musicians are most likely to be mimicking (and sometimes extending and refining and sometimes counterstating) are the

sounds of other musicians who have performed the same or similar compositions" (Murray, *Stomping the Blues* 125).

13. Malone, *Steppin' on the Blues* 2.

14. Chernoff: "Without dancers, many drummers cannot bring forth a wide range of variations, and in this regard we can suggest that dance probably played one of the important inspirational roles in the early development of jazz" (147). See also Wilson, "Association of Movement and Music."

15. Levi-Strauss: "The delight of music is that of the soul being asked to recognize itself, for the first time, in the body" (74).

16. "American social dancing—like the jazz to which it is often performed—has taken on an African-like rhythmic complexity . . . dance cadences in 6/4, or even 5/4, for example, executed to musical measures of 2/4 or 4/4—a fairly sophisticated rhythmic combination" (Stearns and Stearns 14).

17. This ratio is also given in Ralph Ellison's definition of the vernacular: "a dynamic *process* in which the most refined styles from the past are continually merged with the play-it-by-ear improvisations which we invent in our efforts to control our environments and entertain ourselves" (*Going to the Territory* 139–40).

18. Etymologically, ambition ("amb"—about—+"itus"—going) means going about in a social circle to solicit support. One of the things that Hughes does in his novel is to restore the social aspect of ambition.

19. And perhaps personality or style are best thought of as patterns of breaking expectations.

20. Sandy's move from solitude to the pool hall is the opposite of James Weldon Johnson's narrator's desire to remove himself from the South before composing.

21. One indication of the broad significance of the verb "dance" in the tradition that Hughes belongs to is Ellington's assertion that "you can dance with a lot of things besides your feet. Billy Strayhorn was another dancer—in his mind. He was a dance-writer" (Malone, "Jazz Music" 289). (Strayhorn was a composer and arranger who collaborated with Ellington for years.)

22. Like John Rowe, I consider it a mistake to treat "Melanctha" as a separate, free-standing tale. Stein consciously modeled *Three Lives* on Flaubert's *Trois Contes* and, while "Melanctha" points most clearly toward Stein's later style, the three tales are linked by common elements both formal and thematic. See Rowe, "Naming What Is Inside."

23. See De Koven and Ruddick.

24. See Milton Cohen.

25. I disagree with Peterson's conclusions, but it should be pointed out that her article is a fantastically rich source of demographic and geographical details about Stein's Baltimore and its jazz scene.

26. For Stein's investment in typology see Peppis, Charters, and Stimpson.

27. And "always" is the most frequently repeated word in *Three Lives*.

28. Stein: "people do not change from one generation to another, as far back as we know history people are about the same as they were" ("Picasso," qtd. in Webb 454).

29. Snead refers to this form of repetition as "a kind of 'coverage', both in the form

of comforting 'insurance' against accidental and sudden ruptures of the social fabric, and in Swift's less favorable sense of a 'cover-up', or a hiding of otherwise unpleasant facts from the senses" (60). Also see Olsen's article on Stein's attachment to Wiliam James's ideas about habit as a protective and exclusionary form of repetition.

30. Letter to Mabel Weeks (Charters xv).

31. Arrighi draws this distinction from the work of Talcott Parsons.

32. For a careful consideration of the strategies Stein used to configure herself as a genius excepted from the putative weaknesses of women, see Stimpson 497–99.

33. I draw this distinction between the "what" and the "how" from Floyd's description of the jazz imperative in *The Power of Black Music* (97).

34. There are a couple of songs ("Kitchen Man" and "Yellow Dog Blues") in which Smith sings in the third person, but each of these songs also has a first-person section where Smith takes on the troubles of the songs' protagonist.

35. Also: "Poor Anna, . . ." (33, 37); "Poor Lena . . ." (198, 199).

36. Is there any communication between the 1909 publication of *Three Lives* and the 1910 ordinance instituting residential segregation in Baltimore? See Gaines 74.

37. *Three Lives* does suggest the presence of interracial interaction (the "mixed blood" of Melanctha and Rose, and Jane Harden's being raised by white folks) but these are only peripheral to the main movement of the text.

38. Stein's configuration of time in *Three Lives* and dismissal of "syncopated time" in "Plays" is part of a line that can be drawn from the deployment of stereotypes in *Three Lives* to the assertion in *The Autobiography of Alice B. Toklas* that "negroes were not suffering from persecution, they were suffering from nothingness" (238). (Stein is, of course, wrong. In our temporal existence, we all bear the weight of nothingness—whether we "suffer" from it or enjoy it is the question that jazz asks; in the United States, African Americans suffer from the institutional and ideological constructions that attempt to banish nothingness by making it coterminous with blackness.) For an argument about how this line also extends into *Four Saints in Three Acts*, making it into a latter-day "minstrel show," see Webb.

39. Jules Laforgue: "Donc je suis un malheureux et ce / n'est ni ma faute ni celle de la vie" (Thus, I am unhappy and the fault is neither mine, nor life's).

40. One example is Bone, in which Helga Crane is dismissed as "a neurotic young woman of mixed parentage, who is unable to make a satisfactory judgment in either race" (102).

41. It is important that, in the cabaret, Helga articulates herself through her body because the body is that which primitivism and exoticism strain to reduce Helga to. In making the body eloquent, the dance refutes any notion that the body speaks a language less studied, less sophisticated, or less meaningful than the language counted as a marker of rationality by dominant discourses of value. In dance the body speaks, and when it speaks it insists on calling to mind the repressed history of what writes itself on and through the flesh. It presents itself as the medium of a discourse too meaningful and too rich to be figured as merely the object of other, more literate discourses. When it dances, the body presents itself as something always more than mute matter to be

mastered or read. (See also Duke Ellington's interview from 1931: "When we dance it is not a mere diversion or social accomplishment. It expresses our personality, and, right, down in us, our souls react to the elemental but eternal rhythm, and the dance is timeless and unhampered by any lineal form" ["Duke Steps Out" 47].)

42. This is exactly the kind of rich concatenation that Duke Ellington, purveyor of "jungle music," translated into his music in pieces like "Harlem Air Shaft." See Tucker, *Ellington: The Early Years* esp. 255–57, where Tucker describes Ellington as a master of combinations.

43. Morrison: "But jazz unsettles you. You always feel a little on edge. 'Did I catch it?' Then you have to listen again. You're not in control" (qtd. in Carabi 43).

44. For a description of "racist white society's assumptions about black women's sexual availability," see Monda 24–26, and Gaines 80–83.

45. "'Uplift,' sniffed Helga contemptuously" (52).

46. McLendon characterizes this aesthetic sense as "a displacement of her longing for love onto a longing for material comfort in order to ease 'her long trouble of body and spirit'" (79).

47. See Chip Rhodes's reading of *Quicksand*'s initial scene (191).

48. Susan Willis: "The great illusion of commodity capitalism is that, while we may not all be white and middle class, we might (if we have a little cash) trade in its signs" (qtd. in McLendon 78).

49. As Ann Hostetler points out, Helga's aesthetic sense is entirely passive (36). It shapes nothing, but it only selects from among available choices with a strong bias toward inert and undemanding objects.

50. There is a more complicated story to be told about Helga's consumerism; see Muzak. What I am drawing attention to is the imbrication of Anne's and Helga's understanding of themselves as consumers and their suppression of the racial past and of the performance practices that emerge out of this past.

51. Ellington: "the characteristic melancholy music of my race has been forged from the very white heat of our sorrows" ("Duke Steps Out" 49).

52. Koselleck writes that "progress became a modern concept when it shed or forgot its background meaning of stepping through space" (221).

53. A version of this operation can be seen in Nick Carraway's reaction to three African Americans in the back of a limousine. See chapter 4.

54. Larsen makes Helga a figure for one of the most important antagonisms of the period. As Hazel Carby writes, "the twenties must be viewed as a period of ideological, political, and cultural contestation between an emergent bourgeosie and an emerging black working class" (754).

55. Here I am disagreeing with critics like McLendon (82) that read Helga's homesickness for Negroes (or America) as a function of her desire for Robert Anderson.

56. It is worth noting that neither Larsen nor Helga name the performers as minstrels, nor is there any description of blackface or ragged clothing. This is not to say that the two singers are not involved in a form of minstrelsy but merely to point out that the predicament of black culture in the 1920s was inseparable from the legacy of minstrelsy.

This is as true of Duke Ellington as it is of the most pernicious repetitions of minstrel stereotypes. The complexities of this situation is what generates the complexities of Larsen's text. See also Hartman, esp. 223n109, and Garrett, esp. 34, on minstrelsy.

57. Helga's constant return to the Circus obeys what Ralph Ellison calls the "blues impulse," "an impulse to keep the painful details and episodes of experience alive in one's aching consciousness, to finger its jagged grain" (*Shadow and Act* 90).

58. Dvořák does not engage Helga the way jazz had, and this is part of its virtue for her. It does not shake her sense of self but lets her sit passively in the audience and appreciate the music in a manner compatible with her aesthetic sense. Helga hears the "wailing undertones of 'Swing Low, Sweet Chariot'" (92) in Dvořák, but we have to realize how heavily mediated these "undertones" are. See Burgett 30–33.

59. And in between Dvořák and ragtime songs is not a bad way of locating Ellington's music, in a space between harmonic sophistication and demotic rhythms but ultimately superior to both.

60. Irony is always an expression of some form of doubleness. See Baudelaire and, perhaps more pertinently, Gates comments on irony and doubleness in *Signifying Monkey* (89–90, 211–16).

61. Hartman: "acts of resistance exist within the context of relations and are not external to them" (8).

62. Fletcher Henderson provides a different kind of contrast from Ellington. Henderson was the preferred black band for society events (it provided the music for the annual NAACP ball) and was very like Ellington in his attempt to present himself and his band as the acme of sophisticated urbanity. Unlike Ellington, though, Henderson never performed "jungle music" and thus never engaged the contradictions that Ellington's music (and Larsen's novel) negotiates.

63. For discussions of Ellington's irony, see Ellison, "Homage to Duke on His Birthday" (*Going to the Territory* 219–21) and Lock, *Blutopia,* esp. chapter 3.

64. Howard "Stretch" Johnson, one of the dancers who worked with Ellington at the Cotton Club, recalls that "the splendid sound of the Elington organization was not jungle music, but a creative form of irony which masked the commercial pandering to an upper-class white audience thrilled at the opportunity to hear and witness what it though was genuine black exotica. . . . At the club, the sensitivity and lyricism of the Ellington band, even when 'growling,' made it clear that the jungle did not have to be African" (Lock, *Blutopia* 87).

65. In *Reconstructing Black Womanhood* Hazel Carby calls Helga Crane "the first truly sexual black female protagonist in Afro-American fiction" and points out that "the representation of black female sexuality meant risking its definition as primitive and exotic within a racist society" (174).

66. Audrey's dance has both the "loose ease" of the performers in Copenhagen and the grave reserve of Helga Crane (83).

67. Murray considers Duke Ellington to be the paradigmatic performer of blues-idiom dance music.

68. The distinction that Murray makes between the frenzy of Gene Krupa ("possessed by some violent tom-tom oriented savage force") and the "nonchalance" of Chick Webb is very much like the distinction Larsen makes between the dancing of Helga and that of Audrey Denney (Murray, *Stomping the Blues* 106).

69. The term "timbral heterogeneity" comes from Olly Wilson. In "The Heterogenous Sound Ideal in African-American Music" and "Black Music as an Art Form," Wilson argues that a "heterogeneous sound ideal" is central to jazz and other forms of African American music. The example that Wilson uses to illustrate this ideal comes from Ellington. I discuss the heterogeneous sound ideal in chapter 5.

70. Nanton says that he strove to make his sound like that of "a man in a dungeon calling out of a cell window" (qtd. in Dietrich "Joe 'Tricky Sam' Nanton", 11).

71. One can hear Nanton and Miley performing the jungle sound on "Black and Tan Fantasy," "Jungle Nights in Harlem," and "East St. Louis Toodle-oo." For a detailed description of Nanton's contributions to the jungle sound, see Dietrich: *Duke's Bones* and "Joe 'Tricky Sam' Nanton."

72. See chapter 5 for a discussion of the ways in which these kinds of musical performance practices trope on the structures of Western thought and Western music.

73. My formulations here are indebted to Nate Mackey's linking up of Zora Neale Hurston's rhetorical theory and African American musical practices. See Mackey, "Other" 515–16.

74. It is not that Nanton is foreign to the jazz tradition (and he was born in New York), but that this tradition can only become one's own by an approach to it through the dissonant fact that one is never totally inside or totally outside of it.

75. The only vocation attached to Helga's father in the text occurs when Helga tells Robert Anderson that her father was a gambler (21).

76. Hortense Spillers marks how this necessary repetition is more insistent for racialized subjects: "To speak is to occupy a place in social economy, and, in the case of the racialized subject, his history has dictated that his linguistic *right to use* is never easily granted with his human and social legacy but must be earned, over and over again" ("'All the Things You Could Be by Now'" 108).

77. For more on the picaresque and its importance, see chapter 2.

78. This is important because, as Lindon Barrett writes, "to interpose no alternative value in the theoretically moment of calling value into question remains equivalent to strengthening and reincarnating reified, dominant value" (52).

79. Floyd refers to this restlessness as "the driving, *swinging*, rhythmic persistence that we find in all African American music but that is most vividly present in jazz" (*Power of Black Music* 115).

80. Snead: "*transformation* is culture's response to its own apprehension of repetition" (59).

81. Sophisticated was one of Ellington's favorite adjectives, and any music that is tuneless emphasizes those elements most antithetical to possessive individualism: rhythm and harmony. Relevant here are Nietzsche's comments on melody: "For melody delights

so openly in lawfulness and has such an antipathy for everything that is still becoming, still unformed and arbitrary, that it sounds like an echo of the *old* order in Europe and like a seduction to go back to that" (160).

82. "Mutes for brass instruments are inserted into or held over the end of the bell and function by obstructing in different ways the oscillations of the air column inside or outside the body of the instrument (or both)" (Kernfeld 819). For a detailed description of Nanton's use of mutes, see Dietrich.

Works Cited

Adorno, Theodor. *Kant's Critique of Pure Reason.* Trans. Rodney Livingstone. Cambridge: Polity, 2001.

———. *Minima Moralia.* Trans. E. F. N. Jephcott. London: Verso, 1974.

———. *Negative Dialectics.* Trans. E. B. Ashton. New York: Continuum, 1973.

———. *The Philosophy of Modern Music.* Trans. Anne Mitchell and Wesley Blomster. New York: Continuum, 1994.

———. *Quasi una Fantasia.* Trans. Rodney Livingstone. London: Verso, 1992.

———. "The Radio Symphony." *Radio Research.* Eds. Paul Lazarsfeld and Frank Stanton. New York: Duell, Sloan, and Pearce, 1941. 110–39.

Adorno, Theodor, and Max Horkheimer. *The Dialectic of Enlightenment.* Trans. John Cumming. New York: Continuum, 1972.

Aglietta, Michel. *A Theory of Capitalist Regulation.* London: New Left Books, 1997.

Aime Cesaire: A Voice For History. Vol II. *The Strength to Face Tomorrow.* Prod. Saligna and So On. Ed. Catherine Chauchan and Annie Lemeisle. 1994. DVD.

Anderson, Maureen. "The White Reception of Jazz in America." *African American Review* 38.1 (Spring 2004): 135–45.

Anderson, Paul Allen. *Deep River: Music and Memory in the Harlem Renaissance.* Durham: Duke UP, 2001.

Anderson, Perry. *A Zone of Engagement.* London: Verso, 1992.

Andrews, Dwight D. "From Black to Blues." *Black Sacred Music* 6.1 (Spring 1992): 47–54.

Arrighi, Giovanni. "Hegemony Unravelling." *New Left Review* 33 (June 2005): 83–116.

Attali, Jacques. *Noise.* Minneapolis: U of Minnesota P, 1985.

Bachelard, Gaston. *The Dialectic of Duration.* Trans. Mary McAllester Jones. Manchester: Clinamen, 2000.

Badger, Reid. *A Life in Ragtime: A Biography of James Reese Europe.* New York: Oxford UP, 1995.

Baker, Houston. *Modernism and the Harlem Renaissance.* Chicago: U of Chicago Press, 1987.

Baldwin, James. *Conversations with James Baldwin.* Ed. Fred L. Standley and Louis Pratt. Jackson: University Press of Mississippi, 1989.

———. "Here Be Dragons." *The Price of the Ticket.* New York: St. Martin's, 1985. 677–90.

———. "Many Thousands Gone." *Notes of a Native Son.* Boston: Beacon Press, 1957. 24–45.

———. *Notes of a Native Son.* Boston: Beacon, 1984.

———. "Of the Sorrow Songs." *New Edinburgh Review Anthology.* Ed. James Campbell. Edinburgh: Polygon Books, 1982. 85–92.

———. "On Being 'White' . . . and Other Lies." *Black on White: Black Writers on What It Means to Be White.* Ed. David Roediger. New York: Schocken, 1998. 177–80.

———. *The Fire Next Time.* New York: Vintage, 1993.

Balibar, Étienne. "Structuralism: A Destitution of the Subject?" Trans. James Swenson. *Differences: A Journal of Feminist Cultural Studies* 14.1 (2003): 1–21.

Baraka, Amiri. "The 'Blues Aesthetic' and the 'Black Aesthetic': Aesthetics as the Continuing Political History of a Culture." *Black Music Research Journal* 11.2 (1991): 101–9.

———. *Daggers and Javelins.* New York: William Morrow and Co., 1984.

———. "Rhythm and Rime." *XCP: Cross Cultural* Poetics 9 (November 2001): 27–30.

———. *Transbluency.* Ed. Paul Vangelisti. New York: Marsilio, 1995.

Barrett, Lindon. *Blackness and Value.* Cambridge: Cambridge UP, 1999.

Bascom, Lionel C., ed. *A Renaissance in Harlem.* New York: Bard, 1999.

Baudelaire, Charles. "The Essence of Laughter." *Baudelaire: The Painter of Modern Life and Other Essays.* London: Phaidon, 1964. 147–65.

Bechet, Sidney. *Treat It Gentle.* Cambridge: Da Capo, 1978.

Benjamin, Walter. "The Storyteller." *Illuminations.* Trans. Harry Zohn. Ed. Hannah Arendt. New York: Harcourt, Brace, 1968. 83–110.

Benston, Kimberly. *Performing Blackness: Enactments of African-American Modernism.* New York: Routledge, 2000.

Berman, Ronald. The Great Gatsby *and Modern Times.* Urbana: U. of Illinois P. 1994.

———. "Protestant, Catholic, Jew: The Sun Also Rises." *Hemingway Review* 18.1 (Fall 1998): 33–48.

Bernstein, J. M. *The Philosophy of the Novel: Lukacs, Marxism, and the Dialectics of Form.* Minneapolis: U of Minnesota P, 1984.

Bersani, Leo. *The Freudian Body.* New York: Columbia UP, 1986.

Bevan, Clifford, and Alyn Shipton. "Mutes." Kernfeld 818–24.

Blaise, Clark. *Time Lord: Sir Sandford Fleming and the Creation of Standard Time.* New York: Pantheon, 2000.

Bone, Robert. *The Negro Novel in America.* New Haven: Yale UP, 1969.

Brathwaite, Kamau. "Jazz and the West Indian Novel." Bim, 44–46 (1967): 275–84, 39–51, 115–26.

Brown, Scott. *James P. Johnson: A Case of Mistaken Identity*. Metuchen, N.J.: Scarecrow Press, 1986.

Burgett, Paul. "Vindication as a Thematic Principle in the Writings of Alain Locke on the Music of Black Americans." *Black Music in the Harlem Renaissance*. Ed. Samuel A. Floyd Jr. Westport: Greenwood, 1990. 29–54.

Butler, Judith. *The Psychic Life of Power*. Stanford: Stanford UP, 1997.

Byrd, Frank. "Rent Parties." Bascom 59–67.

Callendar, Craig, and Ralph Edney. *Introducing Time*. Cambridge, UK: Icon Books, 2001.

Carabi, Angels. "Interview with Toni Morrison." *Belles Lettres: A Review of Books by Women* 10.2 (Spring 1995):40–43.

Carby, Hazel. "Policing the Black Woman's Body in an Urban Context." *Critical Inquiry* 18.4 (1992): 738–55.

———. *Reconstructing Black Womanhood*. New York: Oxford UP, 1987.

Carroll, Michael. *Popular Modernity in America*. Albany: SUNY, 2000.

Charters, Ann. "Introduction." *Three Lives*. New York: Penguin, 1990.

Cataliotti, Robert H. *The Music in African American Fiction*. New York: Garland, 1995.

Chernoff, John Miller. *African Rhythm and African Sensibility*. Chicago: U of Chicago P, 1979.

Cohen, Milton. "Black Brutes and Mulatto Saints: The Racial Hierarchy of 'Melanctha.'" *Black American Literature Forum* 26 (1986): 112–21.

Cohen, Morris. "Property as Power." *Property: Mainstream and Critical Positions*. Ed. C. B. McPherson. Toronto: U of Toronto P, 1978. 153–76.

Cooper, Stephen. *The Politics of Ernest Hemingway*. Ann Arbor: UMI Research P, 1987.

Cornell, Drucilla. "The Solace of Resonance." *Hypatia* 20.2 (Spring 2005): 215–22.

Cross, Gary. *Time and Money: The Making of Consumer Culture*. New York: Routledge, 1993.

Cutten, George. *The Threat of Leisure*. New Haven: Yale UP, 1926.

Davis, Angela. *Blues Legacies and Black Feminism*. New York: Random House, 1999.

Davis, Miles, and Quincy Troupe. *Miles: The Autobigraphy*. New York: Simon and Schuster, 1989.

de Jongh, James. *Vicious Modernism: Black Harlem and the Literary Imagination*. Cambridge: Cambridge UP, 1990.

De Koven, Marianne. *Rich and Strange: Gender, History, Modernism*. Princeton: Princeton UP, 1991.

de Man, Paul. "Autobiography as De-Facement." *The Rhetoric of Romanticism*. New York: Columbia UP, 1984. 67–81.

———. *Romanticism and Contemporary Criticism*. Baltimore: Johns Hopkins UP, 1993.

Derrida, Jacques. *Margins of Philosophy*. Trans. Alan Bass. Chicago: U of Chicago P, 1982.

———. *Writing and Difference*. Chicago: U of Chicago P, 1978.

Dietrich, Kurt. *Duke's Bones: Ellington's Great Trombonists*. Rottenburg: Advance Music, 1995.

——. "Joe 'Tricky Sam' Nanton: Duke Ellington's Master of the Plunger Trombone." *Annual Review of Jazz Studies 5*. Ed. Berger, Cayer, Morgenstern, and Porter. Metuchen: Scarecrow Press, 1991.

Douglass, Ann. *Terrible Honesty*. New York: Farrar, Strauss and Giroux, 1995.

Du Bois, W. E. B. *The Souls of Black Folk*. Boston: Bedford Books, 1997.

——. "The Souls of White Folk." *Writings*. Ed. Nathan Huggins. New York: Library Classics, 1986. 923–38.

——. "Van Vechten's 'Nigger Heaven.'" *Writings*. 1216–18.

Durkheim, Emile. *The Elementary Forms of Religious Life*. Trans. Carol Cosman. New York: Oxford UP, 2001.

Eagleton, Terry. "Capitalism and Form." *New Left Review* 14 (March–April 2002): 119–31.

Early, Gerald. *The Culture of Bruising*. Hopewell, N.J.: Ecco Press, 1994.

——. "Pulp and Circumstance: The Story of Jazz in High Places." O'Meally 393–430.

Einstein, Albert. *Relativity*. Trans. Robert Lawson. New York: Wings Books, 1961.

Eliot, T.S. "Ulysses, Order, and Myth." *Selected Prose of T. S. Eliot*. Ed. Frank Kermode. New York: Mariner Books, 1975. 175–78

Ellington, Duke. "The Duke Steps Out." *The Duke Ellington Reader*. Ed. Mark Tucker, 46–49. Oxford: Oxford UP 1993.

——. "Interview in Los Angeles." *The Duke Ellington Reader*. Ed. Mark Tucker, 148–52. Oxford: Oxford UP, 1993.

——. *Music Is My Mistress*. New York: Doubleday, 1973.

Ellison, Ralph. *Collected Essays*. Ed. John F. Callahan. New York: Modern Library, 2003.

——. *Going to the Territory*. New York: Random House, 1986.

——. *Shadow and Act*. New York: Signet, 1964.

Fabian, Johannes. "Of Dogs Alive, Birds Dead, and Time to Tell a Story" *Chronotypes: The Construction of Time*. Ed. John Bender and David E. Wellbery. Stanford: Stanford UP, 1991. 185–204.

——. *Time and the Other*. New York: Columbia UP, 1983.

Faulkner, William. *The Sound and the Fury*. New York: Modern Library, 2012.

Feld, Steven. "Aesthetics as Iconicity of Style, or, Lift-up-over Sounding: Getting into the Kaluli Groove." *Yearbook for Traditional Music* 20 (1988): 74–113.

Fell, John L., and Terkild Vinding. *Stride: Fats, Jimmy, Lion, Lamb and the Other Ticklers*. New Brunswick: Scarecrow, 1999.

Fitzgerald, F. Scott. "Echoes of the Jazz Age" *The Crack-Up*. Ed. Edmund Wilson. New York: New Directions, 1945. 13–22.

——. *The Great Gatsby*. New York: Simon and Schuster, 1995.

——. *Jazz Age Stories*. Ed. Patrick O'Donnell. New York: Penguin, 1998.

——. "Majesty." *The Short Stories of F. Scott Fitzgerald: A New Collection*. Ed. Matthew J. Bruccoli. New York: Scribner's Sons, 1989. 464–80.

———. "My Lost City." *The Crack-Up*. Ed. Edmund Wilson. New York: New Directions, 1945. 23–33.

———. "The Offshore Pirate." *Jazz Age Stories*. Ed. Patrick O' Donnell. London: Penguin, 1998. 5–34.

Floyd, Samuel A, Jr. *The Power of Black Music*. New York: Oxford UP, 1995.

———. "Ring Shout, Signifyin(g), and Jazz Analysis." Walser, *Keeping Time* 401–10.

Foster, Pops. *Pops Foster: The Autobiography of a New Orleans Jazzman*. Berkeley: U of California P, 1971.

Frank, Waldo. *In the American Jungle*. New York: Farrar and Rinehart, 1937.

Franklin, Benjamin. *The Papers of Benjamin Franklin*. Vol. 4. Ed. L. W. Labaree and Whitifield Bell. New Haven: Yale UP, 1961.

Gaines, Kevin. *Uplifting the Race*. Chapel Hill: U of North Carolina P, 1996.

Ganter, Granville. "Decadence, Sexuality, and the Bohemian Vision of Wallace Thurman." *MELUS* 28.2 (Summer 2003): 83–104.

Garrett, Shawn-Marie. "Return of the Repressed." *Theater* 32.2 (2002): 26–43.

Gates, Henry Louis, Jr. *Figures in Black*. New York: Oxford UP, 1987.

———. Introduction. *The Autobiography of an Ex-Colored Man*. By James Weldon Johnson. New York: Vintage, 1989. v–xxiii.

———. *The Signifying Monkey*. New York: Oxford UP, 1988.

Gebhardt, Nicholas. *Going for Jazz*. Chicago: UP of Chicago, 2001.

Genette, Girard. *Narrative Discourse*. Trans. Jane E. Lewin. Ithaca: Cornell UP, 1980.

Glick, Elisa F. "Harlem's Queer Dandy: African-American Modernism and the Artifice of Blackness." *Modern Fiction Studies*. 49.3 (2003): 414–42.

Gramsci, Antonio. *Selections from the Prison Notebooks*. Trans. Quintin Hoare and Geoffrey Smith. New York: International Publisher, 1991.

Grandt, Jurgen. *Kinds of Blue: The Jazz Aesthetic in African American Narrative*. Columbus: Ohio State UP, 2004.

Guillén, Claudio. *Literature as System*. Princeton: Princeton UP, 1971.

Gysin, Fritz. "From 'Liberating Voices' to 'Metathetic Ventriloguism': Boundaries in Recent African American Jazz Fiction." *Callaloo* 25.1 (2002): 274–87.

Hammond, John. "The Tragedy of Duke Ellington." Tucker 118–20.

Hanchard, Michael. "Afro-Modernity: Temporality, Politics, and the African Diaspora." *Public Culture* 11.1 (1999): 245–68.

Harris, Cheryl. "Whiteness as Property." *Critical Race Theory*. Ed. Kimberle Crenshaw et al. New York: New Press, 1995. 276–91.

Harris, Wilson. "Introduction." *The Carnival Trilogy*. London: Faber and Faber, 1993. vii–xix.

Hartman, Saidiya. *Scenes of Subjection*. New York: Oxford UP, 1997.

Hays, Peter L. *The Critical Reception of Hemingway's* The Sun Also Rises. New York: Camden House, 2011.

Hegel, G. W. F. *Hegel's Aesthetics, vol. II*. Trans. T. M. Knox. Oxford: Clarendon, 1998.

———. *Hegel's Philosophy of Nature*. Trans. M. J. Petry. London: Allen and Unwin, 1970.

———. *Philosophy of Mind.* Trans. A. V. Miller. Oxford: Clarendon, 1971.

Hemingway, Ernest. *The Sun Also Rises.* New York: Macmillan, 1986.

Holland, Eugene W. "Marx and the Poststructuralist Philosophies of Difference." *South Atlantic Quarterly* 96.3 (1997): 525–41.

Holquist, Michael. "Stereotyping in Autobiography and Historiography: Colonialism in *The Great Gatsby.*" *Poetics Today* 9.2 (1988): 453–72.

Hostetler, Ann. "The Aesthetics of Race and Gender in Nella Larsen's *Quicksand.*" *PMLA* 105.1 (Winter 1996): 35–36.

Hughes, Langston. *The Big Sea.* New York: Hill and Wang, 1993.

———. "Cora Unashamed." *The Collected Works of Langston Hughes: Vol.15* Ed. R. Baxter Miller. Columbia: U of Missouri P., 2002. 21–29.

———. "The Glory of Negro History." *The Langston Hughes Reader.* New York: G. Braziller, 1958. 464–82.

———. Letter to James P. Johnson. 24 January 1937. James Weldon Johnson Papers. Beinecke Lib., New Haven.

———. *Not Without Laughter.* New York: Simon and Schuster, 1969.

———. "Songs Called the Blues." *The Langston Hughes Reader.* 159–61.

Huhn, Thomas. "The Sublimation of Culture in Adorno's Aesthetics." *The Aesthetics of the Critical Theorists.* Ed. Ronald Roblin. Lewiston: Edwin Mellen, 1990. 291–307.

Hunter, Alberta. *Beale Street Blues.* Buckinghamshire: Magnum Music, 1996.

Hurston, Zora Neale. "Characteristics of Negro Expression." *The Jazz Cadence of American Culture.* O'Meally 298–302.

Irele, F. Abiola. "The Harlem Renaissance and the Negritude Movement." *The Cambridge History of African and Caribbean Literature, vol.2.* Ed. F. Abiola Irele and Simon Gikandi. Cambridge: Cambridge UP, 2004. 759–84.

Jaffe, Aaron. "Adjectives and the Work of Modernism in the Age of Celebrity." *Yale Journal of Criticism* 16.1 (2003): 1–37.

Jameson, Fredric. *Marxism and Form.* Princeton: Princeton UP, 1971.

———. *A Singular Modernity.* London: Verso, 2002.

Jasen, David A., and Gene Jones. *Black Bottom Stomp.* New York: Routledge, 2002.

Jay, Martin. *Force Fields: Between Intellectual History and Cultural Critique.* New York: Routledge, 1993.

Johnson, James P. *Runnin' Wild (1921–1926).* Rykodisc, 1997.

———. Letter to James P. Johnson. 1930. James Weldon Johnson Papers. Beinecke Library, New Haven.

Johnson, James Weldon. *The Autobiography of an Ex-Colored Man.* New York: Hill and Wang, 1960.

———. *Black Manhattan.* New York: Arno Press, 1968.

———, ed. *The Book of American Negro Poetry.* New York: Harcourt Brace, 1931.

———. Letter to James Weldon Johnson. 1930. James Weldon Johnson Papers. Beinecke Lib., New Haven.

Johnson, James Weldon, and J. Rosamund Johnson. *Book of American Negro Spirituals.* New York: Da Capo, 1991.

Jones, LeRoi. *Blues People*. New York: Morrow Quill, 1963.

Kawash, Samira. "The Autobiography of an Ex-Colored Man: (Passing for) Black Passing for White." *Passing and the Fictions of Identity*. Ed. Elaine K.Ginsburg. Durham: Duke UP, 1996. 59–74.

Kellner, Bruce. *Carl Van Vechten and the Irreverent Decades*. Norman: U of Oklahoma P, 1968.

Kern, Stephen. *The Culture of Time and Space, 1880–1918*. Cambridge: Harvard UP, 1983.

Kernfeld, Barry, ed. *The New Grove Dictionary of Jazz*. New York: St. Martin's, 1988.

Kinder, Marsha. "The Subversive Potential of the Pseudo Iterative," *Film Quarterly* 43, no. 2 (Winter 1989/90): 2–16.

King, Martin Luther, Jr. "I Have a Dream." *A Treasury of Great American Speeches*. Ed. Andrew Bauer. New York: Hawthorn Books, 1979. 366–71.

Knadler, Stephen. "Sweetback Style: Wallace Thurman and a Queer Harlem Renaissance." *Modern Fiction Studies* 48.4 (2002): 899–938.

Koselleck, Reinhart. *The Practice of Conceptual History*. Trans. Todd Presner et al. Stanford: Stanford UP, 2002.

Kristeva, Julia. "Women's Time." *The Kristeva Reader*. Ed. Toril Moi. Oxford: Blackwell, 1986. 187–213.

Lacan, Jacques. *Ecrits*. Trans. Alan Sheridan. New York: W. W. Norton, 1977.

Larsen, Nella. *Quicksand and Passing*. New Brunswick: Rutgers UP, 1986.

Lefebvre, Henri. *Rhythmanalysis*. Trans. Stuart Elden and Gerald Moore. New York: Continuum, 2004.

Lejeune, Philippe. *On Autobiography*. Minneapolis: U of Minnesota P, 1989.

Leonard, Neil. *Jazz and the White Americans*. Chicago: U of Chicago P, 1962.

Levine, Lawrence W. "Jazz and American Culture." O'Meally, 431–47.

Levi-Strauss, Claude. "Structuralism and Myth." *Kenyon Review* 3.2 (Spring 1981): 64–88.

Lewis, George. "*Gittin' To Know Y'all*; Improvised Music, Interculturalism, and the Racial Imagination." *Critical Studies in Improvisation* 1.1 (2004). University of Guelph. 16 August 2005. http://repository.lib.uoguelph.ca/ojs/viewarticle.php?id=28&layout =html.

Lock, Grahm. *Blutopia*. Durham: Duke UP, 1999.

———. *Forces In Motion*. London: Quartet Books, 1986.

Locke, Alain, ed. *The New Negro*. New York: Simon and Schuster, 1992.

———. "Beauty Instead of Ashes." *Nation* 18 April 1928: 423–24.

———. *The Negro and His Music*. Port Washington: Kennikat Press, 1968.

Lowe, Donald. *The History of Bourgeois Perception*. Chicago: U of Chicago P, 1982.

Lukács, Georg. *History and Class Consciousness*. Trans. Rodney Livingstone. Cambridge: MIT Press, 1971.

———. *The Theory of the Novel*. Trans. Anna Bostock. Cambridge: MIT Press, 1971.

Mackey, Nathaniel. *Bedouin Hornbook*. Los Angeles: Sun and Moon Press, 1997.

———. "Other: From Noun to Verb." O'Meally 513–32.

———. "Sound and Sentiment, Sound and Symbol." O'Meally 603–8.

Macpherson, C. B. *The Political Theory of Possessive Individualism: Hobbes to Locke*. New York: Oxford UP, 1962.

Malone, Jacqui. "Jazz Music in Motion: Dancers and Big Bands." O'Meally 278–94.

———. *Steppin' on the Blues*. Urbana: U of Illinois P, 1996.

Mann, Thomas. *Doctor Faustus*. Trans. H. T. Lowe-Porter. New York: Knopf, 1948.

Marcuse, Herbert. "A Note on Dialectic." *The Essential Frankfurt School Reader*. Ed. Andrew Arato and Eike Gebhardt. New York: Urizen, 1978. 444–51.

———. *Reason and Revolution*. New York: Humanities Press, 1954.

Martindale, Don, and James Riedel. "Introduction: Max Weber's Sociology of Music." Weber. xi–lii.

Marx, Karl. *Capital, Vol. One*. *The Marx-Engels Reader*. Ed. Robert C. Tucker. New York: W. W. Norton, 1978. 294–438.

———. "A Contribution to the Critique of Hegel's Philosophy of Right: Introduction." *Early Writings*. Trans. Rodney Livingstone and Gregor Benton. London: Penguin, 1992. 243–58.

———. *The Economic and Philosophic Manuscripts of 1844*. Trans. Martin Milligan. Ed. Dirk J. Struik. New York: International Publishers, 1964.

———. "The Eighteenth Brumaire of Napoleon Bonaparte." *The Marx-Engels Reader*. Ed. Robert C. Tucker. New York: W. W. Norton, 1978. 594–617.

———. "Toward the Critique of Hegel's Philosophy of Law: Introduction." *Writings of the Young Karl Marx on Philosophy and Science*. Trans. and Ed. D. Easton and Krut H. Guddat. Indianapolis: Hackett, 1997. 249–64.

Mbembe, Achille. *On the Postcolony*. Trans. A. M. Berrett et al. Berkeley: U of California P, 2001.

McKay, Nellie. "An Interview with Toni Morrison." *Toni Morrison: Critical Perspectives Past and Present*. Eds. Henry Louis Gates Jr. and K. A. Appiah. New York: Amistad, 1993. 396–411.

McKeon, Michael. *The Origins of the English Novel, 1600–1740*. Baltimore: Johns Hopkins P, 1987.

McLendon, Jacquelyn. *The Politics of Color in the Fiction of Jessie Fauset and Nella Larsen*. Charlottesville: UP of Virginia, 1995.

Meltzer, David. *Reading Jazz*. San Francisco: Mercury House, 1993.

Miller, Paul D. *Rhythm Science*. Cambridge: MIT Press, 2004.

Miller, Richard. *Solutions for Singers*. Oxford: Oxford UP, 2004.

Moddelmog, Debra A. *Reading Desire: In Pursuit of Ernest Hemingway*. Ithaca, Cornell UP, 1999.

Monda, Kimberly. "Self-Delusion and Self-Sacrifice in Nella Larsen's *Quicksand*." *African American Review* 31.1 (1997): 23–39.

Morrison, Toni. *Jazz*. New York: Random House, 1992.

Moten, Fred. *In the Break: The Aesthetics of the Black Radical Tradition*. Minneapolis: U of Minnesota P, 2003.

Murray, Albert. "The Function of the Heroic Image." O'Meally 569–79.

——. *The Hero and the Blues*. Columbus: U of Missouri P, 1973.

——. "Improvisation and the Creative Process." O'Meally 111–14.

——. *Stomping the Blues*. New York: McGraw-Hill, 1976.

Muzak, Joanne. "'The Things Which Money Could Give' The Politics of Consumption in Nella Larsen's *Quicksand*." *Agora: An Online Graduate Journal* 2.1 (2003): 1–18.

Negri, Antonio. *Time for Revolution*. London: Continuum, 2002.

Ngai, Mae. "The Architecture of Race In American Immigration Law." *Journal of American History* 86 (June 1999): 67–92.

Nietzsche, Friedrich. *The Gay Science*. New York: Random House, 1974.

Nketia, J. H. Kwabena. *The Music of Africa*. New York: W. W. Norton, 1974.

North, Michael. *The Dialect of Modernism*. New York: Oxford UP, 1994.

Ogren, Kathy. *The Jazz Revolution*. New York: Oxford UP, 1989.

Olney, Martha. *Buy Now, Pay Later: Advertising, Credit, and Consumer Durables in the 1920s*. Chapel Hill: U of North Carolina P, 1991.

Olsen, Liesl. "Gertrude Stein, William James, and Habit in the Shadow of War." *Twentieth Century Literature* 49.3 (Fall 2003): 328–59.

O'Meally, Robert, ed. *The Jazz Cadence of American Culture*. New York: Columbia UP, 1998.

Patterson, Orlando. "Toward a Future That Has No Past: Reflections on the Fate of Blacks in the Americas." *Public Interest* 27 (Spring 1972): 45–62.

Peppis, Paul. "Thinking Race in the *Avant Guerre*: Typological Negotiations in Ford and Stein." *Yale Journal of Criticism* 10.2 (1997): 371–95.

Perreti, Burton. *The Creation of Jazz*. Urbana: U of Illinois P, 1992.

Peterson, Carla L. "The Remaking of Americans: Gertrude Stein's 'Melanctha' and African-American Musical Traditions." *Criticism and the Color Line*. Ed. Henry B. Wonham. New Brunswick: Rutgers UP, 1996. 140–57.

Plato. *The Republic*. Trans. G. M. A. Grube. Indianapolis: Hackett, 1992.

Porter, Eric. *What Is This Thing Called Jazz?* Berkeley: U of California P, 2002.

Posnock, Ross. "'A New World. Material without Being Real': Fitzgerald's Critique of Capitalism in *The Great Gatsby*." *Critical Essays on F. Scott Fitzgerald's* The Great Gatsby. Ed. Scott Donaldson. Boston: G. K. Hall, 1984. 201–13.

Pound, Ezra. "Hugh Selwyn Mauberly." *Personae*. New York, New Directions, 1990. 183–202.

Raussert, Wilfried. "Jazz, Time, and Narrativity." *American Studies* 45.4 (2000): 519–34.

Redding, Jay Saunders. *They Came in Chains*. New York: Lippincott, 1969.

Reichardt, Ulfried. "Time and the African American Experience: The Problem of Chronocentrism." *American Studies* 45.4 (2000): 465–84.

Rhodes, Chip. *Structures of the Jazz Age*. London: Verso, 1998.

Ringer, Alexander L. "Assimilation and the Emancipation of Historical Dissonance." *Constructive Dissonance: Arnold Schoenberg and the Transformations of Twentieth-Century Culture*. Eds. J. Brand and C. Hailey. Berkeley: U of California P, 1997. 23–34.

Rogers, J. A. "Jazz at Home." Locke 216–24.

Rosaldo, Michelle Z. "Toward an Anthropology of Self and Feeling." *Culture Theory: Essays in Mind, Self, and Emotion*. Ed. Richard A Shwed and Robert A. Levine. Cambridge: Cambridge UP 1984. 137–57.

Rossing, Thomas D., F. Richard Moore, and Paul A. Wheeler. *The Science of Sound*. San Francisco: Addison Wesley, 2002.

Rouder, Willa. "James P(rice) Johnson." *The New Grove Dictionary of Jazz*. Ed. Barry Kernfeld. New York: St. Martin's Press, 1994. 619–21.

Rowe, John Carlos. "Naming What Is Inside: Gertrude Stein's Use of Names in *Three Lives*." *Novel* 36.2 (Spring 2003): 219–43.

Ruddick, Lisa. *Body, Text, Gnosis*. Ithaca: Cornell UP, 1990.

Said, Edward. *Musical Elaborations*. New York: Columbia UP, 1993.

——. *The World, the Text, and the Critic*. Cambridge: Harvard UP, 1983.

Sartre, Jean-Paul. *Being and Nothingness*. Trans. Hazel E. Barnes. New York: Washington Square Press, 1966.

Schuller, Gunther. *Early Jazz: Its Roots and Musical Development*. New York: Oxford UP, 1968.

Senghor, Leopold. "African-Negro Aesthetics." *Diogenes* 16 (Winter 1956): 23–38.

Shack, William A. *Harlem in Montmartre*. Berkeley: U of California P, 2001.

Shepherd, Paul. *Music as Social Text*. Cambridge: Polity, 1991.

Shipton, Alyn. *A New History of Jazz* London: Continuum, 2001.

Smith, Bessie. *Bessie Smith: The Collection*. CBS, 1989.

Smith, Robert. "Internal Time-Consciousness of Modernism." *Critical Quarterly* 36.3 (1994): 20–29.

Snead, James. "Repetition as a Figure of Black Culture." *Black Literature and Literary Theory*. Ed. Henry Louis Gates, Jr. New York: Routledge, 1990. 59–80.

Southern, Eileen. *The Music of Black Americans*. New York: W. W. Norton, 1983.

Spillers, Hortense. "'All the Things You Could Be by Now If Sigmund Freud's Wife Was Your Mother': Psychoanalysis and Race." *Boundary 2* 23.3 (1996): 75–141.

——. "Mama's Baby, Papa's Maybe: An American Grammar Book." *Diacritics 17.2* (Summer 1987): 65–81.

Stallman, R. W. "*Gatsby* and the Hole in Time." *Modern Fiction Studies* 1.4 (November 1955): 2–16.

Stearns, Marshall, and Jean Stearns. *Jazz Dance*. New York: Schirmer, 1979.

Stein, Gertrude. *The Autobiography of Alice B. Toklas*. New York: Random House, 1990.

——. "Plays." *Writings: 1932–1946*. Ed. Catherine Stimpson and Harriet Chessman. New York: Library of America, 1998. 244–69.

——. *Three Lives*. New York: Penguin, 1990.

Stimpson, Catharine R. "The Mind, the Body, and Gertrude Stein." *Critical Inquiry* 3.3 (1997 Spring): 489–506.

Stuckey, Sterling. *Slave Culture: Nationalist Theory and the Foundations of Black America*. New York: Oxford UP, 1988.

Tate, Claudia. "Desire and Death in *Quicksand*, by Nella Larsen." *American Literary History* 7.2 (Summer 1995): 234–60.

Taylor, Art. *Notes and Tones: Musician-to-Musician Interviews*. New York: Da Capo Press, 1993.

Thompson, Emily. *The Soundscape of Modernity: Architectural Acoustics and the Culture of Listening in America, 1900–1933*. Cambridge: MIT, 2003.

Thompson, E. P. "Time, Work-Discipline, and Industrial Capitalism." *Past and Present* 38 (December 1967): 56–97.

Thompson, Robert Farris. "African Art and Motion." O'Meally 311–71.

Thurman, Wallace. "Fire Burns: A Department of Comment." *The Collected Writings of Wallace Thurman*. Ed. Amritjit Singh and Daniel M. Scott III. New Brunswick: Rutgers UP, 2003. 193–95.

———. "Terpsichore in Harlem." *The Collected Writings of Wallace Thurman*. Ed. Amritjit Singh and Daniel M. Scott III. New Brunswick: Rutgers UP, 2003. 284–88.

———. *Infants of the Spring*. New York: Modern Library, 1999.

Titze, Ingo. *Principles of Vocal Production*. Prentice Hall, 1994.

Tucker, Mark. "Ellington's 'Jungle Music.'" *Duke Ellington and New Orleans: A 90th Birthday Tribute*. Ed. Caroline Richmond. Lugano: Festa New Orleans Music Production, 1989. 13–15.

———, ed. *The Duke Ellington Reader*. New York: Oxford UP, 1993.

———. *Ellington: The Early Years*. Urbana: U of Illinois P, 1991.

Van Vechten, Carl. "Moanin' wid a Sword in Mah Han." *Keep A-Inchin' Along*. Westport: Greenwood Press, 1979. 54–57.

———. *Nigger Heaven*. New York: Knopf, 1926.

Varadharajan, Asha. *Exotic Parodies: Subjectivity in Adorno, Said, and Spivak*. Minneapolis: U of Minnesota P, 1995.

Vincent, Ted. *Keep Cool: The Black Activists Who Built the Jazz Age*. London: Pluto, 1995.

Walser, Robert. "Rhythm, Rhyme, and Rhetoric in the Music of Public Enemy." *Ethnomusicology*. 39.2 (Spring 1995): 193–217.

———, ed. *Keeping Time: Readings in Jazz History*. New York: Oxford UP, 1999.

Washington, Salim. "Of Black Bards, Known and Unknown." *Callaloo* 25.2 (2002): 233–56.

Waters, Ethel. *The Incomparable Ethel Waters*. Sony, 2003.

Watt, Ian. *The Rise of the Novel*. Berkeley: U of California P, 1957.

Webb, Barbara. "The Centrality of Race to the Modernist Aesthetics of Gertrude Stein's *Four Saints in Three Acts*." *Modernism/Modernity* 7.3 (September 2000): 447–69.

Weber, Max. *The Rational and Social Foundations of Music*. Trans. Don Martindale, Johannes Riedel, and Gertrude Neuwirth. Carbondale: Southern Illinois UP, 1969.

Weiss, M. Lynne. "Among Negroes: Gertrude Stein and African America." *Race and the Modern Artist*. Ed. Heather Hathaway, Josef Jarab, and Jeffrey Melnick. Oxford: Oxford UP, 2003. 115–25.

Werner, Craig Hansen. *Playing the Changes: From Afro-Modernism to the Jazz Impulse*. Urbana: U of Illinois P, 1994.

West, Cornel. *Keeping Faith*. New York: Routledge, 1993.

Whiteman, Paul. "Press Release for 1924 Concert." *Reading Jazz*. Ed. David Meltzer. San Francisco: Mercury House, 1993. 116–17.

Wiegman, Robyn. *American Anatomies*. Durham: Duke UP, 1995.

Wilson, Olly. "The Association of Movement and Music as a Manifestation of a Black Conceptual Approach to Music-Making." *International Musicological Society Report of the Twelfth Congress*. Eds. Daniel Heartz and Bonnie Wade. Basel: Barenreiter Kasel, 1981. 98–105.

———. "Black Music as an Art Form." O'Meally 82–101.

———. "The Heterogeneous Sound Ideal in African-American Music." *Signifyin(g), Sanctifyin, and Slam Dunking*. Ed. Gena Dagel Caponi. Amherst: U of Amherst P, 1999. 157–70.

Zamir, Shamoon. *Dark Voices: W. E. B. DuBois and American Thought, 1888–1903*. Chicago: U of Chicago P, 1985.

Zuckerkandl, Victor. *Sound and Symbol: Music and the External World*. Princeton: Princeton UP, 1956.

Index